SNAPSHOTS *of* INSPIRATION

From the Word of God to a Common Man

PETER F. SERRA

www.trafford.com
North America & international
toll-free: 1 888 232 4444 (USA & Canada)
fax: 812 355 4082

This work is dedicated to the glory of God.

TABLE OF CONTENT

Book 2
Spiritual pearls for Natural oysters

Beginning

In the beginning
God made man
Breathed into his
Nostrils and life began.

Secular interests
Worldly affairs
Misguide the lost
Confuse and delay
All who are searching
Seeking the way.

Truth of beginning Christ Jesus King
Sent into the world Life's message to bring
A rainfall in summer a searchlight in dark
A heartfelt reminder of God's proven love.
Amen.

Butterfly

By Rosalie Serra
God says,
"The butterfly is acceptance
Of each new phase of life."
He says,
"Keep the faith
As everything changes."

God is here

By Rosalie Serra
If you breathe
Sigh
Laugh
Or cry
He is our strength
He is our love
And he gave to us
His life.

I Am

I am awesome and smart.
I wonder how I became the person I am?
I hear a bell ring when I get an answer right in my head.
I see a beautiful garden when I think of my BFF.
I want to always stay on top of my schoolwork.
I am awesome and smart.
I pretend to be a dog whisperer.
I feel creative like an artist.
I touch blankets soft as silk.
I worry when the time comes
I might not be ready to grow up.
I cry about not seeing my BFF in school everyday.
(I miss her).
I am awesome and smart.
I understand that everybody has to grow up.
I say, when you set your mind to something
There is nothing you can't do.
I dream about being a singer.
I try always to get good grades.
I hope I can achieve
Always staying on top of my schoolwork.
I am awesome and smart.

By Isabella Serra, age 10.

PREFACE

Let it be said at the outset of Christian discourse that the depth of scripture cannot be encapsulated within the definitions of language and then be regarded as completely exhausted of meaning. Having said this, one can recognize it would be a mistake on our part to assume closure by pronouncing a definitive inhibiting posture upon God's word. The depth wealth and undercurrents of God's word continually offers to us revelation. It reveals to us the great depth that is spiritual weaving, woven from the lives of humanity by the hand of God. We will always find additional understanding, directly in the spoken and printed word, inflection within delivery and fortified strength in the underlying foundations of truth.

We are as small fragments of construction material within a great temple. The wall depth is not given to us and neither is the specification completely understood within the expressions of mankind. Within the word of God lives a language we are capable to express in only rudimentary utterances and vocalizations, within both inward spiritual and corporeal vocalization forms of communication. It is the language of the Holy Spirit.

No matter where we are utilized as building material of said temple, whether, the interior or exterior surfaces, we are accorded access to the sights and sounds of holiness, as well as the reverent attitude that is taking place in the presence of God. Therein we have understanding and potential to increase our communication and comprehensive ability. We can and do learn through visible association, close proximity, and the hearing of God's word. All of the temple material comprises the temple structure in total. We are the temple of God and the Spirit of God lives in us, no matter what denomination or theology we may embrace, because no one can say, **"Jesus is Lord"** without the Holy Spirit. This one defining fact (the presence of the Holy Spirit within us) is the ingredient determining whether or not we are a part of, or separated from, the actual structure of the Kingdom of God.

Barriers are erected when we fail to understand or permit exploration for truth. Like the great temple in Jerusalem during the time of Christ, the existence of barriers, such as the outer court within the structure, made distinction between common man and priest. It also established a false sense of worthiness with regard to the closer one physically came to the actual presence of God, recognized to be within the Holy of Holies sanctuary wherein only the high priest was permitted entrance. This is not the case within Christianity; none of us are worthy to approach God, but all of us can do so because of Jesus. None of us are given more than the next person; in truth, God gives to each of us the necessary grace to allow his peace and presence to be recognized, to the highest point of the individual's desire to understand. As long as the Holy Spirit is in attendance we need only ask seek and knock. Everything is made available to us who desire to know God.

Encapsulation of scripture (not to be confused with wrong understanding) gives way to opportunity for possible descent into division, instead of having God's word as an instrument of unity. At the very least, shallow understanding can become differing opinions, that calcify and separate, ultimately breaking away from the body of Christ. A temple fragmented into smaller parts (denominations) claiming allegiance to the head of the body (Christ), is denied the full strength the body (as a whole) should enjoy. A brittle foundation will break or crumble, as will clay feet unwilling to move into action by the force of truth. Difference of opinion is not necessarily a bad thing, but to close the book on God's word is to invite division and allow pride the opportunity to advance.

Diverse understanding is like a banquet table set before a king, the truly unpalatable will not go unrecognized. Denominational differences in theology and interpretative understanding, at times, lends itself to confusion, while not necessarily intended, can make cloudy the water of life. This then (in part) is the encapsulation of thought and the beginning of stagnant understanding. Perhaps worldly word-combat is man's pride overflowing into the word of God, which unintentionally inhibits fluidity and the depth of understanding we should expect to find within God's *word. Because of conditioning by worldly standards the true depth of focus is not mined and the wonderful gems of wisdom are found by only a few whose desire precludes pride. Truth does not dance around meaning or hide within shadows, but deception is always adept at tiptoe movements and dodge ball maneuvering. Moreover, the one who refuses to move in the direction of understanding may unintentionally deny truth, necessary to be the added strength in the overall construction plan of God. It is my intent to present a common man's journey into some scriptural snapshots, lending a layman's perspective to the panoramic tapestry that is the word of God. There is an abundance of variety within the diet of man, and to some spinach is unpalatable, but to others it is a source of great nutrition. That is to say, we see and hear things, evaluate their nutritional value through our physical and spiritual senses, through the noticeable results brought about by ingestion, and make judgment as to wholesomeness.*

God is the light for us to recognize spiritual language and its constant revelation of meaning. In this light we may pick and choose our fruits and vegetables. However, dietary staples, which are the canons of faith, are on display for all to see, no matter what brand of Christianity we may find closest to our understanding of truth. In these canons we are united within the body of Christ. The intent of this book is not to discuss diversity. Instead, to show that even a common man can find a measure of understanding when God leads his way. All scripture quotations are in **bold italics** *taken from the* **New International Version of the Holy Scriptures, unless otherwise stated.**

Proverbs 3:5-6
"Trust in the Lord with all your heart. Never rely on what you think you know. Remember the Lord in everything you do, and he will show you the right way."

Why is it so many can acknowledge the warmth sight power and need for light and still not know who is the light? There is still darkness in the world that precludes identity until God intervenes into an individual's life. It is not the kind of darkness that blinds the eye to the rays of the sun but the kind that blinds the mind and heart. This darkness afflicts the understanding of man and captures him within the limitations of humanity. It is the finite understanding of man that denounces light and tolerates life as a linear line whose beginning is birth and end is death. It is a concept that eliminates both the promises for eternity and God himself. Without the understanding of God, we have been set loose as children within a candy store. It is perhaps only when this life's offerings have caused us pain and sickness brought about by overindulgence do we begin to recognize a need for a cure. Enter Jesus, who is the light of understanding and source of all healing offered to us in this world of hurt and rejection. The light of this world offers to us security from the deceptions and rejections of a world seeking perfection both externally and internally, within the limitations of man, causing continual far ranging remedial action in order to reach a place unattainable without God. This is the unhappy condition of man, set adrift by his own will only to sail upon an ocean beneath a starless sky, dead in the water, unable to move and navigate between the beginning and end of life itself.

Because of the poor vision inherited within the human condition, regarding our inability to recognize God, he has given to us who have been given sight the status of communicator. God has called all of his children to be communicators. It doesn't matter to him if we are possessors of many lettered titles, or of the common man variety of believer. This is the key, "believer," for whoever has faith in God all things are possible. What matters to him is our desire to commit our lives in this endeavor to share truth. It need not be a ministry as a priest or pastor for the, "all" that God calls, is an "all inclusive all." We may minister by speaking to our friends and family concerning the blessings of truth and freedom, or by just the manner in which we live this life. God is the power to remove deception and permit others to hear the truth that sets free. The content of the book represents both the love and gratitude I desire to share with others. (My only regret is that I cannot express myself in a more legible manner). Having said this, I do recognize that all contained within has been given. Where there may be times you might scratch your head and say, "What did he say?" It's only because I have somehow lost focus and was not listening *as intently as I should have. Of course I could blame it on my wife but I do like living! At the ending of this work there is a poem dedicated to the World Trade Tower's victims who had everything taken away, and also to those who gave everything. In truth this book has been a passion of mine and if only one word finds the heart of a lost soul it was all worth the effort. It is a contrast of night and day light and darkness, understanding and unawareness, truth and lies, life and death that is brought forth in a small way with the small voice of a common man. It attempts to speak to the human condition regarding the spiritual man attempting to reject the dictates of the flesh; the carnal man ruled by his sin nature and the natural man unaware of the word of God, but has been included in the life or death equation nevertheless. <u>Author's note:</u> A number of poems in this work have been reprinted from, "Christian Visions From A Common Man" and in some instances have been rewritten, because, while the original generating thought for such poem was valid, its initial expression failed. It is my hope that with improvement they now may prove viable in God's plan.*

Even the smallest voice
Can impact a life with the message of Christ.
We never know when the call will come.
Mostly it's subtle and placed within our path.
A face that hides inside depression's form
Or one who feels as a castaway in storms.
We never know when God's voice to us will say,
"Go and smile for this one living in the dark.
Show to him the way offered without cost
And speak the words I'll give you
For the troubled and the lost."

OF GODS AND MEN AND DECEPTION'S FRIENDS

*A look into the abyss of deception is the aim of this exercise. For the purpose of making distinction, passive deception is defined as being absent the knowledge of wrong, while aggressive deception incorporates said knowledge with intent to inflict harm. Aggressive deception within nature is found only in human beings. It is the key element for employing evil. Aggressive deception is also found within the supernatural realm declaring itself against God and his creation. In all other forms of life deception appears as passive for the purpose of survival, absent the knowledge of wrong or intent to knowingly do harm. One might attribute the existence of a passive structure a result of the initial fall of man. Given all life is physically interconnected, all life may also have been altered by the sin produced in man. It may be likened to an infection within creation; stamped into and proliferated by man with the onset of sin. With death and decomposition of the body so it may be the returning "**dust of the earth**" was no longer "**good**" as previously declared by God. In this altered state all other life as well as the earth itself became infected or changed in composition from good to something less; moving forward, life apart from man systematically took upon itself the passive or dilute form of deception; after all it only takes one drop of water to change the overall composition of an ocean, perhaps one sin changed all of nature? All life may have suffered from the infection of sin spreading unabated upon the earth as well as in it. When all things are made new, "**the lion will lay down with the lamb.**" This may be more than symbolism speaking within scripture; it may be tacitly reminding us of preexisting conditions that had no need for deception of either passive or aggressive varieties.*

Certainly one can imagine God not needing to incorporate such passiveness within his overall masterpiece of creation. And again, it is not beyond reasoning to imagine God incorporating such passive interplay as a default system for fulfilling his purpose, creation's balance and continued renewal, based upon his knowledge of what would occur regarding man's failure to follow instruction; a default system with consequence.

Genesis 1:31 God saw all that he had made, and it was very good. And there was evening, and there was morning—the sixth day. God declared his creation good and truth stood as a beacon unrivaled by deception, which would come to us causing detraction from God's pronouncement. Perhaps there is no place on earth for truth to be recognized so long as man continues to declare himself supreme. So long as man continues to deny God his rightful place deception will never become homeless. How deception may have come into being within nature, as a passive state, has little consequence for this inquiry. However, aggressive deception is unequivocally stated as not being designed into man. Establishment in man is owing to the practical experience of being deceived and recognition of our failure to heed the prohibition of God. Once man found reason to question visual appearances and oral presentations a negative disposition toward all things came into our determinate capacity. A "prove it" mentality prevailed and cynicism (a byproduct of sin) inhabited the fabric of man. Where once trust stood alone distrust moved in. Wariness became wedded to a predisposed mindset for expecting deceit and calcified into a jaundiced (an attitude of cynical hostility) response. The reaction to an exposed lie will always elicit hostility. Deception is never at ease with itself.

Proverbs 28:1 "The wicked man flees though no one pursues, but the righteous are as bold as a lion." This *"prove it"* operative clearly defined deception as reality, unshakable in foundation and instantly embraced because of its immediate and probable harmful consequence. It was expected and accepted as normal within the mind of man, as truth was reduced in stature owing to our failure to fully recognize its importance. Sin rains down upon the heads of all and is a constant reminder of the struggles we endure for the sake of reinforcing its existence. Sin is a slow death eventually overcoming the body, but the disposition of the spirit in man depends upon whether or not one is saved at the moment the body dies. Having said this, the denial of life after death, or the disbelief in the continuance of the thinking faculty after the body dies, gains acceptance in many as a pillar of deception's power. The ceasing of brain function is looked upon as a sure sign of death, but the spirit is not dependent upon the viability of corporeal life. We have no limitation with regard to human desire, since our desire, emanating from flesh, is likened to the world of the dead, always having room for more. Where there is infinite demand from human desire, emanating from the corporeal existence of man, should we then expect less than infinite from the spiritual? The spiritual aspect of our existence finds limitless the expanse of the mind, absent mile markers defining beginning or end. Our bodily existence is dependent upon our spiritual component but the spiritual needs not the flesh to exist. We fail to recognize God as the hand that frees us as well as the one who made us, and in this failure deception finds the height of its power. In addition, we fail to understand the true impact of recognizing God as a pure spiritual being capable of far greater things unimaginable to us. God existing as a pure spiritual being should convince us as having the capacity to also exist beyond the limitation perceived within the stark reality displayed in bodily death.

Deception's friends

Secularism and false religion find unity within deception woven deeply within its fabric. Within secularism the truth of God finds no place to rest and take root. God is purposely excluded because he is the source of freedom that unravels the knot of secular deception. In this exclusion of God man is made to believe he is independent and self-sufficient. The illusion of independence is promoted and advanced in order to keep man shielded from truth that would set him free. Within the world of false religion man is made to become dependent upon those who would control, approve, or condemn their actions. This is contrary to the freedom purchased for us through Christ's sacrifice. In this need for approval through false religion the freedom God desires for man is denied. Freedom can never be understood within the confines of someone else determining for us what is right and wrong. By reducing man to either illusory independence (secularism) or direct dependency (false religion) the poison upon deception's plate erodes competitiveness within the human condition. Illusory independence nullifies the competitive spirit of man and keeps him focused away from God's truth that permits freedom and abundant life. Providing for physical needs (secularism) will never satisfy the hunger of man's spirit that seeks to be reunited with God. Making people dependent through the illusion of independence, or directly dependent through the fear associated within false religion, removes the competition from those who would be gods in a world dependent upon them, and permits elitism to continue as royalty of old, within the same families. Dependency in both secular and religious offerings is done through the weaponry of fear that fosters control of the individual, and keeps its leaders set apart as significant and indispensable to the lives of those so dependent. *When the competitiveness of man is suppressed freedom falls victim to the hand that feeds him. When man places his soul into the trust of false religion his freedom also falls victim to deception.* In summation, secularism promotes the illusion of independence and simultaneously, through covert incremental phases, forces its victims to become increasingly more dependent. Within false religion the illusion of independence is not necessary. From the outset its members (most of whom are born into such captivity) understand the fear of condemnation is always with them. This *big-stick* approach with external purpose purported to produce perfection in the human condition also has underlying roots that entrench its leadership upon the very treetops of life.

It may be said for everything representing truth there is an effort to replace it with a counterfeit currency. The "bad penny" keeps showing up. It is accepted at face value without examination and when discovered is either passed along discarded or destroyed, leaving us thinking the harm experienced has been negated. With discarding of the coin we may think its cumulative harm has been stopped, but negation of the aggressive deception has not taken place; someone may find and reintroduce the initial intent of deception. The same is true for passing the coin along to the next victim. The only way to be certain of halting the deception is to destroy the coin. Where there is harmful intent there is offense and where there is offense it is first perpetrated against God. While various aspects of life are counterfeited and presented to us as authentic, the real purpose of deception is to deny truth. God is the truth we must embrace in order to live. The ultimate goal of the *creator of deception* is to destroy creation and replace God as Sovereign Lord. This has to be the height of deception's folly!

Deception's affront is aimed at God with the purpose of denying him, and ends in the destruction of all who would embrace and affirm a lie.

Many passive examples within nature show to us a mechanism employed for survival. How this mechanism had come into being is open for conjecture. Be that as it may, (built in by design as a default mechanism, or incorporated directly through the downfall of man), neither avenue contains an end-result, incorporating the knowledge of wrong, or otherwise displays reasoning attributes believed to be found only in the nature of man. We see passive deceptive portrayals in plants and throughout the upward mobility of life, and in this we can see the *competitiveness of nature* as *clearly necessary*. This same competitiveness is shunned by deception desirous of its removal from the nature of man, in order to render him dependent upon the will and benevolence of others.

Purpose

All life has purpose and emanates from God. The purpose of man is to recognize truth and in this observation we are led to God. We can recognize deception within passive structures as either a genetically permitted sin activated default program, incorporated with foreknowledge by God knowing what would occur when sin entered into creation, or a mutant behavior brought into being by the direct influence of sin, absent said default system. No matter which way passive deception was brought into being, we see its family trait absent the potency of an aggressive nature. However, the common cord or underlying purpose of God's intent, for the continuance of life has not been destroyed by sin's influence, even though the primary purpose of sin is to destroy God's creation.

Job: 1:12 The Lord said to Satan, "Very well, then, everything he has is in your hands, but on the man himself do not lay a finger." God placed limitation upon the tests that would come upon Job, who, in this instance represents for us all of humanity, and in the broader sense represents all of nature. Do not touch his life; do not destroy him; do not end the purpose of the man who has placed his trust in me, is clearly the meaning of God's words. Through all of mankind's trials and troubles brought about by deception's evil intent, there is limitation assigned as both a broad based command, such as, ***"Do not kill"*** as well as uniquely endurance specific to each of us. God understands the amount of tribulation we can tolerate, it is not the same for everyone. In this understanding tolerances or thresholds for coping with adversity have breakpoints that may cause us to seek a way out from such trials other than to seek God. In this respect God does not allow evil (Satan) to directly take a life or go beyond the limitation God has declared off limits to evil's designs. The Commandment prohibiting murder is universal extending to all in the natural and supernatural realm. Unfortunately neither existence heeds this command. As such, whoever places their self above God's law will suffer the lake burning of fire and sulfur; serious judgment. If God did not place limitation upon his creation he would have indirectly abdicated his exclusive position as Judge. Such indirect abdication would send a signal to deception that truth is susceptible to attack and can be corrupted within the originator of truth itself. Within deception lives the underlying purpose of distracting mankind away from God and ultimately to deny mankind the knowledge of his true purpose.

If deception is bold enough to attempt to usurp God how then should we treat this warning from Jesus? ***Matthew 5:13 "You are the salt of the earth. But if salt loses its saltiness, how can it be made salty again? It is no longer good for anything, except to be thrown out and trampled by men."*** Clearly we find the meaning in the words of Jesus to imply the saltiness possessed by men is the truth received by God, and if this truth is lost it has then been corrupted and is of no use to anyone. If the truth of God can be corrupted by deception what chance does a man have who has been deceived into accepting a lie in place of the truth of God? ***Matthew 5:14 "You are the light of the world. A city on a hill cannot be hidden. Neither do people light a lamp and put it under a bowl. Instead they put it on a stand, and it gives light to everyone in the house. In the same way let your light shine before men, that they may praise your good deeds and praise your Father in heaven."*** Here again we find our Lord exhorting us to let the truth of God shine in our lives. It is not our truth, as such, we must not think of it as something to be hidden. It is God's truth that set us free from the darkness of sin's captivity, and it is the example of our freedom in Christ that has to be placed on a stand for all to see. All who see it will be drawn by desire for its freedom giving illumination, and in being attracted God continues his frustration of deception's intent. Some may ask, "What is this light that everyone can see?" Simply stated, it is the cessation or permanent discontinuance from our former captivity and involvement in worldly pursuits. In the beginning God called his creation, ***"good."*** Jesus speaks to us in a manner that exemplifies either our compliance or dereliction from this initial pronouncement by God. ***"A good tree bears good fruit and a bad tree bears bad fruit."*** This quote allows us to recognize a direct aspect of fulfilled or unfulfilled purpose. The manner in which we conduct our lives may determine how others view truth. They may find attraction through honesty or be repelled by hypocrisy, if what we profess with our lips is not confirmed by our actions. One main purpose for man is to recognize deception and in this recognition to seek God for the true purpose of our lives. We must remember, when we do not represent truth in all aspects of our life we have directly aided the cause of deception. All of creation was accomplished without a need for deception.

The boldness of deception

Jesus said, ***"Foxes have holes and birds have nests but the Son of Man has no place to rest his head."*** One implication in this statement from our Lord is that there is no place for truth to rest. Truth must always be active and prove itself. Jesus had said, ***"I am the way the truth and the life."*** In his capacity as ***"Truth"*** there is always the challenge of *"prove it"* while deception is recognized as a proven truth! This implies deception has usurped the rightful place of truth, and the lie has attained reality stature within the hearts of mankind.

Failed purpose and deception's friends

Pontius Pilate exemplified deception's blinding entanglements when he asked Jesus, ***"What is truth?"*** Pilate was not interested in an explanation or definition of truth. He had been blinded by the deception that surrounded him constantly. His world was one of ever changing positions that made it impossible for those who assumed an intellectually superior posture, to admit to the reality clearly seen by those whose lives are not trapped by pursuit of position power and greed. Pilate was *above all* a politician who knew Jesus was innocent but acted with political expediency; his was not a moral decision. Scripture gives us some insight into the decision making process.

Matthew 27-19 *"While Pilate was sitting in the judgment hall, his wife sent him a message. Have nothing to do with this innocent man, because in a dream last night I suffered much on account of him."* Not only does Pilate know Jesus is innocent from his own evaluation, but he gets a warning from his wife to have nothing to do with this innocent man. We may want to look into just where this warning originated, that is, how was it Pilate's wife came to have this dream and what was the intent of the warning? It seems to me the warning was meant to persuade Pilate not to interfere with the execution of Jesus. The dream was upsetting to the wife of Pilate and it was fear that moved her to warn her husband that he may be playing in a league way above his position as governor. It is conceivable that God sent this nightmare to her. She suffered greatly and this is what one may expect if God wants to send to us a bad dream. Additionally, it seems to me that a determination of innocence by Pilate may have interfered with God's plan of salvation for mankind. Therein we find the removal of Pilate from the equation removes any chance of Jesus being set free. Nevertheless, Pilate does what is best for Pilate and his political standing. Pilate sends Jesus to Herod who was in Jerusalem for the Passover. Herod is disappointed in Jesus, because he wanted to see a miracle; he mocks him and sends him back to Pilate for disposition of the case. These two foxes had not as yet realized the impact truth would have upon those under their tyranny. But the religious leaders knew full well the threat Jesus presented to their dominance of others and the positions they enjoyed. We can begin to understand the purpose of man for himself and the purpose of man within God's intent to be extremely opposed to each other, as clearly as we can distinguish between good and evil.

Friends

Luke 23:11-12 *"Herod and his soldiers made fun of Jesus and treated him with contempt; then they put a fine robe on him and sent him back to Pilate. On that very day Herod and Pilate became friends; before this they had been enemies."* I suppose, one could look at this and say, the reason they became friends is because they had both concluded Jesus was an innocent man. However, it is more likely they became friends because they both had the common bond of evil at the forefront of their thoughts. ***Mark 3:25-26 "If a household is divided according to loyalties, that household will not survive. Similarly, if Satan has suffered mutiny in his ranks, and is torn by dissension, he cannot endure; he is finished."*** Just as the bond of love unites the children of God, so it is unity is produced when all evil things act in concert against love. While this is not Herod the Great who slaughtered the innocence, this Herod (Antipas) is the one who beheaded John the Baptist, and we can safely say he is evil. What was the meaning of Pilate washing his hands of the whole affair? Did he think he could become ritually clean by his open display of cowardice and inability to make a just decision? In the overall actions of the Jewish council, teachers of the law, and secular rulers there is the understanding they willfully and knowingly executed an innocent man. This is exactly where deception wants to take all of us. Into acts of mind numbing atrocity, wherein we exhibit no remorse for actions executed against conscience, no matter the degree or depth to which we stumble and fall into its alluring traps. No, the washing of the hands by Pilate did not exonerate him from the lesser sin. The greater sin was to hand Jesus over to him in the first place, and in the holding of God's truth in contempt, they shouted, ***"Let his blood be on our hands!"*** is the greater sin. How dark is the darkness of man's soul? Perhaps it is dark enough to permit men to assume the title of gods in a world of men. In a way, both secular and religious spheres of influence found the common ground of friendship within their common enemy of truth.

Sin is progressive

As sin progressed from its inception, the actions of man moved closer to the point of exhausting God's patience. God recognized the behavior of mankind to be, ***"Only and always wicked."*** The great flood consumed everyone and everything with the intent of God to restore and instill in mankind the understanding of God's supremacy in all things concerning what is acceptable to him. We still have not learned this lesson. The impact of sin acts very negatively upon our faith and produces doubt (this will be explored in the next chapter), where once none was allowed. Even when people attempt to find truth within scripture, their intent is off-balance and skewered by deception's influence. Some never make it past creation's narrative because they fail to utilize the common sense made available to all who will but recognize logic.

I must at this point answer the question many suggest has placed a stop sign upon the voracity of scripture. They say, "How can it be from the one couple, Adam and Eve, such variety is contained within humanity?" It is explained through reason. We recognize the example of Adam and Eve as the first of God's creation, given to us as *example* by God. He has highlighted for our edification a given people within the earth's inhabitants from whom we can extrapolate understanding. God had not stopped creating after he created Adam and Eve. *John 5:17 Jesus said to them, "My Father is always at his work to this very day, and I too am working."* Still some will say, "But God rested from his labors on the seventh-day after he completed his creation of mankind and all contained in the earth and the heavens." When we recognize that God can multitask it then becomes obvious to us that the work of God continues on levels we cannot even imagine. This statement by Jesus regarding God always working is enormous. It has been likened to the opening and closing verses in the gospel of John. *John I-5 "In the beginning was the Word, and the Word was with God, and the Word was God, he was with God in the beginning. Through him all things were made; without him nothing was made that has been made. In him was life and that life was the light of men. The light shines in the darkness, but the darkness had not understood it." John 21:25 "Jesus did many other things as well. If every one of them were written down, I suppose that even the whole earth would not have room for the books that would be written."* These opening and closing verses have been likened to great stones being tossed into a lake and the ensuing ripples created cause great movement of thought in the mind of man. They are perfect bookends of strength and mass! And so we recognize diversity accomplished through God always at his work of creation. Wow! This implication of deeds or work accomplished is not limited to earthly matters. It is inclusive of all creation throughout the universe. Man places limitation upon the term universe and he defines it as existing between two points of light, but universe relevant to God is infinite, without a frame of reference for our thoughts to grab hold of. We understand the concept of infinity as reality but we cannot encapsulate or bring closure to the reality of forever. The reality of sin appears as if there is no end in sight, but this is deception speaking to us. Yes, its progression has appeared to travel great distances and seems unstoppable within the appearance of the here and now reality of today, but as all things within nature there is a beginning and end, so too the days of evil's reign will find closure. Sin is progressive, in that, it continually corrupts through deception, until the light of truth is brought into the darkness that did not and would not understand. No one has ever equated deception with logic. Deception is superficial and dependent upon man's failure to seek truth; unwillingness to look underneath the offering presented. A brightly wrapped package is no indication of content and the wrapping with pleasing color may inspire favorable emotion, but emotions can and do fail us. Deception is but one aspect of sin incorporated within the toolbox of stealth-constructed lies.

Numbing

The numbing of righteous anger is brought about through the successive occurrences of sin; this is also deception. The shock that once caused us to shudder, no longer produces its initial impact. The conscience is collectively beaten battered broken and bruised by repeated psychological blows, in effort to have us recognize such behavior as a normal occurrence within the human condition. At some point the result may be to not permit information of this sort to enter the mainstream of society; it will no longer be considered news worthy, and perhaps, at that point in time evil will have free reign, no longer encumbered by the conscience of man. One example of such a separation of conscious awareness is the shockwave of disbelief and outrage, encompassing the world following the kidnapping of the Lindberg child in the first half of the twentieth century, March 1, 1932. Today there are *at least* tens of thousands of children abducted annually, and the outcry is nowhere to be heard. Do we really believe slavery has been abolished, or do we recognize it has changed its shape, is wearing a new suit of clothing and smiling in the brightest of daylight?

At one time in America's history there was an underground railroad transporting people out of the grip of slavery, and now, throughout the world, underground slave-traders are transporting children to the heart of evil. So true are the words of our Lord, **Revelation 2:5 "Yet I hold this against you: You have forsaken your first love. Remember the height from which you have fallen! Repent and do the things you did at first."** Repent and once again recognize the horrors associated with deception! In less than a hundred years sin has produced astounding numbness within the fabric of humanity. Let us remember, in the early twentieth century instantaneous communication was not available, and still the affront to our senses over the kidnapping and subsequent murder of one child, electrified and made us aware of the bold face of evil as it emerged upon the world scene, just a few short years prior to the horrors of World War Two. The clear difference between truth and the lie is the ability of truth to remain constant in its appearance; the lie is continually changing its externally manufactured packaging, designed to disallow the clarity of revelation, in order to capture and render us into disbelieving the atrocities committed, or at minimum, to render us into a state of indifference.

Progressive movement

Here's the word, *Progressive: "Progressing gradually over a period of time. Used to describe a disease that becomes more widespread or severe over time. Advocating social, economic, or political reform."* As the progression of sin advanced all of nature came closer to the limit God would permit, and in this, God commanded Noah to get ready for a sea voyage. All life was destroyed in the great flood.

Let us take a moment to look at the miracle of passive deception's abolition during the construction of the ark, as well as throughout the ordeal. God performed a miracle by arresting passive deception's instinctual influence between all life connected to the rescue effort. Distrust was replaced by trust and deception was replaced by truth, in order to accomplish the rescue mission set forth by God. The progression of sin and its corrupting influence upon those who failed to heed God's warning experienced their own personal destruction and end to the affront to all that is holy.

Once again sin is running unchecked and almost invisible due to the constant deception present in the progressive movement of today, which embraces tolerance in tiny bites that will eventually consume its victims. Not only does the tolerance of today deceive through its message of being sensitive to others, it runs counter to the knowledge of what we know is correct and acceptable to God. Within this progressiveness there is an attempt to ban truth and replace it with *correct thinking* as set forth by men. Not only do we have the *politically correct police,* we also have the *thought police* who are gaining in numbers through deceptive teachings within the educational system of today. We are teaching our children how to think in terms of what is acceptable to others. This is tantamount to placing limitation upon the thought process, or placing the spirit of man within a prison of only acceptable thoughts, as set forth and permitted by the gods of today; while all thoughts of God are denigrated by secular humanism running unchecked within a new age religion, determined to erase God from the language and thoughts of man. Those who have set the curriculum have set the morality of man at all time lows. This is tantamount to a form of post-birth-abortion for the youth of today. It says to them, *"We will erase the conscience of man (because there is no wrong within a godly existence) and in its place leave a vacuum of infinite indulgence answerable to no one but your self!"* It says to all believers of truth, who cannot and will not accept this deception, *"Some of us have evolved at a more rapid pace, and in this, the distinction between gods and men is defined."* It is at times very sad to see the harm deception does while in the motivating forms of position and power; such harm is multiplied when in the company of their sister greed.

Rainbow

⌁

During the deluge cold and pain
Fear and trembling threatened to reign
Noah was steadfast faith filled and bold
And all within the provision of God
Were grateful Noah had heeded the Lord.
Outside the Ark lamenting and crying
Confusion division and sudden the dying
Sudden the breath relieved from its hiding
And sudden the Ark upon water was rising.
Rising to cover the earth
A cleansing of soil toward promised rebirth.
Though awesome the flooding the land was restored
And sunshine was sent as a greeting to all
A colorful rainbow was placed in sky
Never again the waters shall rise.

⌁

Genesis 9:13

I have set my rainbow in the clouds, and it will be a sign of the covenant between me and the earth.

Purpose

What purpose they who think not of God?
Who will save this wanting lot?
A balance beam of right and wrong
Takes not a forward step
Toward he who for sinners kept
The Book of Life
Before man breathe his first breath.
No purpose save receive
The pardon from his throne appear
In flesh and blood behold
The sacrifice of God's own Son
He lives to save our souls.

Ephesians 1:11 In him we were also chosen, having been predestined according to the plan of him who works out everything in conformity with the purpose of his will.

Underground

Someone has to tell me why?
Why lies are lifted up and truth is driven down?
Why honesty's a wanderer and deception wears a crown?
Why deception is a normalcy and truth is rarely found?
Why integrity has its voice suppressed, hidden in a frown?
Why morality is stripped and tossed into a pile?
Why a blade of grass hides fissures deep and wide?
Why stealth and evil doing is applauded not surprised?
Why all that was and all there is amounts to nothing gained?
Why many at the surface are as dead as past remains?
Some invent a smile frontal and profiled
Hinting veiled indifference clinging like a shroud
Skull teeth and bone cannot make a sound
Lies are not permitted in the darkness underground.
All we are and nothing more except the soul so saved
Will enter into darkness grip-renewed in season find
Truth of promise given nevermore denied.
All we are and nothing more except of God survives
Here there is not darkness or fear of underground
Here the river beckons to all except the proud
Here is truth revealed and honesty is crowned.
A plan devised at night will be revealed in day
Facades of glittered gold in earthen vessels crowned
Hear the voice of truth the voice of justice found!
"Where are the lies you spoke in laughter sharpened proud?
Would that you could take a look, you'd find them underground."
Oh, now I know why?

**Romans 3:13-18 There is no one who is righteous, no one who
is wise or who worships God. All have turned away from God;
they have all gone wrong; no one does what is right, not even one.
Their words are full of deadly deceit; wicked lies roll off of their
tongues, and dangerous threats, like snakes poison, from their**

lips; their speech is filled with bitter curses. They are quick to hurt and kill; they leave ruin and destruction wherever they go. They have not known the path of peace, nor have they learned reverence for God.

A voice is heard in Ramah

A large segment of society desires to place limitations upon the fruit of the tree called man. Many within this segment actually masquerade as believers. Knowing God exists and professing belief will not negate their desire to live as gods in a world of self—indulgence. The allurement of the world has captured even some professed believers, aiding the purpose of evil, aimed directly at those incapable of self-defense. The poor and defenseless represent the same people they ardently defend, with hollow words, throughout the halls of government. They have included mankind into the fruit basket of commodities, under the mantle of gods wishing to allow growth of only wholesome products (their selves). Some portions of mankind are just unwanted fruit. Whether a tyrant king, like Herod of old, or a society claiming a right to choose who lives or dies, the underlying evil of deception still remains. We recognize that when Herod had unleashed his armed men to kill the firstborn male children two years old and younger, there was resistance from the parents of these children, and like all parents they defended with their lives the innocence God had placed into their care. Do we really think Herod overlooked the children in the womb? Do we really think there was discernment with regard to the gender of the children in the womb? Do we really believe a limitation was placed upon the destruction of innocence, then or now? Herod of old has been resurrected to once again destroy innocence within the womb of creation. The damage incurred does not end with the killing of the unborn, like all sin it has a progressive propensity to change everything moving forward. Constantly changing what was meant to be safe and secure into chaotic insecurity, through our refusal to comply with the directives set forth by God, as provider of our needs and author of how life is to be lived and cherished. Absent this recognition man is led to believe in limitation of ability and suffers defeat where otherwise victory would prevail. Man taking matters into his own hands and acting as a god will always find deceit at the root of his frustrations and defeats. The voice heard in Ramah has reverberated down throughout the centuries and into our present day. The intent is the same-slaughter of the innocence within the womb of humanity.

Down

❧

Happy voices tiny cheers
Contagious joy from girls and boys
Hearts alert to bursts of fired rounds
Intruding into the children's light
No hoop star shout of hey-hey pump
No jump rope slap with muffled taps
No playground giggles or schoolyard rap
It's darkness spoken
A chalk outline upon the ground captures not a sound
Echoes distant now cascade in memories of a child
As a crowd a cry is sent
Through the clouds and heavens rent
Urgent and exigent prayer
That pounds the chest and rips away pretense
Love's distinctive sound:
O God! Little boy down!

❧

Matthew 2:18 *A voice is heard in Ramah, weeping and great mourning, Rachel weeping for her children and refusing to be comforted, because they are no more.*

Deception in the world parallels God's truth, in that, deception is attempting to accomplish in both man and nature what can only be done by God; restoration to perfection of both man and the world he inhabits. Yes, there is the deeper theological recognition of good being derived through adversity, incorporated through the fall of man, but evil must not be confused with adversity. Hard times for man came about because of evil, the father of deception. In truth, when all things are restored to their beginnings mankind will be perfected, through the added knowledge brought about in part by experiencing adversity; God's love for us comes to us through knowledge existing in sacrifice. Without this knowledge we are destined to become a victim.

All of nature is taught through adversity

A flytrap plant (at minimal) should be assigned a teaching role for us, without prejudice regarding intent. The fly is led to its demise seeking the necessity for its continued existence. In many instances the fly is rewarded within the truthful offering of nature, but it is not cognizant of the deception within the world it inhabits.

Let's look at the wonderment of the spider and its web spinning ability, can we assign intentional deceit through thought? I suspect not. Is this display of web spinning genius a result of a built in mechanism purposely incorporated into creation's design as a means of stability within the continuation of life? This sounds more plausible. Could it be a means of achieving ecological balance and continued proliferation of life? This also sounds like the genius God would incorporate into creation. Unlike the flytrap plant the spider displays the appearance of purposeful thought, but I suspect it is a facet of creation that exhibits serious complexity that must be attributed to God's creative ability. Who knows for sure what thought process is at work? God said, **"My ways are not your ways"** and in this statement we recognize difference of thought incorporating the thinking process.

Should we then assign a non-thinking existence to everything beneath the level of man? Shouldn't we understand we don't know not only God's ways but the ways of nature as well? By our recognition of systemic operation within nature we find there must be intelligent design; a superior thought process at work. It is utterly incomprehensible to assume incalculable accidental derivatives merging to form the entirety of existence as we know it, and then compound these conclusions with hopeless futility, as an end result, makes no plausible sense within the context of genius displayed. Assumptions of accidental evolution are clearly deceptions with intent to deny God, and in turn lead many to their demise. Just like a fly trapped in a web deceit. To embrace hopelessness derived through the denial of God is to embrace the cruelest of deceptions. Not only does it lead to the demise of man, it impacts negatively all healthy aspects of existence within the context of truth suppressed within the fabric of man's soul; the inability to find freedom within the spirit of man, intended to seek God, finds instead, considerable depression and failure to experience true joy. Thus it appears that all of those who profess to be (elite), advanced within the human chain of evolutionary intelligence (their own theory) are not fools at all, rather, they appear to be deceivers.

By virtue of our recognition of good we endorse and advance understanding of holy intent within creation. As long as deception has tricked its way into our existence, we should find a remedial defense aimed at avoiding the destructiveness associated with failing to understand the harmful intent of its being. This is primarily done through the knowledge of God's word. Practical experience also lends to our understanding of life's pitfalls. Truth is the only shield capable to safeguard against lies. When a man expresses a caring position toward his fellow man and in the same breath acts contrary to his expressed beliefs therein lives deception. It used to be very easy to deceive people from one town to another; positions on modern concerns could change like the wind without too many noticing the change. Today, with all of the mind-boggling technology available, it appears to be very difficult to say one thing in California and go unnoticed in New York. Thus deception has had to change its tactics and coordinate its message throughout a worldwide audience; through all of this the common thread used to determine truth is the bible. In this immovable and unshakable truth, which is a thorn in the heart of deception, we find the satisfaction of knowing not only the ways of God, but also the tactics of the enemy.

Common pitfall

We find pitfall because it finds us unaware. Although its appearance seems acceptable to our understanding of truth that often fails us, it is nonetheless the essence of deception's power. Within a context of truth as proprietary (personal truth) deception finds victims by constantly changing its appearance. Deception presents truth as a variable from one person to the next. As such, truth is not a stationary and immovable monolith, rather, it is an evolving resource capable only of self-guidance (mostly incorrect) and restricted to the permissiveness of man's self cognizant sphere; unwilling to intrude upon another's perception out of fear of being denied acceptance, by worldly elite who attempt to bring about a utopian existence in a world absent God. We are unwilling to receive truth as emanating and originating from the beginning in God alone. And light was shone into darkness and darkness did not comprehend its gift of sight; the confines of pride refused to admit something greater than itself. A natural reaction to the unexpected shock of light's intrusion upon the eye is akin to emerging from a darkened movie theater. It is sudden, capturing by its presence, and instinctually our reaction is to recoil. The tiger has no fear or understanding of itself as a possible menu item until it is entangled by the constriction of a great snake. All too often we do not recognize the rationale or our basis for adopting long held beliefs, simply because we have not allowed the light of truth to enter into our existing darkness. Without light to bring illumination we may very well go through life believing darkness to be as good as it gets. But once light enters, there is no recourse but to recognize something outside of formerly held understanding, conclusively opposed to our previously held beliefs and narrowly fixed way of thinking. Yes, in this, *"that is your truth"* declaration, we find differing conflicting theologies within both religious and secular spheres of existence. Yes, there is theology within the secular world and it runs unchecked among the gods. Truth can only be recognized as perfect and immovable when its author is God. Today's manufactured truth offers to all the enamoring title of god, and this somehow is accepted, even when it is proven that man cannot escape the inevitable nightfall of existence.

Deception present within forceful thought

The idea of forceful is evidenced by the action and reaction derived. Whoever has hoped for something and subsequently has seen that hope materialize (this is a form of prayer) has actively sent thought into motion. The amount of force is contingent upon belief (faith) and strikes no allegiance with truth. That is to say, where faith is exercised a response will come irrespective of whether or not such faith is rightly focused; it is a spiritual principle. We may turn on a light switch, and as long as the wires are correctly connected we will get the desired result; turning on a switch with wires making improper contact will cause a direct short circuit, this will also produce a resulting response. Thought coupled with faith is like the light switch, once the circuit is made it will produce a positive or negative result. In the case of misplaced faith (short circuited thoughts) the resulting response can only be deception, designed to keep us away from focusing upon God.

Belief is fuel for movement of thought when focused outside of the natural realm. Within both the physical and supernatural (spiritual), force exerted is either automatic or willful and at times both. I will my finger to move and it does. I breathe as a function of the body and it is automatic. It is only when I am having difficulty breathing does my will attempt to aid in the function. We find prohibitions within scripture *(Deuteronomy chapter 18)* specifically prohibiting us entrance into certain areas, such as, not consulting mediums, magic or witchcraft. The reason is clearly for our good. God does not want us to focus our forceful thoughts in these areas because he does not wish us to enter into places totally devoid of truth. Faith exercised will always elicit a response; we find prohibitions against entering areas whose response will never properly return to us truth. We are told by Jesus, **"ask seek or knock"** and we will receive, find, or gain entrance into the supernatural realm where all things are possible with God. Thus it may be concluded that asking seeking and knocking is a spiritual principle that owes no allegiance to whether or not such faith is properly directed. Therein many are captured by false religions, such as Voodoo or Witchcraft that produces a response through exercised faith, having no allegiance with truth.

Thought has the ability to fatigue as deeply as physical exertion. Mental exercise prompts a desire to stop just as physical exertion produces a slowing reluctance by way of energy expended. There is unwillingness present at the outset of activity. We are reluctant to enter into thoughtful prayer, but like physical exercise, once the unwillingness is overcome the benefits are obvious. **"Thy will be done,"** must be recognized as the pinnacle of hierarchal purpose. Seeking understanding of what we have been given (once understood), removes in us an obstacle against spiritual growth, and we begin to identify purpose, direction and hope, beyond all barriers that were fixed into thoughts limiting man when we were apart from God. My mind wants to cease this exercise and roam free within the comfort zone of complacency, but as with *"pain comes gain"* so too exploration of thought brings forth its reward. In order for force to be present within the transference of thought there must be intelligible utterances. If my thoughts are incoherent my finger will not respond because the thought to move has not been given. The world knows of many languages within various groups of people, but common among all is the language of spirit. The spiritual language is not entirely dependent upon the confines of established word usage. Thought can make known intent that conveys emotion and feeling. Apart from a direct and forward line of communication (thought) to God, we find spiritual language present within parable usage; it incorporates depth of meaning and intent. Within parable usage the underlying depth of truth and its direct impact is expressed through our recognition. In this form of communication deceit has no place of residency. To speak tacitly through common word usage is recognized as a form of indirect communication that has the resemblance of parables. This fabric of thought is not necessarily free of deceitful content, but truth conveyed in scriptural parables cannot be corrupted.

I now begin to understand the words of Augustine. "He who sings prays twice." I find within this statement there is a blending of both internal and vocalized forms of communication that exhibits a most forceful transference of thought. Again, in every form of communication the conveyance of understandable thought must be present in order to encourage a correct or positive result. Herein we find truth in spoken words, symbolic actions or internalized thought. Actions can convey intelligible thought as in, *"I was moved by what transpired."* There are exceptions or fringe interpretative utterances, namely a scream that can convey meaning, dependent upon just how it emanates (immediate urgency, mournful overtones etc.), these are narrowly defined but not limited in force within its content. The cry of a bird in the nest, "Abba, Father!" calls out to the creator of all things and God hears their recognition of dependency. And so no matter the means of communication utilized God not only listens but there is no doubt he fully understands.

Collective forceful thought

1 Corinthians 1:10 I appeal to you, brothers, in the name of our Lord Jesus Christ, that all of you agree with one another so that there may be no divisions among you and that you may be perfectly united in mind and thought. Within the world there are many differing thoughts and many of our observations show to us advantages that may be derived through collective effort as a people and also as a nation or church. Let's look for a moment at two of man's early discoveries of gain through the lever and pulley. We have found the longer the lever or number of pulleys added the capacity for achieving work is increased proportionally in the form of mechanical advantage. So it must also be true with the addition of force (group prayer) to cognitive awareness of God. A voice cries out in the wilderness, how much more will a shout from a multitude? We come to this awareness through God's grace that allows us perception in all areas of existence, experience or intuition, of which, when presented in truth becomes for us illumination, where otherwise darkness will prevail. While it is true that we cannot construct a lever that will move the world, the concept recognized is nonetheless true. Jesus taught,

"A house divided cannot stand," in response to those who had insulted the Holy Spirit within him. The lesson derived is that where there is unity a stabilizing factor exists. Disunity will cause a weakening upon an existing structure, or, as in the case of Jesus, he pointed out to those so easily led to believe that it was the power of evil that enabled him to do good. If truth is to be told these religious leaders were intent to find fault with our Lord no matter what, in order to remain in the spotlight of human accolades. This also is a telling aspect of the ruling religious inasmuch as they readily assumed evil's deception was at work in the miracles performed by our Lord. Would it not have been more natural for the truly religious to recognize the power of God at work? Yes, Jesus was absolutely correct in his labeling them as the children of their father, the devil. So many of us have constructed our own house and live by their own rules of confinement, actively pursuing limitless lives of unfulfilled purpose, all the while never recognizing the inherent ability to venture out into the expanse of eternity and enter into the kingdom of God. We are taught to love God with all of our heart mind soul and strength, but how many of us even take the time to not only understand but to also desire such a love? All too often we neglect recognizing these aspects of our existence and by doing so we lose the collective impetus or energy that is us, the people of God in Christ, resulting in a net loss within the body of Christ. Paul the apostle of Christ had brought into the light, divisions within the church of Corinth, and it appears many today have not heeded his call to unity. Yes, within all banners of Christianity there exists unity of canon law, but the digressive nature of disunity concerning theological division, major and minor, distracts

and otherwise weakens where strength should exist. We often are dismayed by the direction a few people in this world would force us into taking, and still we fail to exercise the voice most potent. Yes, we are told we have a voice in this world but it seems no one is listening to our cry. This world that ignores the voice of truth, fails to recognize censure cannot be accomplished within the thoughts of man and neither can the force of his cry, *"Abba, Father!"* find unresponsive results. When we are united in mind and heart the greatest potential to overcome worldly deceptions, as well as its distractions, finds minimal opportunity to once again intrude upon us. Again, in unity there is collective forceful thought.

Caveman

It takes a lot of faith to believe in random chance.
"Early from the primal swamp emerged that old caveman," they say.
Knuckle dragging hairy cat carnal living brute with bat.
Tiny little pea sized brain hunter of the smaller game.
"Treetop swinging early man had lots of fortitude," they say.
He must have had a real bad day to make him act so rude.
Knuckle dragging forehead slope
I see no resemblance in these caveman folk.

Halls of higher learning echo clarity sincere
Enough to brave an octave strong advancing from the rear
Unaware the willingness of ears
Spoon fed primal soup mixed with lies and fear
By the worldly gods whose motives they keep hidden
For if the truth was told their lies would be forbidden.

"Evolving toward euphoric state,"
So say those who think their great.
Absent road sign warnings or intent to brake
Lacking all stability that only comes through faith.
The gods upon the earth command demand threaten
"We know what is best for you so don't you be forgetting!"
They tell us,
"Only we can solve the problems you perceive."
At least that is what they want us to believe.
They pick and choose who lives and dies
Based upon the wallet size.
Do we wonder why cash is idolized?
"Choose a clinic take a pill don't you worry about the bill.
We will care for caveman needs just remember vote for me!"

Manufactured crisis one after another
Keeping godless gods above the dusty roads
A caveman has to travel and carry heavy loads.

One lie after another piled high and deep
Is weight enough for any man to want to rest and sleep.
Thank God for his clarity that makes them look as clowns
These jesters primp and proper on the outside wearing smiles
But deep inside their blackened core corruption there is found
The haughtiness of pride and silence made from shrouds.

Matthew 8:20 Jesus replied, "Foxes have holes and birds of the air have nests, but the Son of man has no place to lay his head."

Heart mind soul and strength

All of the above must be focused with full capacity upon God, with love. We don't normally separate each aspect of our being and look to see just what is there. However, we should at least have an idea of what it is we are urged to do by Jesus. In order to solidify this united effort of heart mind soul and strength we must be able to recognize what we are looking for within the function of each comprising the totality of man. In fact, that is perhaps exactly what Jesus is referring to by his separation into sections the parts of man, of which both spiritual and physical are implied. There are dual definitions of understanding, inasmuch as a coin has two sides (heads and tails) but the details are not revealed unless there is prior knowledge of its appearance, or else we turn it over to reveal its underlying truth. The heart of man is the physical beating muscle incorporated within the body but the flipside understanding is the place from which emotion is derived. Again, there is duality of understanding within the other aspects of our being. This is perhaps due to the close knit of the fabric itself. It is not strange to find duality within definitions; it happens all of the time within primary and secondary word meanings and usage. Still not many of us venture underneath the projection of deeper underlying understanding until we are found to be misunderstanding, and then it is the seeking force of the mind (spirit) that does the inquiry. And so, I have arrived at the point where I recognize the mind as the thinking aspect of man and this also is tightly woven into the fabric of corporeal existence; the physical brain. I also understand this thinking faculty has ability to exist apart from the body. It is the thinking aspect from which is derived the quality of life. *Soul* is a Greek word meaning, *"life"*. The quality of life is determined by our choice, either to follow the blueprint clearly defined by God, or else, we choose to be a self-directing vehicle absent headlights necessary for driving in the darkness that permeates and detracts from a true vision of reality. It's then that we are faced with the same dilemma that caused the demise of the fly. We must love God with all of our heart mind soul and strength in order to be fully equipped to fulfill our purpose set forth from the beginning. We failed to understand deception is not our friend; has never acted as an early warning system focused upon our good, or made in our image or original likeness. I must at this time conclude there is so much intertwined functionality among all terms and definitions comprising the totality of man, and in this recognition reiterate to myself the understanding that each individual has both a commonality and uniqueness within a singular plurality. This singular plurality is expressed in scripture by recognition from God referring to the first of mankind, ***"Now the man has become like us."*** God's reference was to himself—the Holy Trinity. A singular plurality expressed in the Hebrew word, ***"elohim"*** *or* ***"us."*** In order for us to love God with our entire being we must first of all be honest with ourselves. Jesus said of Nathaniel, ***"Here is a true Israelite, in whom there is nothing false."*** Let's make no mistake Jesus had recognized in Nathaniel a person who had loved God with all of his heart mind soul and strength. It is this that guarantees prayer is not only heard but enters into God's presence with the power of humility. We are basically saying, "God we love you more than we love our self." Moreover, Nathaniel had understood his dependency upon God for all things, and in this he was able to overcome the inherent desire to recoil or run from truth.

All too often we look out into the world of others with a critical eye and without awareness avoid self-examination. When we do look at our self we find a permissive inclination of acceptability present within the awareness of right and wrong, but this is mostly ignored by our unwillingness to comply and our denial of inability to do what is right. That is to say, it may be a subconscious acceptance of defeat. When we honestly look inside our self the light that is shone may cause an acknowledgement of reaction through physical manifestation; a twinge of guilt in the gut or a contraction that shows to us the reality of sin, alive, within the body, purposely attempting to remain hidden. God is, *"I am,"* and evil continually attempts to remain hidden within the encapsulating confinement of, *"I am not."* This coincides with the truth that thought exemplifies for us the reality of life and the absence thereof has a representative in the world of the dead. Again, the twinge or admonishing contraction of sin, being exposed, may not have been made through a cognitive force of awareness. I will my finger to move and it does so with my recognition and expectation, but with the uncovering of sin it is akin to light hitting the eyes upon exiting a darkened movie theater, it is unexpected and the result is reactionary, but nonetheless an action that has to have a cause. The cause may be the light of God's grace bringing exposure to our lives through recognition of sin's existence. Some have understood this truthful grace, but shortly thereafter return to the darkened movie theater and the illusory comforts it provides. Just as Adam and Eve ran from God in recognition that they were naked (exposed as disobedient), the knowledge of wrong when focused honestly upon our self automatically causes a flight reaction away from the light of truth.

A twinge within the pit

A physical twinge of acknowledgement is caused by the appearance of understanding contained in light. Recognition can be advanced to us by physical manifestation brought about by the *Spirit of Truth.* It's the internal searchlight in man-God with us. Reaction to sin's exposure encompasses both physical and emotional spectrums. Awareness causes a reaction that sends that which is hidden into a state of panic and flight. It is surprised and in this there is a recoiling action. *"For every action there is an equal and opposite reaction."* This is applicable within thought as well as physical occurrence. Additionally, there is a transferable medium between both physical and spiritual prime movers. That is, I will my finger to move and it does, additionally the body speaks its own language through both a sense of wellbeing or pain. My foot hurts and in this I am moved to action to find relief. There is duality also within our physical nature that must understand righteous and unrighteous (sinful) behavior hidden in the affinitive relationship with sin. As such, it is also true of the thoughts of man expressed as either good or bad. Negative thoughts cannot be hidden, emotion as well as thought is revealed externally through the eyes, which are the portals of communication. Expression of thought is immediately presented in the spiritual plain of our existence; nothing is hidden from God. How true are the words of the old hymn? *"Rock of ages let me hide myself in thee."*

We cannot run away from our nature but we can give our self away to God, wherein we are assured to not find ruin in the sting of unrighteous thought and deed. And so, I have become aware through the unmasking of sin that lives in me. In this awareness of right and wrong expressed through conscience I have also found communicative speech of deeper implication manifesting itself within a physical twinge of guilt.

The movement of recoil manifesting itself physically through surprise is an indicator of the presence of sin that lives in me. Scripture alerts us to the awareness of all things hidden; the sin in us rules our lives. So sin is alive in us and rules our lives, so what must we say with regard to this force opposed to my will? *"I have seen the enemy and he is me!"* I cannot say, *"The devil made me do it."* This is evidenced by my recognition of Jesus as the **"Son of God."** Since no one can say that Jesus is the **Son of God** without the **Holy Spirit** being in residence, I find there is no room for the devil to inhabit my soul. Thus I must admit that it is *"I"* my physical nature, possessing the corrupting sin of old. In this understanding sin has been exposed and there is no place for it to remain hidden. I recognize now a deeper awareness of the presence of God, without whom the life I now live could not exist. Alone I could not exert the knowledge of right into corresponding action. Therein we find the words of the apostle Paul's recognition of the conflict in man to be correct, **"Praised be the God and Father of our Lord Jesus Christ who rescues me from this body that is taking me to my death."**

Approved status

Today there are many whose denial of God and belief in their advanced state of evolution, awarding god status, do so with understanding and anticipation of the one who will grant to them permanent status of both position and belief. It is as if there is anticipation for the ***"god of this world"*** to show himself and bestow upon them true godlike status. Therein the separation between gods and men will have received authority to their existing belief system. Certainly it sounds as if they are looking for Mount Olympus to be upon the earth, wherein they, the gods, are worshipped and adored by the lesser inhabitants of the land. Many have already received godlike status because of celebrity obtained within the public eye. These are even called, "idols" and "stars" which sounds to me like a prelude or stage setting for what is to come. When the Antichrist does make his appearance upon the world stage there will be eagerness to embrace him, for the sole purpose of maintaining their presently enjoyed positions of authority over others. Just as it is so difficult for many a rich man to lament over impending death, so shall it be for those who have invested in lies that uplift to man godlike status and deny to God what belongs to him.

Insight

I'm in my house but in this room I've never been.
Unrealized potential inside a cobweb door
No sail to catch a breeze, or hammer find a nail
The switch for casting light into this room has failed.
Length without width, hope without cause, echo without volume
A voice inside a book, no one hears its call.
A blank unwritten page, future without past
Time without meaning and sentence never grasped
Like drifting in a dream and never seeing self
Like finding need for action past the time of doubt
Like opening of the blinds made of synergistic haze
Like falling in a dream and never touching ground
Like paint thrown at a canvass is splattered all about
Like speech that is confusing without clarity defined
Like swirling blizzard snow conceals what's inside
Like a beating heart whose rhythm sees a line
Sudden is the present strong the view we find
Inside the door so shielded by cobweb thread so fine.
Away the props and scripted nays-coveted and saved
Away debris of cluttered past where now we stand amazed
Away to thoughts unfathomed—beneath dust of errant care
Away the empty darkness denying sight to stares
Away to coinage absent depth and signposts thin and flawed
Away to clouded meaning absent ardent force
Away to veiled concealment in journey dark with gloom
Away to all that littered and cluttered up this room
With lamp now at my feet I see a shadow's bones
A serpent in a pit awaiting dinner's bell
This is not my room! It's a tomb, on its way to hell!
I'm listening now, O God of Light, Savior King.
"My son
Inside all tombs captives find
A wall they cannot climb
A top they cannot reach

A bottom that's unending
A place echoes can't speak
A path without beginning
Dark that never ends
Until one is forgiven
The cobwebs of their sins."

⤙ ⤚

John 18: 37-38 "You are a king, then!" said Pilate. Jesus answered, "You are right in saying I am a king. In fact, for this reason I was born, and for this I came into the world, to testify to the truth. Everyone on the side of truth listens to me." "What is truth?" Pilate asked.

Government gods

A dictator's slogan: No man no problem.
A government god: No man no cost.
A dictator's title: Dear Leader.
A government god: Servant Master.
A dictator's scheme: Brown shirts.
A government god's dream: National police force.
A dictator's solution: Firing Squads.
A government god: Death panels.
Numbering of man's days had already been decided by God.
Apparently deception has an insatiable appetite.
Permissiveness is illusion's song when right's denounced instead of wrong.
When sensibility no longer shocks shakes or tumbles political stock.
Dependency is slavery to the hand that writes the check.
Honest men still say, "I worked for this!"
Society has labored long to bring us laws of good.
"We care for you with many allotment beats per heart."
Generous are the limits the new government gods set forth.
A rooster crows with each new day waking us from sleep.
A factory whistle signals work and a time to cease.
A government god pretends-unknown is the language that we speak.
A school bell sings a special song serving food so bland
And nothing on the cold steel tray speaks of God's great plan.
A government god speaks "hope and change" nothing has depth and all is staged.
Nodding cheers canned approval cardboard stares
Prison walls with windows made of lies
Beautiful landscape paintings with mechanical breeze
Woven as if mortared sewn and weaved as thread
Blinded by illusion and all within are dead.
A servant denies his master and his worth plummets like lightning falls.
Surely the master's spoken but he does not heed his call.
We call them politicians but that's much too kind.
Leeches have a nature and parasites we understand
Government gods have a choice bend a knee or upright stand.

35

To be blind makes not a fool but a fool is surely blind.
His hand can feel the fire sending truth up to the mind
Still he can't withdraw while immersed in flames of pride.
A gilded cage denies flight.
A beautiful prison appoints inmate guards.
What has changed?
Freedom.

Revelations 13:16 The beast forced all people, small and great, rich and poor, slave and free, to have a mark placed on their right hands or on their foreheads. No one could buy or sell without this mark that is the beast's name or the number that stands for the name.

SIN AND DOUBT

In this chapter a correlation between the sin nature of man and the impact it has upon faith will be examined in an effort to overcome the negative aspects of doubt. Intent is to build awareness of the forces or tendencies drawing us away from God. Once recognized, we may then minimize the negative consequence hindering spiritual growth in both faith and understanding of our relationship with God. Spiritual growth should not be looked upon as something that increases as one can imagine a plant sprouting, rather, it may be better understood by the absence or diminished frequency of sin. With the absence of sin, good fruit will come forth to inhabit the place formerly occupied by weeds.

Matthew 28:16-17 Then the eleven disciples went to Galilee, to the mountain where Jesus had told them to go. When they saw him, they worshiped him; but some doubted.

The above scripture quote takes place after the resurrection of Jesus, and still some doubted what their eyes clearly saw. Apart from the expression of doubt exhibited by some of the disciples, also included in the above scripture is the worship of Jesus. I point this out to those who doubt the divinity of Christ. Jesus did not stop the disciples from worshiping him. As such, his acceptance is answer to those who would reduce his stature below equality with God. Apologetics in this area is not the aim of this chapter, however, because within this depiction we find both acceptance and doubt it is important to understand that all of the disciples are depicted as worshiping Jesus, even though some clearly doubted what was self evident. When we find our self in doubt it is then we must resort to worship; in worship we are given the necessary spiritual structure that overcomes our natural inclinations to deny truth. Sin is more than a conscience headache. It continually attempts to make dull the sword of the Spirit. It cradles the denial of God and inhibits truth. Our human nature is sinful. This should not be confused with the various kinds of sin. Rather, it is our very existence that has been corrupted. The redemption of man is a two-part process. First we are born again and receive a new spirit, the bible calls this receipt a ***"down payment"*** that assures us of our salvation. However, the body is awaiting renewal that will come through being resurrected to life everlasting. Man disobeyed the command of God and the consequence of disobedience was absorbed into our total existence as human beings. We were changed. Imperfection became the reality of our existence. When a substance is incorporated into another a different reality comes into being and the former will no longer exist. In the disobedience of man his totality was changed from a state of holiness to that which is denied the claim of belonging to God. Man's days no longer equaled eternity. Like an untreated infection sin lives in us. From the moment of disobedience declivity was established and struggle began, sin seized opportunity, and we, like lightning falling were destined to return to the dust of the earth. We were denied access to the ***"Tree of Life"*** and dispossessed from paradise, but God went with us in the knowledge gained through disobedience. We then began to understand the cost associated with sin. The condemnation of conscience mocked our failure to trust in God's prohibition, and all things were then subjected to doubt, brought about by the advent of deception's emergence from the shadow of evil's intent. Right and wrong is not just conceptual, it is fact. We recognize stealing is wrong and murder is wrong, even those who murder and steal do not want to be murdered or have their goods stolen. It will make even those who commit crimes angry to be a victim. Therein we see truth in its universally unshaken undeniable strength, not only conceptual but actual fact. One consequence of sin is called conscience. All of us, either victim or criminal find agreement within conscience. It brings to us the awareness of evil in the world. It established a questioning posture, asking if things presented to us are true. From the moment of deception's birth the doorway of doubt was brought into existence and has continually forced us to divert our focus in order to weigh and consider consequences of a failure to recognize its appearance. By opening the doorway through disobedience doubt took-up residence within our thinking faculty and it became a part of our reality. The word of God has been given to us as the antibiotic against this condition; it is pure and complete truth. By doubting God's pronounced prohibition we entered a downward spiral culminating in the actual act of disobedience. By accepting doubt, sin seized its opportunity for fruition and we made it a companion and component of our existence.

We had never been exposed to the curveball of deception and like trusting children we listened to the voice of sin without doubting. We doubted God's word simply because we heard the corruptor's voice present to us the promise of things unknown. What horror must have invaded the hearts of those (so trusting), at the recognition of deception? Certainly this serpent, this great deceiver, was not unknown to them, for he had access to the garden of God. Trusting children, listening to the voice of a corrupt adult. Conscience is a nice word that literally means, "With the knowledge or understanding of what is right and wrong." "Con" from the Latin meaning "With" and "Science" meaning "Knowledge." Some ask, "Why did God allow man to sin?" Certainly, "He could have shielded us from the Evil One's deception and protected us from ourselves." The answer may simply be, it was necessary for mankind to fall upon hard times, because God wanted instilled in us the character traits that can only be appreciated through overcoming adversity. Tough love? Was God complicit in our downfall? Not really, we were fully aware of the prohibition set forth, and in this awareness we rejected obedience for the allurement of the unknown. Prior to disobedience we were not burdened with the knowledge of right and wrong. It was not until we began to contemplate the actual act of disobedience did the slithering encroachment of sin find footing of possible surety. However, God knew beforehand how we would choose regarding his prohibition. As such, within the plan of God for us, we lost temporarily our immortality and gained added awareness necessary for the finishing aspects of creation. Deception threw us a lemon and God made lemon juice out of our injury.

Without the first of mankind falling into sin what need would we have for courage? Who's threatening us? What need for mercy and forgiveness? Who did wrong? What need for compassion? Who's suffering? Appreciation of God's love for us, without adversity entering into our existence was an equation we could not understand. Those who receive mercy are grateful and only the recipient fathoms the gift. God loved us and still he allowed us to be separated from him for our own good. Much later it was Jesus who suffered the ultimate separation from God as he took upon himself the sins of the world. By doing so, reclamation of what belonged to God began (in the formal sense of purchase price paid) and the learning of hard lessons set-forth by hard times and struggles was initiated. We understood the pronouncements of good and the denouncements of evil but it was not until the advent of Christ's victory over death, did we receive the ability to not only hear but to heed the inner voice of truth that cost so much for us to acquire.

Even with redemption the sin that lives in us has the penchant ability to erode our faith. Just as the first creation ran-off and hid after recognizing their sin of disobedience, we also have an instinctual or reflexive response (closely associated with self-preservation) to flee from holiness. Sin cannot approach God and so our nature is continually pulling us away. This fleeing is done on a conscious level, but is also taking place within the automatic mechanism incorporated within the body, not dependent upon conscious thought. When people are held within darkness, they are denied the light of truth, and remain unaware of light's freedom-giving qualities, that dispel imaginations produced within a world without light. Sounds may be heard in the dark but no one can be sure of the cause unless light reveals the surroundings. Our nature embraces lies (strongly hides from the reality of consequence) rather than come into the light of truth. Sin repels us away from God and this causes us to doubt. The further we are pulled into darkness the more we are given to be unsure of grace, and fall victim to doubt. Even we who have been allowed into the light are not immune to the natural instinct to flee from holiness when we sin. While we are consciously aware of being clothed with the righteousness of Christ and permitted into the presence of God, our nature makes it impossible to remain sinless in thought and/or deed, thus a tug-of-war is established between body and spirit. Our physical nature will produce the fruit of its existence and our new spirit, received at rebirth, will produce the good things of God. As such, we must recognize our need to run toward God and never to allow the condemnations associated with failure to place distance between God and us. Perhaps this is one reason why Paul writes, *1 Thessalonians 5:16-17 "Be joyful always; pray continually; give thanks in all circumstances, for this is God's will for you in Christ Jesus."* The one who is joyful signals to all the knowledge of God, and the one who prays constantly, will never succumb to the eroding aspects of sin and doubt. We will holdfast to the surety that is God's grace. Most of us have experienced the reflexive response of shielding our eyes, when emerging from darkness into the brightness of the sun. Our response to the light is quick and determined after only a few hours of darkness, say, within a movie theater. A lifetime within the darkness of unknowing is dispelled by the joy of truth as its light enters through the doorway to our hearts. God's light, does not repel us, it surrounds and protects.

Apart from the first of God's creation, let us take a moment to look at the biblical account of Job, in order to exemplify what must have been an excellent relationship between both God and Job, made strong through communication established in prayer. What happened to Job was not exclusive to him and his family. Satan tested him (extremely) because God had declared him to be his servant, and because God approved of him. On several levels Satan wanted to disprove the pronouncement of God concerning Job as a faithful servant, but suffice to say, Satan was probing and tormenting him in order to find or produce doubt, centering on God's friendship, that he knew must accompany the sin nature of Job. There is a great difference in the approach to Job as opposed to Adam and Eve. Satan's antagonisms compared to the enticements accompanying the first of God's creation is tantamount to the usage of a sledgehammer in place of a feather. Adam and Eve did not have a sin-nature they had to be attracted to sin through deception. Job was cognizant of the consequence of sin, while the first of mankind had no concept of wrong. As such Job was treated harshly due to the belief of Satan that Job would not serve God without the blessings he enjoyed. It was inconceivable to Satan that Job could remain faithful. The first of mankind doubted God but Job did not. Because of Job's close connection to God (prayer life) he was able to withstand the erosion of faith that normally would accompany hard times and struggles. Satan had thought his destructive work upon mankind was total and complete, within the context of damage achieved through original sin. He (Satan) is shocked, by the awakening of his wrong assumption. He finds God approving the man called Job, even with the knowledge that Job is a man whose nature has been corrupted. So we see, that for us who are also tested and probed by evil's intent, there's a desire on the part of evil to have us denounce the grace and love we have received, in order to return us to the hidden agenda we formerly found ourselves inhabiting. On a deeper level it is evil attempting to find fault with God, in order to remove the barrier of God's perfection. That is, if he (Satan) can prove God's determination concerning Job to be incorrect, he will have removed the barrier of perfection baring him from making challenge to God's throne. The coexistence between sin and doubt and the corrosive aspect upon belief is woven deeply into the fabric of man. There really is no difference between us, and Job, God has declared us to be family. This status will always attract testing. It is up to us to prove God correct to bestow upon us his mercy.

Recognition of need

Mark 9:19. "O unbelieving generation," Jesus replied, "how long shall I stay with you? How long shall I put up with you? Bring the boy to me." Jesus had come upon some of his disciples and teachers of the law arguing. The disciples of Jesus could not drive-out an evil spirit from a boy. The father of the child wants Jesus to help. He asks for help and adds to the request, **"If you can?"** Jesus replies, **"If you can?"** and continues by saying, **"Everything is possible for him who believes."** Within that statement by Jesus we see the potential for our own faith. The man laments his condition by stating: **"I do believe; help me overcome my unbelief!"** In this statement by the man we see the conflict of belief and disbelief simultaneously present in all of us because of the sin nature seeking to hide from truth. It is no wonder Jesus quantifies the strength of faith in terms we can understand; faith the size of a mustard seed can accomplish the impossible, sadly, doubt the size of a mustard seed can prevent it. So true is the scripture that says, **Matthew 15:8 "These people honor me with their lips, but their hearts are far from me."** We can now begin to appreciate the meaning of a double-minded man. He is a man exhaling the truth of God with his intellect and simultaneously denying this truth within the darkness of his heart. The men arguing with the disciples were teachers of the law. They had seen or heard of the miracles performed by Jesus and still their sin-nature (perhaps the repelling thorns of jealously and pride) kept them blind to the truth before their eyes. There is always the exception, some know truth but consciously align themselves with evil in order to gratify their own desires. This is the case with the Evil One and all of those who make the decision to rebel against God, with knowledge of his supreme authority. How great then is the pull of desire that will knowingly rebel against God, fully aware of ultimate demise? Yes, in many there is a non-belief in God, and subsequently they fail to recognize the need to have their sin nature arrested by grace. In many, anger is produced over the mere mention of the God they do not believe exists, this contradicts logic, highlights the lie they live, and heralds the truth living deep within their core but adamantly refuse to admit! Truth will always rattle the cage holding mankind captive. It's no wonder, "bad news sells." We have an attraction for sin it's our nature. It's not counter to the grain of desire pulsing within our veins. Thus there's a struggle within us to do what we know is good, but we cannot do it until the knowledge of God permeates our lives and sets us free to be what God intended. Conscience is an intricate part of our judgmental process. Like a navigational compass pointing us in the direction God wants us to travel. It may be accepted as the very voice of God instilled within, from the inception of hard times and struggles.

Understanding desire controls the fire

The spirit is supernatural in creation's origin, as such, was never intended to be dominated by the subordinate nature of the flesh. The spirit in man is God giving of himself, but the flesh was created from the earth. The flesh is subordinate because it is created and the spirit is of God himself. The potter can never be subordinate to the pot. I do not think with my foot, but the foot can communicate to me an ailment. The flesh is not the thinking faculty of man, rather, it is the aspect of man that makes us human and contains an alert mechanism installed by God, bringing to us awareness of hunger, thirst, pain and other aspects of life. If allowed to rule, excess will always be demanded by our human desires. Like a raging fire that will never say enough, so long as fuel, oxygen and temperature are present, desires and dictates of human nature cannot be removed from a leadership role until truth sets us free; until truth puts out the flames. With truth there is understanding and in understanding there is God's light illuminating his grace. Sin is the monkey wrench that is thrown into God's creation, placing us into an out of order condition. Incorporated into the design of man is an automatic system that brings attention to our bodily needs. This is a good system and when working properly maintains bodily functions at optimum abilities. However, like a failure of a governor that controls and regulates the speed of a turbine the needs of man can be thrown into unwanted and dangerous operation when the thought process is overridden, that is, when the thought process is not in control. Want and desire can be mistaken for need and in this failure to discern, excess will never find satisfaction. When we know the warning or alert mechanism is not working properly we may then take action to repair the condition. Understanding our propensity toward wrong, when ruled by the corrupt nature of the body is a great step toward achieving victory. In addition to recognition of sin's rule we must also realize we need help to defeat this body that has usurped the rightful place of our thinking faculty.

The fire of God is greater than the fire of desire

Regaining control and lessening human desire is accomplished by realizing something is not working properly, and it's not our thinking faculty. It's not we making poor choices in our lives, it is the sin that rules and dictates. Let's look for a moment at the prophet Jeremiah, he had become reluctant to do what God required and declared his intention to not mention God any longer. He is then compelled to do what is right because the very presence of God had become a permanent part of his being, it was like fire imprisoned within his bones. As such, he had no choice in the matter. The presence of God within his life shattered the rebellion emanating from a desire of flesh to once again rule in his life. In actuality, Jeremiah had given admittance (his reasoning) to the natural desire to repel from God, under the excuse attributed to his personal troubles associated with all who point-out the failures of others. In this case his thinking (intent) and corporeal desire was in agreement. The fire of God is greater than the fire of intent and desire. God's fire destroys the duality of outward physical presentation and inner hidden agenda, attempting to deceive others as well as our self. Rebellion is a veil designed to obscure and deny the reality of man's helplessness. It is the outward expression of sin that desires tenacious control through an alert system never intended to rule. Doubt, brought about by sin's deception, stokes the flame of desire, targets the core of our being, and attempts to destroy our freedom to choose. This is the true intent and depth of darkness, but God's light emanating from within radiates outward and restores a broken system, that has impulsively reacted to constant signaling stimulants presented externally and from within. Until our hearts are focused upon God the lip service reality prevails. The apostle Paul inquires, *1 Corinthians 3:17 "Don't you know that you yourselves are God's temple and that God's Spirit lives in you?"* He is asking this question of us who have recognized God and have been born again, because many have found themselves slowly returning to a former way of life. He recognizes that while our conscience is making us aware of right and wrong, he could not, and neither could we adhere to the warnings of conscience, because we were ruled by our sin nature. And so we have within us the struggle to do what is right. Anytime we place ourselves at the pinnacle of importance we invite erosion of the character traits gained by sacrifice and adversity. When we dilute the character of virtue we invite sin and doubt to erode the fabric of freedom and faith. Through external means there is an abundance of struggles that continually attempt to distract us from the truth that God exists, and he has not left us. Through all of our struggles God has always remained with us. *Matthew 28:20 "And surely I will be with you always, to the very end of the age."* The message of Christ that continues to reverberate is one in which he continually states the reality of God. All of the prophets proclaimed this message but they were not heeded. As such God sent his Son and still people refused to render to God that which belongs to him. The disciples and all who call upon the name of the Lord in good times and in times of struggle proclaimed the reality of God. So must we, for even the smallest of voices can impact a life with the message of Christ.

Now, back to the failure on the part of the disciples to drive out an evil spirit from a boy. We find that Jesus is successful. He frees the child from the evil spirit's influence and the disciples ask, ***"Why is it we could not?"*** Jesus tells them, ***"This kind requires prayer."*** What Jesus may actually be saying is that it takes more than words to drive out the bad influences in our lives, more than lip service. The child who heeds the advice of his parents will not find himself exposed (as was the first creation) by the deception present in this world. Listening is a form of communication. It's a form of prayer.

Doubt is persistent

Let's look at the story of the rich man and the beggar named Lazarus, as told to us by Jesus in the gospel of ***Luke (16:19-31).*** It is my guess that this account is a depiction of what is to come, in general terms, because Jesus places the rich man in the circumstance of eternal damnation, clearly post-judgment, and it centers on the consequence befalling those who fail to see the hardships of the poor. However, the example showing the persistence of doubt within the story is supportive of the attributes of doubt. In death the rich man has no identity, while Lazarus enjoys not only the surroundings of paradise but he has his identity intact. In life the rich man had everything he wanted and obviously was not burdened with the struggles that accompanied Lazarus. Even in death the rich man still did not understand Lazarus was no longer his servant, or dependent upon the crumbs that fell from his table. He was asking Abraham to have Lazarus bring to him a drop of water to place on his tongue, but was told, a great divide separates them and no one can crossover. He then entreats Abraham to allow someone to, ***"return from the dead"*** to warn his brothers of the place he now found himself in. There's little doubt the rich man would have volunteered his services. Abraham responds by stating, ***"Your brothers have Moses and the prophets and even if someone were to come back from the dead they still would not believe."*** Here again, is the doubt that persists, even if we should see truth raised from the dead! As in the subject verse of this chapter, Jesus had been resurrected from the dead and his disciples (brothers) still had doubts. Even if someone were permitted to return from the dead to tell of the hardship that befalls those denied the presence of God, people would still find doubt present, and injecting itself into the reality of what is clearly seen. The purpose of sin is to destroy, to deny God his rightful place of leadership, and to deny the penalty attached to its stigma through doubt. Erosion of faith through doubt, created by sin, can manifest itself within innumerable actions, aimed at the continuance of captivity and all of its accompanying baggage. These erosive distractions, away from reality, are sometimes called addictions or compulsive behavioral dictates. Our captivity prior to salvation was acutely terminal, so much so, we sought to find release from the condemnations of conscience within the shadow of doubt, made manifest by sinful lifestyles that offered to us the illusion of peace, through drugs and activities designed to distract us from the reality of our condition.

Shadow

Get behind me, O doubt!
Your time has ended.
Your shadow is transparent.
Your whisper wanes and fails.
Your attachment is severed.
Your song of mourning, sorrow, impending doom and death
Has sung its last at dawning, as truth appeared so blessed!
Your twisting mist of shadow obscures no longer sight.
You stand in abject narrows from which you cannot hide.
Now doubt-yourself, within your darkest glare
And hear the voice of laughter where once there lived despair!

Psalm 23:1-4 "The Lord is my shepherd, I shall lack nothing. He makes me lie down in green pastures, he leads me beside quiet waters, he restores my soul. He guides me in paths of righteousness for his name's sake. Even though I walk through the valley of the shadow of death, I will fear no evil, for you are with me; your rod and your staff they comfort me."

Recognition marks a turning point

Recognition of our condition comes about through the light of grace received. Freedom requires commitment to the way of God's intent, otherwise a foundational shift will occur causing erosion of faith, lending courage to an already defeated enemy, ever seeking to dominate and destroy. We cannot do both, a foot in heaven and another in the fire-fueled by human desire. This will eventually leave us exhausted from the revolving door activity, that brings us into proximity of finding truth believed, but never permits exit to know it for sure. There are many things we do not understand and cannot comprehend. As slaves ruled by our sin nature we cannot understand the ingrained and undeniable internal conflict completely, but we know something is not right. We cannot fathom the enormity of eternal life or God's everlasting love. We try to encapsulate eternity within the rearview mirror of our lives and continually find ourselves wanting. We sometimes do not understand why it is bad things happen to people who really don't deserve the cards life has handed to them. We do not have the ability to understand how God knew all of his children before he created the foundations of the world, but we believe it to be true. We believe that God is always with us and in control, no matter how terrible slings and arrows of this life may sting and hurt. Ultimately God will make all things right, in this there is no doubt! ***Galatians 6:9 "Let us not become weary of doing good, for at the proper time we will reap a harvest if we do not give up."***

Gentle Malady

~⌒⌒~

If this faith of mine is false I must be nuts!
If truth trust and love is a sickness, I must be nuts!
What medication did I take to end up wanting good?
Going from aggressive insanity to passive peace
Everyone loved my lobotomy of the heart.
There's a divide called good and bad
Happy and sad night and day wrong or right
These are not concepts but actual fact
But with a concept I am convinced
God is! God is! God is! Who he says he is.

~⌒⌒~

Exodus 3:14 God said, "I am who I am. You must tell them: The one who is called I AM has sent me to you."

<u>*Lack of immediate consequence emboldens and encourages doubt*</u>

When we know what it is that hinders our faith we then have the ability to remove such obstacles and once again we become powerful witnesses for truth, as on the day we first believed. On the day we first believed there was *no doubt* in our minds and hearts that God's presence in our life was made known, and in this knowledge God took his rightful place of reality within which freedom is gained. On the day we first believed the flesh bowed to the appearance of God in our lives and was removed from the unlawful position of dictator of our life. What has happened since then is the slow erosion of sin that continually injects doubt through the insistence of the flesh, to once again rule in our lives. So true is the scripture that says: **Rev. 2:5 "See how far you have fallen."** *Again,* **Rev. 3:5 "Strengthen the things that remain."** There is apparently a natural falling away from the truth we have received. Within the context of having one foot within the promise of eternal life and the other in the grave the struggle between true and false continues until we are made whole once again. **2 Corinthians 4:16 "Therefore we do not lose heart.**

Though outwardly we are wasting away, yet inwardly we are being renewed day by day." On a fundamental level this is the conflict in man (the struggle between good and evil) and the remedial provision of God. Within this struggle lives the sister of sin, the cloud of doubt that attempts to reinstate the darkness of despair that formerly inhabited our lives. Doubt gains assurance within our reasoning because there is not always an apparent immediate consequence to sin. Lightning does not fall from the sky and render the offender to a charcoal gray puff of smoke. Not at all, the consequence for sin seems far from justice. Lawbreakers seemingly escape the justice most would expect should occur. This then probably reinforces a belief in the, "Sin does not exist" doctrine within secular humanist declarations. It would also add doubtful impact to those wanting to do right and live according to both conscience and God's pronouncements. It may also seem at times to be folly to live a righteous life. *Jeremiah 12:1 "Lord, if I argue my case with you, you would prove to be right. Yet I must question you about matters of justice. Why are wicked men so prosperous? Why do dishonest men succeed?"* Jeremiah may very well be asking God for understanding within the confines of his struggles. He sees the wicked prosper and the unrighteous succeed and he wonders why? He understands that a malady has infected the thoughts of the people who pay lip service to the established acceptance of God, but underlying their outward position, say to themselves, *"God does not see what we are doing."* It is apparent to us today that many have adopted the position of those in the time of Jeremiah. The sin nature has cast sufficient doubt to actually deny the existence of God. Inward denial and outward expressions of disobedience are encouraged to increase in potency, where the illusion of justice-denied is present. It is indeed a downward spiral that leaves little room for handholds of escape once we allow doubt to gain a mustard seed of weight; it pulls us down and further from truth. The mental tug-of-war is only offset and won through the strength of prayer. Connection with God allows men to run with horses and not become weary.

Jeremiah 12:5 "If you have raced with men on foot and they have worn you out, how can you compete with horses?" The erosion of faith through sin giving birth to doubt, may be so subtle that we need to be reminded of the depth of our fall and the weakened state it has left us in. Thus the admonishment by Jesus to strengthen the things that remain and to recognize how far we have fallen. With this admonishment we are able to gain strength through knowledge and recapture our true position of faith within the core of our being. *What goes on within the core of our being is reflected in the outward expression of our lives.* God's question regarding Jeremiah's racing with men, may actually be encouragement for him and for us to understand our adversarial encounters are not only rooted in human beings. If we get tired of the struggles against men and wish to throw up our hands and deny God his voice in our lives, how then can we ever hope to find victory over far greater enemies within the spiritual realm? Paul the apostle tells us basically the same thing when he instructs us to put on all of the armor of God. The armor of God transforms us into the equivalent of the armor plating of tanks-it makes us bulletproof! Not only from external deceptive attack but also from the internal struggles and condemnations of conscience littering our present day. If we permit sin's internal condemnation opportunity, it will produce the negative response that causes us to seek the illusion of not being seen. Just as corrosion will eventually eat away at the most reinforced armor plating the influence of doubt will erode the armor of God. We may convince ourselves that certain things are kept private within us, but we cannot deny the way in which we live to those with eyes to see. God does see and hear everything spoken in the heart and everything vocalized by the lips of man. Perhaps when the struggle to gain sufficient faith is achieved we may then also be empowered by prayer to actually make a difference in the lives of others as well as ourselves.

A need to be vigilant

Mark 14:37 "Then he returned and found the three disciples asleep. He said to Peter, "Simon are you asleep? Weren't you able to stay awake for even an hour?" And he said to them, "Keep watch and pray that you will not fall into temptation. The spirit is willing but the flesh is weak." Jesus returns (this takes place before the crucifixion) to the place he had left his disciples and finds them asleep. He expresses his disappointment in their inability to stay awake and to pray. Jesus points us to our weakness. He really is warning us not to relinquish our vigil to do the will of God. To do so gives confidence and strength to the flesh that desires a dominant position over the will of God. Again, this is the withdrawal of our nature from the holiness of God and in turn dilutes our faith through disassociation. A relationship with others means involvement. We cannot go to sleep and claim to be involved in the activities of God or others. When we lull ourselves into thinking all is well and peace is within us, we may find suddenly there is an eruption that had been building beneath the surface of conscious awareness. We may find ourselves adrift in a place of confusion brought about by the slow advancement of a complacent heart. The soldier of Christ must remain vigilant and ready to serve with the weaponry given to him upon the day of enlistment into the Army of God. It may be sufficient to say that in most things involving human desire, wanting to do a thing, is probably a thing that should not be done. The desires of flesh are mostly in opposition to the will of God. Is it a mystery that we become weary and seek sleep? We know the struggle within us has the proclivity to rage contempt, as much as a prisoner's failure to reject memories of liberty lost. The prisoner may be in the cell but he is always thinking of a way out. Vigilance is paramount if we wish to keep wrong confined and the spirit of truth vibrant and actively running toward God.

Struggles

It seems when we master the walk along comes the struggle to talk.
There's a struggle outside of the gate and a struggle within
Companions of sin bringing welts filled with pain.
Like the wobble of a top at the end of its spin
We struggle to remain upright.
As a ship listing we look for a pier of support
As would a ghost slanted and bent
Diminished by every breath.
Like the advent of troubling days
And water rushing the shore to lord over sand
We struggle with footing that's wet
And struggle sometimes to forget.
At times we struggle to recall
A time when struggles were spent
And always we wonder just when
When the struggles will end?

Isaiah 65:16 Anyone in the land who asks for a blessing will ask to be blessed by the faithful God. Whoever takes an oath will swear by the name of the faithful God. The troubles of the past will be gone and forgotten.

You of little faith

Matthew 14:28-33 "Lord, if it is you," Peter replied, "tell me to come to you on the water." "Come," he said. Then Peter got down out of the boat and walked on the water to Jesus. But when he saw the wind, he was afraid and beginning to sink, cried out, "Lord, save me!" Immediately Jesus reached out his hand and caught him. "You of little faith," he said, "why did you doubt?" And when they climbed into the boat, the wind died down. Then those who were in the boat worshiped him, saying, "Truly you are the Son of God." It is not only frustrating for us to be confronted by this unwarranted doubt but it has to be frustrating to God also. In that moment, immediately following the miracle of walking on water, and the wind bowing to the Savior's will, we find understanding recognizing Jesus as, God with us. This same recognition of untarnished faith appeared to us the moment we received God's grace; the veil of deception clouding our lives was lifted. In the above scripture there are many things that come to mind as we picture this portrayal but the thing that should be fixed into our higher level of perception is Peter crying out, *"Lord, save me!"* Peter did not need the empowerment of the Holy Spirit, who would come to them much later on the day of Pentecost, in order for him to understand his need for Jesus, to save him from being captured by the uncaring water surrounding him. All too often we are confronted by the storms of life, we know we need help, and perhaps we also may be sinking into depressing and dangerous surroundings, so let us remember Jesus is always reaching out his hand for us to grab hold of, and in this there is the surety of deliverance from seemingly impossible conditions. When we are threatened on any level of life it is not a matter of how much faith we have, rather, it is understanding that Jesus at that point in time is not placing us on a faith scale to determine if our trust in him is sufficient enough for him to act in our behalf. No parent would act in this, *are you deserving fashion.* Jesus is called, *"Eternal Father"* and in this capacity we must never doubt his willingness to come to our aid.

Fabric Testing 101

⌒‿‿‿⌒

"Attention class, I am proud to introduce to you, Dispatcher Grey.
He is your deceiver for tonight."
"Goodnight students, pay close attention.
In the daylight you'll need stealth.
A test a grab a grip
Pull apart, tear divide, snatch, injure and strip.
All of these will come in time
Patience is the hunter's bow that causes man to slip.
A peck a rip then shreds
Lift him up knock him down
Stay deep behind the set
Daze the man all you can
The rest cannot resist
The fabric of family enters the abyss.
Big fish eat
Big cat bites
Big dog barks at night
The shark don't miss with his kiss
Little ones can't hide.
Study hard within the dark
Avoid light.
Class dismissed."

⌒‿‿‿⌒

Mathew 12:29 Or again, how can anyone enter a strong man's house and carry off his possessions unless he first ties up the strong man? Then he can rob his house.

The tourist

The negative aspect of sin and doubt (disbelief) can persist for a short period of time even within the throne room of God. The prophet Isaiah finds himself out of contact with reality. He is swept away by the sights and sounds of the throne room, but is not made aware of his particular role within the assembly. Like Isaiah we must overcome our halfhearted belief in the existence of God, in order to become the emissary of his message and truth. He is an observer of reality and not a part of it, until he's forced by holiness into the truth made manifest in the presence of God. In the sixth chapter of the book of Isaiah the prophet is acting like a tourist as he takes in the sights and sounds of the throne room. He says, *"I saw the Lord seated on a throne, high and exalted, and the train of his robe filled the temple."* Isaiah snaps out of his tourist mentality as soon as he hears the seraphs announce the holiness of the Lord: *"Holy, holy, holy is the Lord Almighty; the whole earth is full of his glory."* He realizes he is a sinful man in the presence of God and laments his forthcoming destruction. It is then that one of the seraphim takes a live coal from the altar and touches the coal to his lips, saying, *"See, this has touched your lips; your guilt is taken away and your sin is atoned for."* Here's what happened. Contact with holiness transformed his unholy condition of disbelief into that which is acceptable to God. His failure to recognize the presence of holiness was set aside and forgiven through recognition. This sounds quite just. His guilt is removed and his sin is atoned for by the touch of holiness. Many of us have been touched by the hand of God, if this were not the case our worship would be in vain and we would be no better off than our previous focus (lost in darkness) residing in a land offering no hope. The universal reality of right and wrong (truth) would then be reduced to just a concept limited to only the individual, without substance, for no matter which side of the equation we may be attracted, the sum would always equal the permanence of the grave. Within this deception of false understanding, insanity would then become our closest relative, from whom it would be impossible to flee. In this we would find hopelessness, desperation and despair, within the children of man, and wars, greed for power, and the illusion of wealth would be enhanced through our belief in the finality of man's existence. Seems to me much of that still abounds. *Isaiah 22:12-13 The Lord, the Lord Almighty, called you on that day to weep and to wail, to tear out your hair and put on sackcloth. But see, there is joy and revelry, slaughtering of cattle and killing of sheep, eating of meat and drinking of wine! "Let us eat and drink," you say, "for tomorrow we die!"* The failure to recognize the commands of God will always lead to the disillusionment associated with false beliefs, causing us to deny truth, and in the process disobey God. Isaiah was awakened to recognizing truth and within his realization all of the baggage of guilt contained within his life was exposed for all to see, and therein the statement, **"your guilt is removed"** is necessary for the prophet's wellbeing. His sin of not recognizing the presence of God and holiness is atoned for, but the baggage of guilt must be removed from the one who serves God. In the presence of holiness everything hidden is brought into the light of truth and can no longer ambush us with guilt and remorse of past failures. It has been exposed by the holiness of God who accepts us the way we are, at the moment we recognize that he is correct and we are not. Those of us who continually dwell upon the past are destined to relive the distasteful moments within the painful clarity of truth. This then is one reason we are to keep focused upon what lies ahead, for what is in the past cannot be changed. We cannot completely forget but to have something removed is to be able to view it from a distance. *Memories are like a passing cloud that triggers thought through its portraits, then quickly dissipates from view. To remain focused upon its movement and projection prolongs the dissipation and brings more details to mind. Dwelling upon the past is to keep hurt within us and to attempt denial of the healing touch of holiness. Remaining focused upon the past distracts us from the present.* Isaiah was permitted into God's presence and shocked into reality by the awareness of everyone around him. Unless we are touched by holiness and made aware of our woefully imperfect condition we will never be permitted to attain the true potential God desires for us; peace from condemnation and abundant life. The recognition of holiness made amends for Isaiah's lack of understanding, removed his guilt and atoned for his sins. From the throne room and the altar that the seraph took the burning coal is brought to us the need to recognize the sacrifice of Christ. Isaiah was about to embark upon a mission of God's intent. There would be no room for past baggage. *Sin and guilt have a tendency to chase after us, and keep us focused upon the past. Sin and doubt make a blur of reality and can turn our worship into meaningless repetitions, having lost the truth of the presence of God. These can lull us into a,* **"God does not see what we are doing"** *mindset, which really is a loss faith.*

Matthew 5:14-16 "You are the light of the world. A city on a hill cannot be hidden. Neither do people light a lamp and put it under a bowl. Instead they put in on its stand, and it gives light to everyone in the house. In the same way let your light shine before men that they may see your good deeds and praise your Father in heaven." We may see the loss of light (truth) in many ways, brought about by the slow erosion of sin and doubt. In addition, seemingly repetitive imperceptible aspects of our lives, denied sight to others (usually those aspects we do not want seen in the light of day), can lead us into increased degrees of sin. These can become a seedbed of sin, watered by acceptable internal compromise that will eventually add to the already existing doubt, to the point of believing, *"God does not see what we are doing!"* Clearly this kind of erosion marks for us a need to stay focused upon God, who is ever before us. Sin and doubt is like a shroud blocking the emanation of light, but also is muting the sounds of joy that must naturally emanate from the living. Whole congregations can be silenced into mechanized worship, because sin and doubt have so clouded the reality of the presence of God. And so, not only must we be on guard against those slings and arrows shot at us from external sources, but we must also guard our heart against the denial of truth by the internal influence of our nature, that seeks to run and hide from God.

Sustaining Grace

O Lord,
Find my helmet dented
My shield bruised and worn
See the tatters in my clothes
And scars upon my bones
See the sharpness of my sword
And find me ever watchful
In the day of your return
I have watched in readiness
The hail of sling and dart
But you, O Master
God and King
Have preserved
My heart.

Luke 12:37-38 It will be good for those servants whose master finds them watching when he comes. I tell you the truth, he will dress himself to serve, will have them recline at the table and will come and wait on them. It will be good for those servants whose master finds them ready, even if he comes in the third watch of the night.

High Fire

*There's power
In the day mercy enters in
Announcing to the spirit
"A new life now begins."
There's power in the day
Freedom's breath we take
To do the things we knew as right
But we could not break away.
There's power in the knowledge
Of he who sent his flame
To burn away deception
Allowing truth to reign.
Like sanctifying embers
Engulfing us with love
You sent to us high fire
Your presence from above
O burning flame of power
Containing torrents
Of God's grace
Saving rain from heaven
Wash upon this place
Strength within us dwell
And a fortress make.*

Acts 2:1-4 When the day of Pentecost came, they were all together in one place. Suddenly a sound like the blowing of a violent wind came from heaven and filled the whole house where they were sitting. They saw what seemed to be tongues of fire that separated and came to rest on each of them.

Renew

⌒⌣⌒

Renew the moment of your grace
That brought me to my knees
Renew the childlike faith
Of when I first believed
Joy was in my heart
Like finding a lost friend
See how far I've fallen
How I've failed to grow
See how weak and feeble
I stand before you, Lord.
Draw close to me.
Although I seek
My faith is weak
Like fire that's grown cold
As coal turns gray around its edge
And is forgotten at the core
Somewhere I lost my way
Somewhere I lost my cross.
In the knowledge of my loss
My voice cries out with pain
"I cannot live with halfway home
Or halfway in the grave!"
Send the fire lost
Into this waiting heart
Renew the faith with binding cord
Renew this man, O Lord.

⌒⌣⌒

Ephesians 6:18 And pray in the Spirit on all occasions with all kinds of prayers and requests. With this in mind, be alert and always keep on praying for all the saints.

I AM

⌒⌒⌒

Without the eyes of faith
Who can really see?
Some never understand
Life is in he who is
I AM.
Character must be built
To awaken from dreams
In some the dream continues
Deeper until death
Great is the blindness
That shrouds the soul
Veils of layered darkness
Denying life complete
Rejecting the mind of good
To end up in defeat
If you heed the Word of God
Know this:
Passing may envelop all the senses
And darkness can sweep vision from the eye
Stilling the heart when the final beat arrives.
But we shall continue on
As light from the beginning
As eternity's persistence
Knows not a final dawn
Of praising and exalting God
With thunderous applause!

⌒⌒⌒

Psalm 46:10 Be still, and know that I am God; I will be exalted among the nations, I will be exalted in the earth.

Matthew 18:1-4 At that time the disciples came to Jesus, asking, "Who is the greatest in the Kingdom of heaven?" So Jesus called a child, had him stand in front of them, and said, "I assure you that unless you change and become like little children, you will never enter the Kingdom of heaven. The greatest in the Kingdom of heaven is the one who humbles himself and becomes like this child." Unless you change and become like little children you will never enter the Kingdom of heaven. Now, that is a powerful statement by our Lord. This does not mean we are denied salvation, rather, it points us to the lost of this world who have denied and doubted both the existence of God and the penalty associated with disbelief. For those of us who have been born again, we have received a new spirit of faith and trust, found only in the innocence of a child. When the truth of God was revealed to us through God's grace, whatever pride present in our lives was removed, and the humility necessary for entrance into the Kingdom of heaven was added. There was *no doubt* in our hearts and minds that the presence of God was made manifest in our lives. We were born again, made new, just as little children and we believed and trusted in God implicitly. We were not affected by any doubt or uncertainty!

We must always be on guard against the natural aspects of our existence that seeks to challenge the truth we have been given. It is not that we can *never* enter the Kingdom of heaven rather it is the understanding of foundational drift that seeks to remove us from the reality we have been blessed to recognize. Again, it is our sin nature that seeks to hide from truth and in this aspect of our present life we must be vigilant against this repelling force.

One final thought, apart from the subtle erosion of faith brought about by our sin nature, there may come a sudden shock to our existence (such as the loss of a loved one) that impulsively, through our emotions causes us to repel and rebel against God, this is a failure on our part to recognize the reality of death within this corporeal existence we all share. This kind of emotional shock is understood, it sends us into places we hope will shield us from such reality. Unfortunately within this emotional upheaval and otherwise panicked state we often do not run toward God. It is also a failure to recognize that at the proper time God will restore to us the righteous desire of our hearts. Just as in most cases of salvation, the sudden appearance of truth rapidly changes the direction in which we were traveling, so too, a sudden onset of sorrow or other damaging occurrence can cause us to not only question our faith, but to discard or place it into a state of suspension that has lost its meaning. Fortunately for us, while we may think we have abandoned our faith in God, he has never abandoned us to our hurts or sorrows; he remains faithful. Just as a parent will allow his child to run off into his room to sulk, over what is important to him, so it is, God allows us to run off and hide but he never leaves us alone. Amen.

Innocence

Sermon and Homily are my two best friends
When we go to sleep
Sermon guards the window
And Homily the door
Both of them love to bark
But Sermon loves to roar!
Mother says,
"Okay, they can sleep in your bed."
You see, my friends have button eyes and tails of fluff
They can never cause a fuss.
And so,
Jesus, on you I will depend
You are my real best friend.

Luke 18:16-17 Jesus called the children to him and said, "Let the children come to me and do not stop them, because the Kingdom of God belongs to such as these. Remember this! Whoever does not receive the Kingdom of God like a little child will never enter it."

Advanced Training

⌒‿‿⌒

The fishing hole mysterious and safe
For us to cast a line in search of the "big one"
We were sure to find.
The flattened rock and old tree stump
Were the favorite spots for launching expeditions when days were very
hot.
The fishing hole wasn't very deep
Sometimes we would swim around or just wet our feet.
Amazing how the legend of the "big one" could persist
When no one saw him throughout all our childhood bliss.
Such faith adds excitement to children's hearts at play
Perhaps it's all in training for faith in God one day?

⌒‿‿⌒

2 Corinthians 13:5 Examine yourselves to see whether you are in
the faith; test yourselves.

BODY SOUL AND SPIRIT

This is an effort to find tangible understanding within the intangible. I suppose given the enormity of unknown factors complete definition may not be possible. Having said this, all I can hope to unveil is truth God allows. Attempting to separate the components of man and view each individually is a daunting thought, nevertheless by scriptural pronouncements, logical assumption and otherwise common sense, some answers are hoped for.

Ecclesiastes 12:6-7 **"Remember him-before the silver cord is severed, or the golden bowl is broken; before the pitcher is shattered at the spring, or the wheel broken at the well, and the dust returns to the ground it came from, and the spirit returns to God who gave it."** Remember God before you die. Remembrance takes place in the spirit/mind of man. We have an excellent understanding of flesh and bone. Medical science has made wonderful progress because of the dedication and desire of those gifted to heal. So much understanding for the physical existence of man but when it comes to understanding soul we drift off into gray areas that do not satisfy our need to confirm. Spirit/Soul is not of this world with regard to the material of creation. While it is true one needs sand and water to make a sandcastle, it must be recognized not only sand and water but external thought and work must accompany creation. The thought that permits shape and articulates individual characteristics associated with sandcastle architecture may be likened to the "breath of life" that produced man as a living being. The life-force producing animation is the soul of mankind and is integral to the fabric woven into the finished work; without which there would be no work of art. ***Genesis 2:7 "And the Lord God formed man from the dust of the ground and breathed into his nostrils the breath of life, and man became a living being."*** We have no adequate gauge for measurement of this breath of life within the context of our five senses. We can view the animation of man, the accompanying signs of life, but when we attempt to define that which is intangible our language fails us. We can see the effects of this life but trouble arises when we seek to find the cause. It is not as if we can separate this intangible component, hold it up to the light and then examine the contents. There are no qualities for us to grab hold of, but still, this spiritual component (that is us) has substantive independence apart from all other components recognized as dependent upon its presence. Within our senses there is duality that indisputably recognizes that which cannot be seen, but still it is projected into thought. For instance, with our eyesight we are able to view all that is before us and with insight we can perceive that which the eye cannot. We can touch the fabric of physical existence and we can also be touched through our feelings that are the fabric of thought. We can hear the sounds both pleasing and disturbing through ears and we can also listen to the inner voice that can recognize right and wrong danger or safety. We can taste the goodness of food and the goodness of God. If we check the dictionary for definition we find a somewhat adequate description. *Soul: "The animating force in the human being often thought to survive death."* This definition by Webster leaves one with the impression soul is separate and distinct from man, but it fails to give origin and clarity to just what produced said animation in the first place. It is thought to be separate because it is perceived to have the ability to exist apart from corporeal existence at the time the body dies. This is partially true, because not all bodily death will see a continuance of life. Continuance of life after death is dependent upon the condition of the soul at the time of death (saved or not). One reason for this belief in automatic continuance in all instances of death may be attributed in part to the "often thought to survive death" injection of immortality, into the equation of the physical mortality of man. This understanding is clarified somewhat by the bible that states, "and man became a living being" from the fact that God breathed into the building material of dust the "breath of life." However even with this pronouncement from scripture we are still left without a gauge for measurement or a light strong enough for viewing. All of our physical approaches for study seem to fail us when it comes to something we know to be us, but we cannot grasp because it exists outside of physical determinates. Understanding soul becomes more complex when we add the word spirit. *Spirit: "A vital animating force, soul. The part of man being associated with feeling and mind."* On the surface it appears soul and spirit are one, and while this is true in the totality of a living being, there is plurality within the singularity of man. Soul is a Greek word that literally means life. Spirit is the thinking faculty of man, and soul is life in its entirety, allowing the completeness of man and is not dependent upon the body to exist. It's interesting that man understands himself within the context of body soul and spirit and in this understanding we remain one. This is somewhat similar to Father Son and Spirit. Like a diamond having facets we are endowed with complexity and yet we remain one. In the one (soul) all things pertaining to the operation of the body and the thinking faculty are permitted to function because of the presence of this animating force. In the other (spirit) is derived the quality of life based upon the direction in which one thinks. While soul is constant in its ability to power the body, spirit is an ongoing process of adding understanding to the initial blank slate existing upon our birth. There is perhaps inherent knowledge within the spirit at our birth simply because the spirit is of God, but we may not be aware of it, and perhaps we do not become aware of it until we die; upon our death there very well may be an explosion of understanding only available to those within a pure spiritual existence, only achieved when out of the body. Revelations of a sort, we could only see as reflections but not in actuality. *1 Corinthians 13:11-12 "When I was a child I talked like a child, I reasoned like a child. When I became a man, I put childish ways behind me. Now we see but a poor reflection; then we shall see face to face. Now I know in part; then I shall know fully, even as I am fully known."* Paul says we shall know to the degree of perfect understanding, just as we fully understand now that our thinking faculty proves our own existence. It is not enough to just think but thinking must be correct in order to fully understand and appreciate life (soul) itself. The Holy Spirit searches even the deep things of God, and we, through our thinking faculty/spirit are made aware through spiritual recognition or thought. In the physical presentation of man there is the clear recognition of animation, and mortality is most evident upon death of the body. Within the initial creation (the installation of said force for animation or commanded life) was incorporated immortality until the poison of sin infected the totality of man. It makes sense that death would then encompass or deny every aspect of life. Ecclesiastes states, ***"the spirit returns to God who gave it."*** That is to say the thinking faculty with accompanying animation remains intact. We would at this point in time have left one order of creation, and entered into another, the pure spiritual. If it is true ("the spirit returns to God who gave it") for everyone then belief in the immortality for the soul is correct. However, Ecclesiastes is not done relating to us the truth contained in wisdom. ***Ecclesiastes 9:5 "For the living know that they will die, but the dead know nothing; they have no further reward, and even the memory of them is forgotten."***

Is this a contradiction of the words expressed by Ecclesiastes in the subject scripture quote? If the aforementioned is true ***"but the dead know nothing"*** it would then follow that the immortality of the soul thought to be an automatic continuation of life may not be the case at all. Ecclesiastes has made an explicit statement, and in this ***"dead know nothing"*** pronouncement the totality of man ends at the moment of death. This is total death for even the memory of them is forgotten. Jesus had referred to some who had died as ***"asleep"*** these he remembered because they had been predestined and designated as belonging to his flock. Therefore if we look at both scripture quotes ***("The spirit returns to God who gave it"*** and ***"the dead know nothing")*** in the context of what we know of the promises of Christ, we find both to be true. Simply stated, for those who are not in Christ there is no afterlife. For those of us who have received a *new spirit* we shall return to God upon death of the body. That is to say, the thinking faculty that is uniquely us continues on. Everything becomes a bit clearer when we recognize God as Father. The apostle Paul clearly says that he would prefer to be out of this earthly tent (body) in order to be home with the Lord. Jesus says that whosoever believes in him ***"even if he dies yet shall he live."*** Again, not every soul returns to God, for life that has not been sanctified (set apart by God) cannot approach God. Moreover, it makes no sense that the unsaved should approach God prior to the judgment. ***"What good is it for a man to gain the whole world, yet forfeit his soul?"*** What's interesting is most if not all of the world's religions incorporate some form of belief that embraces the immortality of the soul. This belief may be a subconscious yearning for a restoration to what was the initial condition of man. Perhaps the only belief that does not identify with a continuance of life is the non-belief called atheism. In this obstinate stance they are most correct, upon their death they will no longer exist. The real question should simply ask, "Is there a continuation of life after physical death?" We may want to rearrange the question by asking, "Does the thought process continue after the body dies?" We may cut through the haze by simply asking, "Does God exist?" If our answer is yes, it follows that thought exists within the pure spiritual realm, and it becomes incumbent upon us to find out who is the originator of thought. If on the other hand we deny the existence of God what will be found upon the death of the body is, ***"the dead know nothing."***

ONCE WE ACCEPT THE SPIRITUAL EXISTENCE OF MAN IT FOLLOWS WE MUST RECOGNIZE A CREATOR OF MAN. THERE IS NOTHING CONTAINED WITHIN THE ACCIDENTAL EVOLUTIONARY THEORY THAT COULD EXPLAIN THE SPIRIT/SOUL COMPONENT. THERE IS NOTHING HERE THAT COULD PRODUCE THE SPIRITUAL INGREDIANT NECESSARY FOR MAN TO BE COMPLETE. IT IS WHAT'S NECESSARY TO GIVE HIM LIFE. GOD IS SPIRIT. ANIMATION OF MANKIND REQUIRES MUCH MORE THAN FLESH AND BONE. THIS IS EVIDENCED IN THE THOUGHT PROCESS-THE SPIRIT OF MAN.

Matthew 16:24-26 Then Jesus said to his disciples, "If anyone would come after me, he must deny himself and take up his cross and follow me. For whoever wants to save this life will lose it, but whoever loses his life for me will find it. What good will it be for a man if he gains the whole world, yet forfeits his soul?" Jesus is saying, if someone wants to follow his example of life he must deny the sinful ways of this world, and in doing so God recognizes the heart that desires him and his truth. Jesus is saying we must undergo a spiritual change; our thinking must no longer be focused on earthly things. We must be penetrated by truth, like a spiritual bullet straight to the fabric of our thoughts, in order for us to be born again with a new way of thinking. The new man is rewarded with life and the old man that loved his life dies when the body meets the grave. This translates into *life-gained* for all who believe the appearance of truth, and life forfeited for those who do not. There is nothing to take with us to the grave, other than our identity. So whoever wants to preserve his soul must acknowledge that God is right and we are not. With receipt of a new spirit we are given not only a new way of thinking but also the power to say no to that which is wrong. As the scripture says, **"Your attitude must be Christ's,"** this then is the renewal of spirit or transformation of one's mind, given life and ability to choose between what *God wants* for us, instead of what we want. This sounds like basic parenting and completely expected from God, who is our Father. Jesus in teaching us how to pray incorporated, ***"thy will be done on earth."*** He alerts us to the fault within our thinking process and allows us to recognize God's ways as correct, and the ways of man are not.

The Better End

Cling not to me endurance friend
For gray the hairs upon the head
Point clearly toward a better end.
Holdfast not days of youth, it's better now with nuisance aches
Better now at reduced pace, far better now with love and grace.
O flesh and bones to no avail your moan, conformity is right.
With hands upraised to God in praise goodness is in sight
All our cares are washed away by the promises of Christ.

Ecclesiastes 7: A good name is better than precious ointment, and the day of death is better than the day of one's birth.

Solo flight

Because so much of our gained truth is life experience a level of belief or trust in God, as well as in life after death, may be directly witnessed proportionately to such experience, by individuals whose experiential truth builds upon an existing foundation of faith given by God at the moment of rebirth. Death or near death experiences can also be a solidifying confirmation not only directly, but also indirectly for those who have had similar experiences within the context of afterlife or near death moments. As such in an effort to support belief in a continuation of life after the body has died I'll relate a truthful experience. I know a man who thirty years ago was heading home. I don't know if this man had died or not (only God knows). This man was among the stars and heavenly bodies moving at what can only be described as incredible speed-the speed of thought. Along his way there appeared to him large mathematical equations as signposts or directional markers. These were instantly understood as easily as one would recognize a traffic signal. Along his way he was turned around. When this man returned to the normality of corporeal existence, awake in his bed, he was tremendously disappointed because of the quickly dissipating knowledge of the night's experience; dumb again, if you will. Again, I do not know if this man actually died (only God knows), but the accounts of afterlife experience enjoy numerous personal testimonies. Just as numerous are the accounts that relate a void of experience from those pronounced dead by medical doctors and have later been found alive. Others have had horror stories and upon returning to the body completely turned their lives around. For the one whose experience is firsthand the foundation of faith finds exceptional renewal, and to the one hearing of another's witness similar to their personal experience something is also added. As for the one who has nothing to report this also tells us something relative to the condition of the soul, saved or otherwise.

Sand Vision

꩜

Each day the grain of sand by nature's wear diminished
Less and less until nothing save the breath of man
Heavenly lights instantly discerned in spirit flight
Beginning of perceptions not learned always present in the breath
"Home," the insistent urging-direction known
Across the universe the light of understanding flies
Imparting direction in the breath of a newborn's cry.

꩜

The postmortem of Jonah

Jonah 2:1-10 From inside the fish Jonah prayed to the Lord his God. He said: "In my distress I called to the Lord, and he answered me. From the depths of the grave I called for help, and you listened to my cry. You hurled me into the deep, into the very heart of the seas, and the currents swirled about me; all your waves and breakers swept over me. I said, 'I have been banished from your sight; yet I will look again toward your holy temple.' The engulfing waters threatened me; seaweed was wrapped around my head. To the roots of the mountains I sank down; and the earth beneath barred me forever. But you brought my life up from the pit, O Lord my God." In some there is the belief that Jonah did not die bodily and as a consequence was not resurrected. Jonah is not only drowned but he is placed on the menu as dinner for a big fish. Jonah is hurled into the sea, he has drowned, and from the depths of the grave (the pit) he calls to God. Jonah falls to the root of the mountains, to the base of the undersea mountains; a long way down. It's interesting that scripture should describe undersea mountains before the science of undersea mapmaking existed. I can remember from my childhood a cartoon depicting Jonah alive in the belly of a whale, sitting at table under candlelight lamenting his condition. But that was a child's cartoon. The story of Jonah is important for us to understand because Jonah prefigures the death and resurrection of Jesus. Jonah is the only sign that would be given to those who had demanded of Jesus a miracle. It is the resurrection miracle that is important and germane to the example that Jesus offered to those seeking a sign. If Jonah had not experienced bodily death the example given by Jesus would not be completely accurate. Thus the spirit of Jonah persisted after the body died, and after three days deep in death Jonah was resurrected out from the tomb that was the belly of a big fish. Jesus also spent three days in the grave and during this time he proclaimed the good news to all. *1 Peter 3:18-20 "For Christ died for sins once for all, the righteous for the unrighteous, to bring you to God. He was put to death in the body but made alive by the Spirit, through whom also he went and preached to the spirits in prison who disobeyed long ago when God waited patiently in the days of Noah while the ark was being built."* All who had been predestined by God to be saved heard the good news of salvation and were set free from the deep sleep of the grave. For those who look for reasons to deny the death of Jonah through modern day reports that purport, "Men have been found alive within the belly of a shark or some other sea creature," therein is the disbelief factor that was also present in the minds and hearts of those seeking a sign from Jesus. Man is always looking to find answers for miracles within the world of limitation, rather than to recognize God. Many deny God and some aspire to be gods. It is interesting that those who would be gods aspire to a level of existence that they do not recognize to exist? What is also interesting is the difference of opinion concerning Jonah's death or his non-death exists within theological circles. It is certainly not a question in the minds of those who do not recognize the existence of God. They have resigned themselves to a here and now existence only. However, praise God, because our salvation is not determined by a passing grade in theology; in large measure it is determined by us through acceptance of truth.

The Barrier

∽‿‿‿⌐

Human ability and natural laws place limits upon our thoughts
And form for us a finite view giving power to what's lost.
The greatest of these barrier stones present themselves in caskets.
The seed must be transformed into something it was not
And cease to be a seed but not to be forgotten.
Loss of limbs will not reduce my mind
Will not diminish spirit now or over time
And when my losses mount and body meets the grave
I still shall not diminish, no, not even for a day.

∽‿‿‿⌐

2 Corinthians 4:1 Therefore we do not lose heart. Though outwardly we are wasting away, yet inwardly we are being renewed day by day.

<u>Deep in the grave asleep</u>

Well we see and hear a lot of dialog from those who have left the body and then continue within the spirit (thought process), and we have established that thought exists outside of the body through the ultimate recognition that God is. Now let us look at what it could mean to be deep in the grave asleep, devoid of thought. Prior to the sacrifice of Christ there was nowhere for mankind to go **("the dead know nothing")** upon the death of the body except for a few exemptions like Moses and Elijah, we see them very much alive at the transfiguration of Christ. They are exceptions because prior to the cross there was nowhere to go upon death of the body; the spirit could not as yet **"return to God who gave it"** because the sacrifice of Christ had not as yet atoned for the sins of man. Thus humanity remained deep in the grave asleep. In some there is biblical interpretation expressing belief that Elijah did not experience death and further advance he may be one of God's two formidable witnesses we see described in the Book of Revelation chapter eleven. The belief that Elijah did not see death coincides with the biblical pronouncement that man is to die once.

This thought, that Elijah is one of the end-time witnesses stems from the fact that *"the beast that comes up from the abyss will attack them, and overpower and kill them"* thus Elijah will have satisfied the *die once* pronouncement in scripture. *Hebrews 9:27 "Just as man is destined to die once, and after that to face judgment, so Christ was sacrificed once to take away the sins of many people; and he will appear a second time, not to bear sin, but to bring salvation to those who are waiting for him."* As such, there are some who point to Elijah as being one of the two witnesses mentioned in the Book of Revelation. Of course there are exceptions for the purposes of God; Lazarus died was resurrected by Jesus and presumably he died again. At the death of Jesus, *"The tombs broke open and the bodies of many holy people who had died were raised to life."* These also are presumed to have died again. As for Moses we know that he passed away as evidenced by the quarrel between Michael and Lucifer over his body. It is recognized they argued over whether or not the spirit of Moses would continue after the body had died and return to God who had given it. Lucifer, the accuser of man had wanted him buried deep in the grave asleep. We know who won the argument as evidenced by the appearance of Moses at the transfiguration of Jesus. Jonah was an exception to *"the dead know nothing"* pronouncement because he was an example (sign) for the purpose of God. There are other recorded exceptions to the *"die once rule"* in both new and old testaments but for the remainder of multitudes who slept deep in the grave nothing could awaken them until the sacrifice of Christ freed them from darkness. I suspect there is not much difference from those who slept in the grave and those of us who heard the good news proclaimed while still alive. That is to say, Jesus proclaimed salvation to those asleep in the grave and those of us alive and unsaved; in both cases the individual is awakened to life. He awakens consciousness and presence of mind; he holds the keys to both heaven and hell offering life to the living and dead! It is these (held deep in the grave asleep) that ascended with him to heaven spiritually, consciously aware of themselves once again. Jesus returned to his Father's house with all of those predestined and identified by God as his children. Jesus did not return home to his Father's house empty handed; he returned in triumph with multitudes! Perhaps now we can understand more clearly why it was necessary for God to know us before he formed the foundations of the earth.

A nothingness existence (nothingness existence sounds contradictory but as long as God remembers us there is always a shred of existence) is exemplified by the words of Christ as he refers to the dead daughter of the synagogue leader as being asleep. Jesus tells the dead girl to wake up and then he instructs the parents to give her something to eat. How many of us have upon awakening from a deep sleep found hunger foremost in our thought process? Talk about being in tune with humanity from the Creator's point of view. It is also presumed that this young girl also saw death a second time. But it was for the glory of God (as was the case with Lazarus and all who were resurrected by Christ) the ***"die once"*** pronouncement was circumvented. Jesus healed on the Sabbath and according to the religious of his day he had broken the Sabbath Law, but Jesus is Lord of the Sabbath, as such, he cannot break that which is subordinate to him.

Dry Bones

What is left of man can fill the Canyon Grand
And continue to heaven's door
Have mercy, O Sovereign Lord
For we are
No more.
Dry bones buried deep
Reach up in silent chorus
Soar to mighty heights
Though enveloped by the grave
Lay gentle at your feet O Lord, songs of praise.
Have mercy on the captives Lord, held within the night
Have mercy, for the darkness has a hold so tight.

Ezekial 37:1-3 The hand of the Lord was upon me, and he brought me out by the Spirit of the Lord and set me in the middle of a valley; it was full of bones. He led me back and forth among them, and I saw a great many bones that were very dry. He asked me, "Son of man can these bones live?" I said, "O Sovereign Lord, You alone know."

THE PERMANENCE OF HELL OR NONEXISTENCE

Within the words of Jesus there is implied a degree of punishment to be determined by the judgment of God. To be placed into the fire of hell should not automatically be considered a permanent state of torture; it should also be recognized as the means by which God can totally destroy both body and soul. The pronouncement of the existence of hell comes to us through the word of God, as such there should be no doubt among believers concerning this truth. However, most of the world's population has placed this truth into the category of fantasy, along with the understanding of eventual judgment for evildoers. Because many in this life escape the punishment of man there is this belief that death is final and all evil done in this life, upon death, is without consequence. This also is deception, seeking to deny truth to those lost within worldly pursuits. We know that God can do whatever he wants with the element of fire. The burning bush was not consumed; the burning coal from the altar of God did not render Isaiah into a torturous state of being and the fire within the cruel furnace of king Nebuchadnezzar's pride did not harm Daniel, because God would not permit the fire to destroy him. It appears the fire of hell will become an eternal sentence no matter which extreme is so judged appropriate by God, eternal torture or nonexistence.

Matthew 10:28 *"Do not be afraid of those who kill the body but cannot kill the soul. Rather, be afraid of the one who can destroy both soul and body in hell."* The permanence of hell is not in question rather it is the *option* of God that should be considered in order to understand the place called hell as either eternal torment or a second death from which there is no return. It would appear

God has the option to send to hell those he deems worthy of eternal torment, or else, for some, there is total destruction. In the above passage Jesus is basically saying, this life of ours will come to an end in its corporeal existence. As such, fear of those who can kill the body and then do nothing else is misplaced. We must recognize the one who has power over us, whether in or out of the body. By Jesus saying God *"can"* destroy both soul and body he leaves open a sentencing to eternal torment or destruction in the lake of fire, which may very well be the place called hell. Certainly there are those who deserve to be tortured forever, and then, there are those whose existence is worthy of a quick burn, or even varying temperatures and degrees of torment proportional to the deeds in life. In essence, God will dispense the perfect punishment to fit the sin. It does not take a great imagination to recognize some serious candidates for eternal torment. One would think those demonic forces arrayed against God would be on the list, and all of those who knowingly worshiped the Evil One. As for those destined for the lake of fire, in specific terms we know all liars, murderers, perverts, and everyone whose name is not written in the Book of Life are destined for the aforementioned lake. This sounds like a large number of candidates but it has been said, the road to heaven is narrow. Because scripture implies that some of the unsaved will be *better off* than others on the Day of Judgment the question begs to be asked, how so? I don't know if there is an answer but let's look closer at the words of our Lord.

<u>*Murderous thoughts and adulterous hearts*</u>
<u>*Are always married to lies*</u>

Matthew 5:21-22 "You have heard that it was said to the people long ago, 'Do not murder and anyone who murders will be subject to judgment.' But I tell you that anyone who is angry with his brother will be subject to the judgment. Again, anyone who says to his brother 'Raca' is answerable to the Sanhedrin, but anyone who says, 'You fool!' will be in danger of the fire of hell." To kill someone is murder, but Jesus places murder anger and contempt, into the category of being worthy of judgment and in danger of hell's fire. The only issue remaining is whether the fire offers death or eternity on the grill? We should not fast forward the

implication of eternal torture administered by the hand of God. It is an awesome thought for us to contemplate, the God of Love bringing about eternal pain in perfect proportion to the gravity of one's sins, or nonexistence. By contrasting actual murder with a desire to see its fruition, Jesus is placing thoughts and acts into the same vein of seriousness. Jesus is treating the physical and the spiritual with equal weight. Of course this must be so. If we look at the words of Jesus as he accords intent, equal in culpability to the actual act, he leaves no room for sin to slither free. Jesus is bringing all aspects of sin into recognition and is not permitting a loophole for those within the pure spiritual realm. If all of the unsaved are going to hell and they are to endure eternal torment, what then is the meaning of Jesus when he states, *"It will be better"* for some on the Judgment Day than for others. Self indulgence, violence, maliciousness and damaging others bodily, or through character assassination are highlighted by our Lord to be worthy of severe punishment. Reasoning suggests if there is severe punishment there may very well be punishment to a lesser degree. Having a choice in the matter, I suppose, everyone subjected to judgment would choose to be totally nonexistent rather than to be tormented throughout eternity. Nonexistence is pronounced without ambiguity in the Book of Revelation because it refers to the lake of fire as the *"second death."* In the same breath, the lake of fire is where the devil and others will be tossed into for eternal torment. We can understand why the devil will be tormented (in fact we applaud and praise God for this), but what about others? Are there some instances where people will be judged as harshly as those demonic beings? I can imagine one conversation, "Adolph this is your cell and Satan is your new cellmate." Will there be a lesser degree of punishment? I do think that the lesser punishment is total destruction. The lake of fire, announced as the *"second death"* may imply destruction to the point of nonexistence, and also, since the devil is tossed into it (for eternal torment) there is a duality of purpose suggested, as presented by Jesus in the subject scripture quote. All sin is related to the lie and has no constraints, by which it is inhibited, because, with the advent of the lie all manner of sinful manifestation was and is brought into being. Because of this, liars have been placed into the category of murderers and perverts worthy of the lake of fire. The lie is made manifest in every imaginable form. Seemingly innocuous lack of truth in advertising, or, spin doctors attempting to whitewash crime, or, the tyrant given free reign in the name of religion, are all nourished in the same garden of plausible deniability, rooted in the constantly shifting positional change associated within the uneasy presentation of the lie. The world we live in has the illusion of light, but the true darkness is pervasive. The light of Christ is the only illumination given to us that is totally pure and can never disappoint us who follow.

They wanted to be gods

Genesis 6:4-5 "The Nephilim were on the earth in those days—and afterward-when the sons of God went to the daughters of men and had children by them. These were the heroes of old, men of renown. The Lord saw how great man's wickedness on the earth had become and that every inclination of the thoughts of his heart was only evil all the time." Nephilim is the Hebrew name given to the offspring produced by the union of fallen angels and the daughters of men. This does not necessarily have to be the first recorded demonic possessions, because they may have not been of the kind that we might initially think of (purely spiritual). You see, while we understand angelic forms of life as either angels of light or darkness, we should not automatically think that demonic possession has to be of the purely spiritual kind. There is the possibility that other life forms (created by God) having physical characteristics were the cause of both the so-called giants upon the earth and an attempt to recreate in the image and likeness of evil. This may very well account for the void of life we perceive in our own universe? As such, what we may be seeing is beings (non human) having contempt for God's creation called mankind. They not only had contempt for God but they lusted after his creation. In this lust we can see why Jesus finds adultery of the flesh equal to adultery of the mind (spirit). This was a corrupting of the children of God by rebellious beings, whose pride would not submit to the reality of God calling his creation sons and daughters. This is truly contemptuous and worthy of eternal punishment in hell. Moreover, this corruption and subsequent proliferation, led to the flood with devastating results for mankind. It was as if the sin of man was not enough for those corrupting influences, they had to hurry the death sentence along the path to the grave. Mankind was in his infancy, so one may conclude the first demonic possessions inflicted by fallen angels or beings of flesh, was child abuse in its worst form. This may have been a desire by demonic beings to destroy what God had created and an attempt to recreate within the image of all that is unholy. Thus God began again after the devastation of the flood. This desire by fallen angelic host, to become gods has not drifted away into history. Today there are many who believe they are gods; all nice and comfy within the non-consequential world of, *"God and sin does not exist."* This new-age concept is at least equal to the stupidity first displayed by those who thought they could rebel against God without consequence.

Jude 1:6-7 And the angels who did not keep their positions of authority but abandoned their own home, these he has kept in darkness, bound with everlasting chains for judgment on the great Day. In a similar way, Sodom and Gomorrah and the surrounding towns gave themselves up to immorality and sexual perversion. They serve as an example of those who suffer the punishment of eternal fire. The angels who did not keep their positions of authority and the immorality and perversion of Sodom and Gomorrah *"serve as an example of those who suffer the punishment of eternal fire."* Within this expression by Jude we can see the most extreme forms of worthiness for eternal fire. This is the permanence of eternal damnation and not the quick burn implied by being tossed into the lake of fire, referred to as the *"second death."* Although, for now these are being *"kept in darkness, bound with everlasting chains for judgment on the great Day."* By Jude giving to us these two examples (demonic possession and the total depravity of Sodom and Gomorrah) we are alerted to the depths to which both the supernatural and natural world had defiled both God's sensibilities as well as the design and intent for mankind. One may conclude that all sin will be judged, but not all will be pronounced as worthy of eternal fire. If we fast forward to the time of Jesus we find many representations of demonic possession and in the one called, *"Legion or Mob"* there is the pronouncement from them that their *"time had not come to be tortured."* The admission by those called *"Mob"* leads us to the understanding that they were indeed cognizant of their impending doom, and somehow knew it to be not their time. They knew Jesus and they knew it was not their time for judgment, and so, they were aware of their guilt and they knew they had no excuse!

We cannot conceive of torture infinitely accurate and proportionately fair, but God knows everything. They knew they would be tortured! Perhaps now we can get a clearer picture of one aspect of the brilliance of our Lord, as he teaches the disciples how they should pray. ***"Thy will be done on earth as it is in heaven."*** In that one sentence is summed up the complete purpose of creation. When we place our will and purpose ahead of God's intent we fail to follow design criteria. Jesus reiterates throughout his ministry for us to follow him. In so doing we will follow the will of God.

It will be better for some

Luke 17:1-3 Jesus said to his disciples: "Things that cause people to sin are bound to come, but woe to that person through whom they come. It would be better for him to be thrown into the sea with a millstone tied around his neck than for him to cause one of these little ones to sin. So watch yourselves." Once again Jesus displays to us the severity of sin of our own volition, and that of being caused or encouraged by those who intentionally set out to bring about the downfall of others. Jesus says to us, it is better to be drowned in the depths of the sea than for some to face the eternal torment God has in store. He is making a distinction with regard to those responsible for the downfall of others; nonexistence is too good for them. For those who would deliberately corrupt for personal gain or satisfaction, Jesus highlights their disregard and he holds them to a greater degree of responsibility for their contempt and uncaring attitude. It is one thing to find yourself trapped by any number of worldly designs but to be responsible for designing and building such traps, knowing they will bring about the fall of others, is to invite eternal confinement and torment. God holds them in contempt. In some, whose desire promotes and otherwise demands the proliferation of evil, God finds them to be abominations equal to the first demonic possessions and the total abandonment of morality displayed in Sodom and Gomorrah. Only God knows for sure what actually happened in those places and only God can judge accurately the punishment deserved.

Individual judgment

Revelation 20:13-14 "The sea gave up the dead that were in it, and death and Hades gave up the dead that were in them and each person was judged according to what he has done. Then death and Hades were thrown into the lake of fire. The lake of fire is the second death. If anyone's name was not found written in the book of life, he was thrown into the lake of fire." Here we see the conquering of death and the land of the dead (under the earth and under the sea), death and the place that held the dead captive is no longer in existence. Hades or the land of the dead (the underworld) is banished from existence. **"Each person was judged according to what he had done."** Well it looks to be one coin with two sides. Perhaps the second death really is a total termination from existence, while for others a total death would be too lenient a sentence. The Book of Life is singular and contained within it are the recordings of God himself; he made the entries before he began to create this world. However, the judgment books are many. Whether life or judgment, we are these open books. The spirit of man records everything we have ever done in our lives. As we grow old we may mercifully forget certain aspects of our lives, but what has been imprinted on our spirit is like indelible ink, very long lasting. Just as those pure spiritual beings cannot keep hidden their thoughts and actions, so it is with the spirit of man. The individual is to be judged for the deeds of his own life, there will be no such thing as, "The devil made me do it" defense. Actually I believe that while there will be much gnashing of teeth, I don't think that anyone will venture into any kind of defense, since our lives will be like a crime being captured on a video recording; undeniable. I am at times just dumbstruck over the sheer power of God to reach into the grave, resurrect, judge and punish. Wow! There really is no hiding place that will elude the justice of God.

More or Less

Matthew 11:20-24 "Then Jesus began to denounce the cities in which most of his miracles had been performed, because they did not repent. "Woe to you Korazin! Woe to you, Bethsaida! If the miracles that were performed in you were performed in Tyre

and Sidon, they would have repented long ago in sackcloth and ashes. But I tell you, it will be more bearable for Tyre and Sidon on the day of judgment than for you. And you, Capernaum, will you be lifted up to the skies? No, you will go down to the depths. If the miracles that had been performed in you had been performed in Sodom, it would have remained to this day. But I tell you that it will be more bearable for Sodom on the Day of Judgment than for you." Here again, we find Jesus making comparison with the most extreme sins of immorality and disregard for God, by those who knew truth based upon their own eyewitness to the miracles performed, and he judges those who knew with greater severity, than those whose depravity was disgusting and reprehensible in the sight of God. The words of Jesus do not imply that all will be punished equally. No, quite the contrary, Jesus states, it will be better for some than for others and he does not keep secret that which will cause severe treatment. *"But I tell you it will be more bearable for Sodom on the Day of Judgment than for you."* Unwillingness to submit to the will of God is right at the top of the list of those worthy of eternal torment. Jesus went about his work on this earth performing many miracles, healing many, and freeing all who were held in the grip of evil, so, what Jesus is saying regarding those towns where many of these miracles were performed (but did not change their disregard for God) is that those who were living in total depravity within the cities of Sodom and Gomorrah would have more readily received the good news of salvation, because, at least within Sodom and Gomorrah there was no pretense of righteousness. Certainly those fallen angels (like the unrepentant towns) had access, to not only witnessing God's miracles but they had access to God as well, which should have cured even the most severe case of rebellion. *"Fear of the Lord is the beginning of wisdom."* These former angels had fallen into a realm of stupidity that has no equal! As such, their punishment will be most severe. Unbelief and unwillingness to come into compliance with God's will is something that has (I suppose) mystified the saved and blessed among us for all time. There is the belief by some that God does not exist and there is no judgment. Others know that God will do everything he says in his own time, but they still rebel, because they discount the punishment as being so far off that when the time comes they will have at least lived a life that was in accord with their own desires.

This is seduction by illusion. Big mistake. Many are the lamentations at the appearance of a hangover. God is more than a hangover for the defiant, he is their worst nightmare personified. No one can imagine what God has in store for those who love him, and no one can imagine the torment God has in store for those who do not. For those who knew God and knew his existence to be the eternal giving of love, for these, who harbored a traitorous rebellious and hateful agenda against him and his creation, there is no way we could ever imagine his wrath.

Woe

Matthew 23:15 "Woe to you, teachers of the law and Pharisees, you hypocrites! You travel over land and sea to win a single convert, and when he becomes one, you make him twice as much a son of hell as you are." Wow! Jesus really unloads both barrels at those who cause others to sin. Again, we see the severity of judgment for those who cause others to sin. It is so true that to those much is given much is expected. These teachers of the law and Pharisees were treated to a snapshot of what they can expect at the judgment. They were hit with seven woes pronounced from the mouth of Jesus and there was nothing they could do about it, except to listen and inwardly foment at the truth burning into their façade of outward piety. Jesus called them, **"Whitewashed tombs, which look beautiful on the outside but on the inside are full of dead men's bones and everything unclean."** Most men faced with this tidal wave of truth would wither and fall to their knees in repentance at the sheer exposure of their hypocrisy, but not these self-righteous, they refused to bend to the will of God. What is amazing is the fact that those worthy of eternal fire are the ones who had professed being the closest to God. Breaking a sacred trust, whether vows of ministry or allegiance, always will find the woes of the Lord waiting to pronounce their judgment. Indeed, there will be much gnashing of teeth. The Pharisees and teachers of the law had won converts through deception. They knowingly misled new converts, and prevented others entry into the Kingdom of God, by denying the truth of God. Omission of truth is no less a lie. When truth is denied the lie is presented. The Pharisees and teachers of law were likened to the children of their father, the devil. Jesus called him a liar and murderer from the beginning, having no truth in him at all. It was the lie that enticed the first creation to doubt and disobey God's command. We can now begin to understand why it is all liars along with murderers perverts and others are slated for the lake of fire. The devil attacked mankind in his infancy with lies, and those demonic beings also preyed upon man in his infancy. Woe to them! To lie is an instant death sentence to be carried out at the appointed time the Judge so sets. Deceiving others is looked upon as a prime candidate for eternal flame, but to deceive one's self into thinking that a chance in hell exists, or a chance to dethrone God exists, is pure foolishness. The lie is so strongly abhorrent to God that even for someone saying, ***"Thus says the Lord"*** (and the Lord did not say it) a death sentence is attached for misrepresenting God. With respect to the Pharisees and teachers of the law they not only misrepresented truth but they knowingly misrepresented God. They did what they did in order to maintain their positions of authority and status over the common man. I guess one could say they loved to lord it over others. When people covet their positions of authority over others, and attempt to control even the knowledge of right and wrong within the individual, it is equivalent to a vicarious or substitute misrepresentation of God.

Insomuch as the conscience can be looked upon as the voice of God within us, directing us to right and wrong, others have no right of denunciation, for with the *mind of Christ* there are no gray areas for needed light. Attempts aimed at subjugating conscience (to impose your will upon another) are really disguises designed to remove the freedom given by truth. It's also a veil designed to obscure and denounce the will of God. To deny truth is to deny freedom on an individual basis. Whosoever the Son sets free is truly free and able to determine what is right and wrong, in general understanding, as in the commandments as well as on an individual basis. There are situations and activities that for some are not considered sinful, while to others their conscience or religious teaching declares it to be a sin. One example of this is Paul eating meat offered to idols, his faith permitted him to do so, but others saw it as a sinful act. If we are to be judged on an individual basis we must never relinquish our ability to discern right and wrong as it applies to our own life. Thus we are told to not judge others. As for those denied the truth to recognize what God requires of us, by those who wish to keep themselves in controlling positions as spiritual guides dwelling in a land of darkness, they are destined for the lake of fire. No matter how a lie is presented it will always have a faulty disguise. Fancy suits and robes or ornamentations of gold cannot distract away or hide the dirt and grime of the lie. It may not immediately be recognized, but will always be unveiled by the light of truth. It will always be clearly seen with the unveiling of time.

The loser

Revelation 20:1-2 *"And I saw an angel coming down out of heaven, having the key to the Abyss and holding in his hand a great chain. He seized the dragon, that ancient serpent, who is the devil or Satan, and bound him for a thousand years."* So much for tough guys whose bark is much bigger than their bite. Can we imagine the servants of the Lord waiting such a long time to be given the green light to chain up this devil? The angel is carrying the key to the Abyss and a great chain. This is the authority and power of God on display. I can almost see the hands being raised and the cries for attention, to be the one who snatches the devil by the neck and tosses him into the abyss. Finally, no more diplomacy as was the case with the conversation between Michael and Satan as they ***"quarreled"*** over the body of Moses. At that time Michael ended the debate and deferred to the Lord by saying, ***"The Lord, rebuke you!"*** No more debating with God or questioning his judgment as was the case of God declaring Job to be, ***"blameless and upright, a man who fears God and shuns evil."*** Satan had replied to God's comment concerning Job in a manner that suggested Job's motives for being a good servant were not at all of the goody-two-shoes variety. ***"Does Job fear God for nothing?"*** Satan wanted to be God. He places himself into the seeker of truth role of the Holy Spirit. It is the Holy Spirit who searches even the deep things of God, (motives and truth), and Satan was certainly probing and searching for any misstep he could possibly find, in order to claim imperfection in God himself. His backhanded slight against the Holy Spirit was an unpardonable sin. To search is to look into a matter, to examine or to discover truth. We may search with honest intent to discover truth or probe with maliciousness. The devil had assumed the role of malicious prosecutor in his case against Job and by doing so he cast doubt upon the pronouncements of God himself, which reflects upon the role of the Holy Spirit. The Holy Spirit is known as the *"Counselor"* (as is Jesus). *Isaiah 9:6 "And he will be called Wonderful Counselor, Mighty God, Eternal Father, Prince of Peace."* Again, *John 14:25-26 "All this I have spoken while still with you. But the Counselor, the Holy Spirit, whom the Father will send in my name, will teach you all things and remind you of everything I have said to you."*

Jesus had warned the Pharisees that to sin against the Holy Spirit was unpardonable. By attempting to sift through the motives of God in the Assembly of God, he (Satan) was presenting his case to be God. The accuser of man is not about to limit his accusations to just mankind. He is looking for fault in everyone in order to claim the status of God for himself. He had set himself up as judge and is attempting to prove that his verdict is correct, and God is not. The devil did not care about Job and he tormented him in order to elicit anything that would prove God to be wrong in his declaration concerning the character of Job. The devil had used cunning and lies against the first of mankind, but now he is going to use brute force in order to make his point. He fails, as Job is everything God had credited him to be. In another place in scripture we see Jesus making a similar pronouncement about Nathaniel. He says of him, *"He is a real Jew, there is nothing about him that is false."* This kind of evaluation is one we all would love to hear the Lord pronounce concerning ourselves, and in a way the grace of God has said the same thing. The account of the seizure and imprisonment of the devil with relative ease by an angel of the Lord, begs for an answer as to why it is God had tolerated this arrogance in his presence for so long? It may be for the benefit of the onlookers who had gathered to *"present themselves before the Lord." Job 1:6-7 One day the angels came to present themselves before the Lord, and Satan also came with them. The Lord said to Satan, "Where have you come from?" Satan answered the Lord, "From roaming through the earth and going back and forth in it."* If there was ever a non-answer this is it! Satan injects doubt in the pronounced judgment of the Lord (concerning Job being blameless) and if, at that time God were to just deep fry the devil out of existence the question would have remained unanswered leaving everyone with a different impression of just who God is and what he is all about. It was an attempt to malign and it needed to be set right. God's policy has always been for us to reason with him. Transforming the devil into a crispy critter at that time may have left the impression that God is a dictator and unwilling to have his judgment questioned. But God allows this negative in order to prove his position. It may be true that the closer we are to the Lord the greater are the attacks of the enemy. Certainly it was that way for Job. This would certainly make sense, because Jesus is the Good Shepherd who leads his flock from the front, and not concerned at all with the war before him, he will care for all who will follow no matter what adversity is placed in our way.

Black

Black the widow's cloth like sack of old
Declaring undying love to a starving world.
Black the hole in space theory thought accepted
Blacker still the place of love rejected.
Black the ancient plague feeding need to flames
Blacker still the mountains filled with man's remains.
Black the beggar's bowl grasped by outstretched hope
Blacker still, the heart that fails to see the soul.
Black the tie of formal wear
Corruption dressed to hide, knit one purl two, snares.
Black the secret veiled by the coffin pall
Black the sailor's sea and black the eye of war.
Black the robes in rooms of hearing worn
Deaf as death itself to graceful wisdom borne
Upon the rushing wind that sings her righteous song.
Black the hearts of men blindness captive scorn
Chains of prideful thought invite, lightning fall!
Black the day when night is no more
Justice and judgment is at man's door.

Luke 10:18 I saw Satan fall like lightning from heaven.

Might

The potter breaks the clay for the defects it presents.
The creator shall send injustice into flight
Smashing it to pieces by the power of what's right.
The lofty pride of man the evil in his hand
The hidden things of hearts and plans produced at night
Will all be brought to justice by the power of his might!
Run to the mountains seek shelter in caves
Now the latent isles thought absent from his gaze
Reveal the foolish measures of man in his last days.

The Lord of all creation has called an end to days
Of thought without the heart and of hearts absent praise!
Look to the heavens.
He comes upon the clouds.
His kingdom to sustain
O man of foolish pride repent!
It's your life to gain.
Before it's too late, before the trumpet sounds
Before the seal he breaks.

Revelation 19:11 I saw heaven standing open and there before me was a white horse, whose rider is called Faithful and True. With justice he judges and makes war.

Harvest

❦

Growth of blackened core leafing silent corridors
Pride from lofty vantage spreads latent rain poisoned breath.
Darkness creeping within keeping
Works of malice wrought
For naught its flood caustic touch
Viper's cunning plan ensnared
Deceptive hiss of ignorance
Silenced by the Judge.
Tonic sweet a gallant feat
Of blood upon a tree
Weeds to wheat blissful passing
Death to life everlasting
A river passing desert ways
Rejoice filled transformation
Holiness the healing kiss awakens hidden life.
"Keep the wheat!
Take the weeds to fire's strife!"

❦

Matthew 13:14 "The reason I use parables in talking to them, is that they look but do not see, and they listen but do not hear or understand. So the prophesy of Isaiah applies to them." It can be safely said, based upon scriptural analysis, that God can destroy body and soul in hell or he can torment for eternity those he deems worthy of such torment. Either way, we know the decision made is correct and just. We don't know how God can both destroy and/or torment in the one place called hell, but it's only one mystery we cannot fathom. I suspect it is not so difficult for God to accomplish either a living hell or total demise in one place. Mankind and supernatural beings have limitation and prohibitions placed upon their existence. We are given responsibility and are expected to fulfill our purpose. Life is not *"duty free."* Life is both taxing and rewarding. How we conduct ourselves determines the quality of life *here and now* but more importantly after the body dies. We were created for the purpose of God and to deny or deliberately refuse our purpose is to risk his judgment. Remember the fig tree that did not bear fruit (fulfill its purpose), Jesus cursed it and it withered and died. So it is with us who do not complete the purpose for which we have been brought into existence. We can be destroyed at the root like the fig tree (cursed by Jesus) and tossed into the fire for consumption, or else, we may taste the pain of hell's fire and its torment knowing there is no reprieve. We have no real concept of what God can conceive as punishment. It need not be the physical pain we envision, it could be mental (spiritual). Just as the wife of Pilate said she suffered greatly in a dream because of Jesus, does anyone *doubt* God can be a nightmare of unimaginable magnitude, throughout eternity for those he has judged to be worthy?

Let it Go

Guilt of the mind
Sighs of the heart
Thoughts of intent
Acts without love
Let it go and make a new start
Now is the time for repentance and grace
Think not of tomorrow it will not save
There's no hiding deep in the grave
It will not forestall destiny's rage
Let it go and make a new start
God is forgiving up to a point
Reach for his pardon or spend life in the joint.

Daniel 6:26 I issue a decree that in every part of the kingdom people must fear and reverence the God of Daniel. For he is the living God, and he endures forever, his kingdom will not be destroyed, his dominion will never end. He rescues and he saves; he performs signs and wonders in the heavens and on the earth.

Having taken a superficial peek into the options God has, with respect to total destruction or eternal torment, let us now take a closer but deeper look at one who is the recipient of eternal torment.

The Rich Man and Lazarus

Luke 16:19-24 "There was a rich man who was dressed in purple and fine linen and lived in luxury everyday. At his gate was laid a beggar named Lazarus, covered with sores and longing to eat what fell from the rich man's table. Even the dogs came and licked his sores. The time came when the beggar died and the angels carried him to Abraham's side. The rich man also dies and was buried. In hell, where he was in torment, he looked up and saw Abraham far away, with Lazarus by his side. So he called to him, 'Father Abraham, have pity on me and send Lazarus to dip the tip of his finger in water and cool my tongue, because I am in agony in this fire.' But Abraham replied, 'Son, remember that in your lifetime you received your good things, but now he is comforted here, and you are in agony. And besides all this, between us and you a great chasm has been fixed, so that those who want to go from here to you cannot, nor can anyone cross over from there to us.'" The discourse between Abraham and the rich man is one that brings our attention to the dismal finality awaiting those who have failed to recognize the chasm of separation existing in this lifetime. While Abraham rightly makes known to the rich man the barrier existing between them and the connotation of great separation existing within the context of distance, there is also the subjective recognition implying substance between good and evil. This separation begins within the heart and becomes clearly defined as one moves through this allotted portion of life. While the discourse centers on Abraham and the rich man, we should not assume that all of the departed-poor find an open door leading into paradise. Not at all, but what we may infer is it will be much easier for the rich to become distracted by all of the so called, "good things" life has to offer, and in the distraction miss the ultimate good that is God. Abraham was a very rich man.

Genesis 13:2 Abram had become very wealthy in livestock and in silver and gold. But he did not permit himself to become distracted by his wealth, which has a tendency to build into a man an independent attitude that forms a great divide of pride. Abraham is thought to be a symbolic representation in this parable presented to us by Jesus, but it may also represent the organizational chain of command within the kingdom structure. Sadly for the rich man, it represents a total disconnect from God. God does not get involved with conversations with the condemned. He is concerned with the living; they are enjoying his presence and eternal life, as well as all of the good things God has to offer. Abraham imparts a bit of dignity to the rich man by addressing him as "son" but within the designation there is the stark truth that clearly defines the category within the title of son as either good or bad. In this life all children are born into family and the title of son or daughter is given. Nothing can ever change that birthright. As such, the designation of son, accorded the rich man, is accurate and akin to a father speaking to a condemned criminal through the fixed barrier erected by ruling authority. We should also recognize for us to be viewed by God as his children we must also be born into his family; we must be born again as Jesus explains to Nicodemus in the third chapter of the gospel of John.

The place called hell is widely recognized as the place denied the presence of God. This is a profound statement inasmuch as we openly admit to the omnipresent ability of God throughout all of creation. Clearly the place called hell must be a new creation, wherein God has decided he will not be found. What does this place offer absent God's presence? Agony and nothing good are the two main ingredients that come to mind. With respect to the, "nothing good" aspect we should understand that from God's perspective justice is a definite good. However, from Abraham's viewpoint he rightly describes the condition of the damned. Agony is something we cannot imagine, because no one can imagine the torment God can and will impose on those who have chosen to align themselves with a self-centered existence in this lifetime.

The rich man was not asking for much, just a drop of water to ease his pain. Of course water represents to us life and in this condemned condition there can be no life offered. No reprieve, no parole, no commutation of sentence, God's judgment is final. In life the rich enjoy a certain amount of fame. They are accorded the best of life's offerings. Materialism and the coveting nature money engenders attracts many to those possessing such wealth. It is the blind leading the blind syndrome. Who is this rich man? He could be anyone, perhaps an ancient king. Perhaps modern man whose thirst for acquisition of the world's offerings no longer finds his self captured by wealth exclusively. Instead, power and position is sought in order to impose upon others the godlike attitude within the individual whose self-reliant demeanor has demanded a bolder and brighter spotlight. Such demands can and do carryover into all kinds of acquisition designs, the range of which finds residency within business to dictatorial evil. All pride finds a common thread to pronounce itself. The identity of the rich man doesn't matter. He represents multitudes that have found damnation. They may be likened to a mountain of bones that share only death-death on display in the heat of naked exposure. We may also envision the *"valley of dry bones"* as seen by the prophet Ezekial. The impression is monumental and lasting. Throughout all of mankind's shared existence of mortality we find two complete end results. Both are derived from either the adherence to good or the capturing allurement of man's nature, which rejects even the notion of an authority beyond self. ***Psalm 42:2 "My soul thirsts for God, for the living God.*** From the depths of desperation we may now see the true agony of one who is separated from God. It is one thing to not know God while we are living this life of ours, but it is a completely different situation when one finally comes into direct proximity with God only to find it will be the last time to ever lay eyes upon he who is completely pure and good. This separation, complete with the lasting image of the one true God burned into the memory of the condemned, can cause one to cry out for just a drop of the previous reality; too no avail. While we are still alive in these bodies, our focus upon the things that last and bring to us good, throughout eternity, must not be distracted or lost in the activities that capture and make demands upon our time, to the extent we no longer have time to associate with God. Let us, like the psalmist, seek "streams of water" while we can still be nourished by its life giving qualities within the here and now of our lives. To do so is to guarantee we will not become beggars, lost in a place offering nothing but the failure and regrets of a life wasted in the vain pursuits of sin and death.

"Even the dogs came and licked his sores." This statement is basically an indictment of guilt looming heavily above the head of the rich man. To say even the dogs recognized the agony of Lazarus, and attempted to alleviate some of his suffering through the licking of his wounds, is to pronounce the most damning of evidence against the cold and callous heart of the man finding himself within the same inescapable predicament experienced by Lazarus during his life of misery. What we sow so shall we reap! Is most evident in this depiction of God's justice. ***"The time came when Lazarus died and angels carried him to Abraham's side."*** This added ingredient within the story highlights truth of the existence of angels. During the time of Jesus a portion of the ruling religious rejected the existence of angels, while still another party had held to the belief in such heavenly beings. It is difficult for us to understand how such a separation could occur since angelic appearances within Old Testament writings are clearly documented. As such this addition to the teaching of Jesus also makes clear the truth concerning the angelic host. Lazarus went in style to the bosom of Abraham. He was carried, given a personal escort into paradise. One has to think that this Lazarus person was one who knew God and still he had not blamed God for his sufferings.

"At his gate was laid a beggar named Lazarus. Within this statement we find a twofold meaning. Lazarus was physically placed outside of the home of the rich man and in many instances within scripture we find the meaning of the word "gate" to infer the opening of one's mind to something that is happening. As such we can safely assume that the rich man was fully aware of the presence of Lazarus, perhaps Lazarus could actually see the rich man's table filled with the best of culinary delights. But all he hoped for was the crumbs that fell to the ground; reduced to the level of a dog.

"There was a rich man who was dressed in purple and fine linen and lived in luxury everyday." Purple is not only the color of royalty but it is symbolic of those who could afford clothing of color. This made the rich more pronounced and afforded to them the spotlight of recognition they craved from those who were of lesser value in their assessment of the human condition. One might conclude that he was damned if he did and damned if he did not wear such expensive attire. To dress in royal display would accord to him acceptance among his peers, while to dress down like a common man might very well have been received negatively by this same peer group.

There is no doubt that during the time of Jesus there were those of means who had not fallen to the depth of uncaring ascribed to the rich man within the setting of hell. But these may very well have been few. This rich attire, display of excess while surrounded by such suffering and deprivation, as was the experience of Lazarus, only added to the mental agony of a beggar's condition. Virtually nothing was granted to the man who begged outside the gate of this earthly paradise-the rich man's home. It is fitting that this rich man finds himself outside the gates of heaven where not even the dogs can lick his wounds or relieve his agony. No not even the company of dogs is permitted to him. *"Father Abraham, have pity on me . . ."* Poor Lazarus had to beg for but a short period of time compared to the eternity facing the rich man's eternal punishment. His reward for greed and uncaring appears to be one of the poorest of investment returns, that will shake the godless to their core from everlasting to everlasting.

What was the cause of Lazarus's death? Was it malnutrition? Did he just desire release from his torment so badly that his survival-instinct failed? Along with his hunger for food did his desire to live fail to compensate for the severe nature of his sufferings? Perhaps it was a combination of all of the above? Still, we have to wonder why it is he was brought to the rich man's home, and who are these Good Samaritans who transported him? For the answer to these questions we must look to the surroundings of the time. Certainly there was no social security system that provided for the indigent. A man's social security system was his sons and daughters. To be without family was looked upon as falling under the curse of God, (God had not provided for this man's old age). Truth is we do not know how old Lazarus was when he died. Obviously we can assume he was an older person but that would be to negate the reality of his declining physical health. Moreover, what we find is the underlining reality of one being totally dependent upon the good graces of the rich. It is apparent to us that the rich man in this town was not one endowed with kindness and compassion. As for the identity of the people who brought Lazarus to the attention of the rich man, seeking his favor toward Lazarus, we can only surmise that they were unable to care for him out of their own resources. Great was the responsibility of the rich. The rich were looked upon as favored by God's blessings. As such, they were thought to be pious and elevated above the common man.

Let us remember that the mindset at the time of Jesus was such that as long as one adheres to the law, salvation with respect to acceptability by God was then guaranteed. Unfortunately for many their thoughts in this matter were shattered against the cold hard wall of reality and left to agonize in the hopelessness of despair; just as Lazarus had come to realize in his lifetime, and as the rich man discovered in the afterlife. Jesus points to the way of redemption, but is rejected by those whose self-righteous corruption of truth, regarding one's true condition (sinful) falls upon ears that understand his message but refuse to acknowledge his truth. To these whose priority finds acceptability within their reasoning, that elevates self above truth, the reality of God's supremacy presented to them at the final judgment is tantamount to the light of truth that penetrates and saves those who believe the message of Christ. Unfortunately for them this revelation comes to them at the recognition of the undeniable truth of God, as they stand in awe of the justice administered with perfect precision.

Rich Poor Man

❧

The life one leads is reflected in the end.
Find a resting place of peace
Or agony that lasts.
Find a judgment no defense can beat
Or find the Tree of Life whose fruit is fresh and sweet.
Find the darkness absent light
A blend of screams regret's bite
A taste of just the smallest thing
Cannot be brought to land forlorn
Where lives awaken to past wrong.

All the while it's made known
What remains is bone
Spirit tied into a knot
Finds great the space
Across above it matters not
Rich man poor man without names
Are bound together by a flame
Burns forever without end
How great the chasm deep divide
As deep as thought and twice as wide
What good is it to gain and find
All has been in vain?

❧

Proverbs 16:5 The Lord detests the proud of heart. Be sure of this: They will not go unpunished.

The Rich Ruler

Luke 18:18-25 A certain ruler asked him, "Good teacher, what must I do to inherit eternal life?" "Why do you call me good?" Jesus answered. "No one is good—except God alone. You know the commandments: 'Do not commit adultery, do not commit

murder, do not steal, do not give false testimony, honor your father and mother." "All these I have kept since I was a boy," he said. When Jesus heard this, he said to him. "You still lack one thing. Sell everything you have and give to the poor, and you will have treasure in heaven. Then come, follow me." When he heard this he became very sad, because he was a man of great wealth. Jesus looked at him and said, "How hard it is for the rich to enter the kingdom of God! Indeed, it is easier for a camel to go through the eye of a needle than for a rich man to enter the kingdom of God."

I have read this account of the rich young ruler many times, and in some instances I find a degree of self-righteous pride emanating from this rich young man. He has already been apprised of his non-good status; Jesus revealing to him, none are good except for God. Still, the young man makes the declaration pointing to his adherence to the commandments and within this statement he seeks additional hurdles to overcome that would assure him of eternal life. *"Sell everything you have, give the proceeds to the poor"* and then do what your initial instinct had led you to do. Seek out the truth of your life by following the example of Christ. Become dependent upon the mercy of God and not confined to the false dependency of riches; riches will not gain for you the kingdom of God and the prize of life. This young man did not hear what he was expecting. He may have been so blinded by his own appraisal of himself, expecting to gain accolades from Jesus that lauded the good life he had led. Instead, he is told he needs to make a sacrifice of all he held most precious; of what he had judged most needed to maintain not only his status within society but also the appearance of one willing to do what God requires. His attention is heightened only to be dashed upon the rocks of reality clearly making it understood, what he sought cannot be bought! He wants this challenge, to do more, because his riches are such that it is unimaginable to him that he could not accomplish whatever it was Jesus had found lacking in him. He is saddened to learn, is greatly disappointed by hearing it is not something he can accomplish with his wealth, except to get rid of it! When Jesus tells him he still lacks one thing, he never imagined how poor he really was; his wildest dream could not have taken him to the depths of poverty presently surrounding his life. This reality was too much for him to understand, for in the mindset of those who have always found and expected deference from others, not only respectful of their opinions but their wealth, it was impossible for him to hear the truth spoken deep into the darkness of his unwillingness to change from ruler to servant. In many ways within today's reality we find a servant-master's mindset, especially within those elected to represent others, affording to them a voice that's so often denied the individual without wealth in both riches and /or celebrity status. Even the foolish among the wealthy and celebrated find avenues to project their thoughts into the minds and hearts of others. How sad it will be for them who do not hear the voice of Jesus saying, *"Come follow me."*

We have now taken a look into two conditions suffered by the rich. One of which is inherent in the class of the wealthy, which forms a malignancy of thought that produces a callous barrier around the heart of one so afflicted. We see this clearly in the story of the ***"Rich man and Lazarus."*** The other is exemplified within the discourse between the rich young ruler and Jesus. His need to divest himself of the idolatry associated with his wealth and the power to make changes within his environment is all too much of a sacrifice for him to even begin to fathom. As such his callous attitude is displayed in the unwillingness to find dependency upon God for his daily bread. His reliance upon worldly wealth to maintain an appearance of division between himself and the masses, to the exclusion of himself from the sinner category, based upon his determination regarding worthiness of the kingdom of God. Interesting is the fact that neither the rich young ruler, nor the rich man who finds himself in hell are afforded an identity. Even the little they had was taken away from them. In the one he has found the eternal surroundings of hell. In the other he only imagines hell to be upon this earth, absent the security of his wealth. Neither one is found to be acceptable to God.

There is another form of idolatrous behavior associated with displacing the provision of God with worldly wealth. This is found in the desire to acquire. So alluring is this desire that the results one would usually associate with wealth-acquired, are also found in individuals whose attention is fixed upon achieving satisfaction in the offerings of the world. For this example from scripture let us take a look at a man called Gehazi, the servant of Elisha the prophet.

2 Kings 5:19-21 "Go in peace," Elisha said. After Naaman had traveled some distance, Gehazi, the servant of Elisha the man of

God, said to himself, "My master was too easy on Naaman, this Aramean, by not accepting from him what he brought. As surely as the Lord lives, I will run after him and get something from him."

Gehazi's Price

Gehazi is a servant of the prophet Elisha. As the story is told, a man named Naaman (one who is wealthy and a commander in the army of the king of Aram) is seeking a cure for his leprosy in the land of Israel. He is referred to the prophet Elisha by the king of Israel and his (Naaman's) expectations are that Elisha will come out to meet him and call upon the name of the Lord his God and in this he would be healed. Instead, Elisha sends his servant to him with instruction for Naaman to go and bathe seven times in the Jordan River and he will be healed. Sounds all to simple to Naaman whose expectations are such that given the letter of introduction he had carried to the king of Israel, along with those who accompanied him and the gifts of treasure at his disposal, he had thought the prophet would put on a display of great power in honor of his arrival with credentialed request in hand. Naaman finally follows these simple instructions and is healed. He attempts to bestow payment to the prophet with many gifts, but is told in essence, it is not necessary to do so.

It is then that the avaricious juices within the character of Gehazi begin to spin the lie he understands will gain for him the wealth and position he had inwardly always craved. Ultimately Gehazi is reduced to the fate one should expect from God. He had placed a price tag upon the free gift of God and in so doing had reduced God to the level of one whose motivation for doing good is profit. And so we see that the desire for wealth can also make it impossible for the poor man to enter into the kingdom of God. Not only did Gehazi find a living hell on earth by acquiring the disease of Naaman, but he also had caused a cloud of despair within himself continually forecasting his future on the great Day of Judgment. And speaking of future, not only did Gehazi doom himself to a life of misery from that day forward, but he also caused all of his descendants to live under the curse of God. One could say this form of greed displayed by Elisha's servant attaches with it hereditary impact of lasting proportion, from which there was no cleansing available. However, it is safe to assume such a judgment upon Gehazi and all of his descendants (this can mean all of those directly descended from him, and in a broader sense all of those whose greed equals or surpasses Elisha's servant) will follow them into the grave and to the ultimate judgment of either an eternal sentence of torment in hell or else total destruction of both body and soul in the lake of fire also known as the second death. There is a time in a person's life that he finds it necessary to gather together the things of this world, and this is not usually a bad thing. It becomes bad when the desire to acquire trespasses across the barriers of legally acceptable and morally correct activity. Greed is bad and uncontrolled greed is even worse. For the one who remains fixed in this state of mind there is no redemption. However, many a rich man has found the error of his ways and repented. There was a chief tax collector that Jesus honored by spending time in his home, the man was so grateful he made restitution to everyone he had cheated and salvation had come to this man. And so, for God all things are possible, even bringing salvation of a rich tax collector, which is as difficult as placing a camel through the eye of a needle.

TROUBLED WATER

Wherever people gather there is potential for corruption. Where the purpose for gathering is self-preservation, desperation and need, corruption's potential is increased in proportion to motivation. Thematic occurrences within scripture are the norm and exemplify for us our need. The condition of man is highlighted throughout the history of God's chosen people. The recurring themes of corrupt behavior, rebellion, chastisement and judgment all signal to us our need for vigilance to remain faithful to God. Woven throughout the magnificent tapestry that is the word of God we find good and evil, success and failure, truth and deception, exemplified in those who have had firsthand tutoring from God. The behaviors spotlighted in scripture, having failed or succeeded in the ways of God, hold multipurpose lessons for us that will stand out as beacons throughout the existence of man.

So many illnesses and so little cures, such was the time of Christ. It was a time of faith and a time of hope. There was hope in the faith that had proved to be viable within those who sought a healing from God. Many seeking a cure had gathered regularly at the healing pool in Jerusalem. Perhaps some were unable to leave the pool confines and were regarded as so much human suffering, handed over to the mercy of God. There is much within this gathering of faithful that runs counter to the love of God, and so we must consider what may have actually been taking place. The following is an attempt to explore what appears to be a deceptive endeavor within the human condition of corruption.

John 5:1-9 Some time later, Jesus went up to Jerusalem for a feast of the Jews. Now there is in Jerusalem near the Sheep Gate a

pool, which in Aramaic is called Bethesda and which is surrounded by five covered colonnades. Here a great number of disabled people used to lie-the blind the lame and paralyzed. One who was there had been an invalid for thirty-eight years. When Jesus saw him lying there and learned that he had been in this condition for a long time, he asked him, "Do you want to get well?" "Sir" the invalid replied, "I have no one to help me into the pool when the water is stirred. While I am trying to get in, someone else goes down ahead of me." Jesus then said to him, "Get up! Pick up your mat and walk." At once the man was cured; he picked up his mat and walked. Apparently faith was alive and well in Jerusalem. It had become common knowledge and traditional belief that a healing could be obtained at the Sheep Gate pool for anyone swift of foot. This Sheep Gate lottery appears to have the underpinnings of opportunism aimed at enriching the established religious of the day. Many people gathered at the pool in the belief that periodically God would send his angel to stir up the water, and whoever got into the pool first (as the water was stirred) would be healed. Healing on a first come first served basis places people into a mindset believing God is too busy and impatient to heal all, thus, "Get on your mark, get set, go!" And just like a race there were those who signaled the first sign of the water's turbulence and perhaps, also determined the winner. There were those who not only encouraged the spark of hope, they aided and abetted the production of and continued belief in the purported miraculous healings. Choice locations affording best chance of first entry may very well have been sold at a premium to the newly infirmed (rich) seeking a quick fix. Otherwise how can we account for thirty-eight years of faithful hope present in the one Jesus healed? For those unable to walk or run men could be employed to carry them to the desired finish line at the moment the water was troubled.

Thus the response, *"Sir, I have no one to put me in the pool."* Certainly one would think after thirty-eight years of seeking a cure, attrition alone should have gained him a choice position where he could just fall into the pool at the first sign of the angel's presence. This man had no such luck. Those who could pay for a hired hand may have been fortunate enough to hire the swift of foot entrepreneurs. It follows the cynicism of this observer that the winners of this lottery may very well have been no more than nuggets placed into an old gold mine, or healthy individuals masquerading as the infirmed, no different than the healing tents of charlatan preachers capitalizing on the desperate within the theater of troubled water. And yes, just like the tent healer revivals provided shelter from the elements the "colonnades" provided a sense of security reminiscent of the homes they may have lived in. With respect to tent revival healings, mostly it was the preacher who received a communication from God involving a person with a specific aliment, and as he describes the ailment he also selects the afflicted and selected by God from the crowd. He prays over the afflicted and instantly the afflicted is miraculously transformed and made whole. The packaging of these deceptive affronts to God may appear different but the content is the same deception of old.

Others who had hired men in hope of a healing had such hope dashed upon the rocks of cruel disappointment, and as the so-called newly healed recipient openly praised God for his mercy, a renewed hope in the next race to restoration was born. I'm sorry to say, this situation *does not* sound like God's love, it is identical to circumstances we must conclude to be a scam. It's inconceivable to think the power of God was at work within such a cruel context. One can be persuaded to believe this pool *business* was just that, a business designed to impoverish the sheep even more. This pool focus, (even though the story incorporated an angel of the Lord as instrumental) failed to focus upon God. Certainly God would not play this cruel game with the children of Israel. Certainly this pool practice did not reflect the compassion of God. Enter Jesus. Our Lord sees the man and asks, **"Do you want to get well?"** It is almost laughable to hear Jesus ask this question of a man he knew to be long suffering, and who has had tremendous faith in the prescription available for those seeking a cure within an atmosphere of desperation. Outside of the concrete truth contained in scripture, traditional beliefs are born, and many have flirted indirectly or otherwise with unfaithfulness to God. In other words, all that is contained in scripture is true, but not everything of truth is a depiction of good. As such, throughout God's word we find good and evil, success and failure, truth and deception in order for us to be made aware.

An interesting observation within the context of this healing pool of religious oversight calls attention to the beliefs of some and not others. The Pharisees held belief in angels while the Sadducees did not, thus one might conclude this healing pool business was strictly a Pharisee run operation. *2 Corinthians 11:13-14 "For such men are false apostles, deceitful workmen, masquerading as apostles of Christ. And no wonder, for Satan himself masquerades as an angel of light. It is not surprising, then, if his servants masquerade as servants of righteousness. Their end will be what their actions deserve."* "Sure, I want to be healed, says the man," but look at me, I don't have anyone to pick me up and put me into the pool. Jesus sees the faith of the man, knows of his long suffering and has compassion on him. Okay, says Jesus, you're healed get out of here. He picks up his mat and walks away. This is where the waters of tradition are troubled. The religious observe the man carrying his mat on the Sabbath. They notice this thirty-eight year veteran of the pool brigade has been cured by means other than the traditional prescribed authorized method. They stop him and ask why he is carrying his mat. They are not interested in his cure and how that may have come about. No, they are interested in the outward expression of enforcing the law. At least it may appear to be the case, but like a minor traffic infraction can open the door to further investigation by a police officer, so it may be with these religious police. They knew he was healed, he had been hanging around the pool for thirty-eight years, but they had nothing to do with his healing and this must have been perplexing to those operating a scam. One has to wonder how they picked him out of the crowd while all other activities went unchallenged? These religious police were quick to see an infraction of the law; a man carrying his mat working on the Sabbath, meanwhile everywhere about them there is sanctioned work being performed for a price. The man replies, *"The man who made me well said to me, "Pick up your mat and walk."* Of course, this was an affront to the Sabbath law as interpreted by the religious. There's a curious thing about religious rulers, they have very little tolerance for those who dare infringe upon their controlling grip. This coveting of power makes plain their intent to exploit faith and deny truth to those most desperately seeking God. It reveals an attitude of disrespect for the things of God by replacing him with the counterfeits of tradition and manmade rules. It shows a willingness to exploit for profit that which is offered free of charge to those whose faith recognizes and seeks God. The healing pool practice has not been done away with. Faith has nothing to do with chance. *"Woe to you shepherds!"*

Hurry-Hurry

❧

Step right this way folks
Special dispensations for all who have the price
Cures for all your hurts, peace of mind and light!
Do your limbs fail to function?
No problem we can't solve we have the healing water
And no sins we can't absolve.
It is we who hold the power to permit or bind your faith
Hurry-hurry before it is too late.
It's not the age of grace but splash for cash we're hawking.
Is your body weak and broken?
Do you want to walk?
Smiles are cheap my friend but it's cash that talks the talk!

❧

2 Kings 5:9-10 So Naaman went with his horses and chariots and stopped at the door of Elisha's house. Elisha sent a messenger to say to him, "Go, wash yourself seven times in the Jordan, and your flesh will be restored and you will be cleansed.

Fat Cats

The love of power is a product the pride, power of love speaks gentle and
wise.
The love of standing applause cannot hear truth calling out to the lost.
Jets and limousines not bothersome lines for kings and queens.
Titans of industry tycoons and heirs show us a picture absent cares.
Facades of perfection faces aglow behind the projection lives darkness
below.
Hollywood hammers celebrity nails erecting the sets designed to fail.
Seekers of office like sails of a ship dip into the wind and flow with its
grip.
Deceiving pulpits lofty as sky declare to the masses financial praise.
Demons plaguing our days are not conquered by prayer but with capital
raised.
Everything has a price it is said but some things should never be sold.
The faith of a friend, the bond of love, the soul of a man and a child's
trust
The gift of wisdom and knowledge of plans should never be passed from
pocket to hand.
An atmosphere free of shallow thoughts sees a border that must not be
crossed.
Some cats are wearing really thick glasses still everyone gets his cut
It's not vision needing correction it's the heart.
Many fail what is just and ignore the law they acquire positions and
manipulate flaws.
Never addressing sidestepping ways but pack opportunity as a bigot stores
rage.
Greed builds great walls and erects circles absent only is the barbed wire.

The homes of some are beautiful prisons.
We reap what we sow, nothing is for keeps, time drifting toward
tomorrow
Suddenly arriving to collect what is borrowed.
Not power coin or pride can revive a silent heart.
Cold cash in a freezer no matter how many grand, will turn over

As clothes in the dryer, as combat demands, hand to hand.
The cycle ending according to plan mercy accepted or fiery end.

～ ～ ～

***James 3:13-16 Who is wise and understanding among you?
Let him show it by his good life, by deeds done in humility that
comes from wisdom. But if you harbor bitter envy and selfish
ambition in your hearts, do not boast about it or deny the truth.
Such wisdom does not come down from heaven but is earthly,
unspiritual, of the devil. For where you have envy and selfish
ambition, there you find disorder and every evil practice.***

Do you want to get well?

Jesus knows he is addressing a man who has suffered for a long period of time. Jesus is not attempting to stir up the faith in the man and have him focus it on God; he is simply asking the question in order to point the way to becoming whole. The invalid man, upon hearing the question asked of him immediately responds by stating his poverty has prevented him from claiming the remedial cure. ***"I don't have anyone to help me gain entrance into the pool when the waters are stirred up,"*** is his reply. Upon hearing this Jesus just tells the man to, ***"Get up! Pick up your mat and walk."*** At once the man is cured; set free from the pool brigade of narrow-minded expectations regarding the God who loves him.

What was it that caused the man to immediately find healing? What must have been going through his head at the moment of his first step? I can imagine the look of patience upon the face of Jesus as he awaited the reality of his question to sink into the man. There must have been a perfect meeting of the minds as the words of Christ dug into the reality Jesus wanted the man to recognize. "Yes! Yes! Yes! I want to be healed" may have been the mental explosions erupting in the heart and mind of the man as he raised himself from the position of wanting to the reality of life he formerly could only imagine.

No hoops to jump through and no race to run, he now realized he had only to desire the freedom present in healing in order to claim it for himself. Like a child asking a parent for food so it is with us who seek a miracle from the God who loves us. Jesus points to the spiritual

111

principle of asking seeking and knocking and permits the man to recognize what he had been searching for all of his life has always been available to him. ***"Do you want to be healed?"*** is the question asked of us all, regardless of the condition we seek to be freed from. Could it be that simple? Surely the man who was now walking and carrying his mat out from the confines of depression and hopelessness must have been asking himself this very thing. No doubt his steps were bold and confident as he strode before those who knew of his thirty-eight years long confinement. It was now his turn to praise God with a boldness that only comes from knowing God has touched and healed him on every level of existence.

Naaman seeks a cure

Let's look again at the story of Naaman the Syrian who comes to Israel seeking a cure for his affliction. Naaman is the commander of the Syrian army and is highly regarded by the king of Syria. Despite being a great soldier, he sufferers from a dreaded skin disease. Anytime we see the descriptive "dreaded" we know it is more than a bad case of acne. It is one that invokes fear in the afflicted and causes one to seek a cure through that which is not available within the normal healing remedies available to man. When all hope is lost it is then mankind lifts his eyes to a higher level of existence, and in the case of Namaan he travels to Israel to find the prophet of God called Elisha. Naaman brings with him a small fortune in anticipation of a cure. Elisha does not go out to meet him despite his letters of recommendation and excellent reputation. Elisha sends his servant to speak the words that will gain for Naaman the cure he seeks. ***"Go wash yourself seven times in the Jordan River and you will be cured."*** At this point Namaan becomes enraged and begins his return to Syria, perhaps thinking to his self, "I could have done this in a Syrian river and the water there is cleaner!" The people traveling with Naaman, persuade him to try the prescription, he does and is cured.

Unlike the healing pool there is no mad dash to the finish line. But like the healing pool there is the question in the minds of those seeking a cure. Can it really be this simple? In order to conflate these two activities (the healing pool waters and the Jordan River) we must look to see what it is that hinders healing? Underlining both situations there is human reasoning that places known limitation into the realm of the impossible. It is only when authority outside the confines of the individual pronounces a way to that which is sort after does the light of reality shine forth its ability to cure. The authority spoken to the seeker allows the one who receives it to open the door from within his self. This authority is truth. Jesus spoke truth to the invalid, ***"Get up! Pick up your mat and walk."*** The truth present in the authority of Christ opened the door to belief and in this belief the power of God (always present in his creation) was unleashed to overcome that which was formerly believed to be impossible. This is an intriguing and gripping statement wherein we have only to believe in the ability of God and such belief will then be transformed in us as power! Power not only to cure the afflictions plaguing the flesh but also to remove the horizons of limitation present in our thoughts as they apply to what is impossible for man. So true are the words of scripture: ***"All things are possible for those who believe"***

It now becomes evident that the problem with inability lies in the heart of man who will not or cannot believe in the ability of God to cure all of our illnesses and to solve all of our problems. The inability to believe God's power can overcome anything stems from our very own nature. It is the *"sin and doubt"* condition that is only overcome within a born again or similar occurrence. It is within these moments or windows of clarity that we are able to say without the nagging background of doubt, "I believe." It is this total belief that opens for us the doorway of infinite possibility. No longer are we hindered by the disbelief that denies truth. At these times in our life prayer is approached with not only confidence but with surety! For anyone who has tasted such truth, the faith established is unshakable. Still, over time there is the tendency for us to drift away from the monolith of established faith and once again find that nagging voice holding us back from the infinite realm of God. This is not as bad as it may sound, because, who can say they can be trusted with such power? I certainly cannot, many times my first inclination is impulsive and fueled by emotional reaction. Thank God for his checks and balances hindering our ability to move mountains.

And so as we look upon the Sheep Gate pool we may find there may have been instances where both desire and faith find unity unlocking the doorway to that which is sort after. For the most part the actors in the healing pool are all powerless to achieve due to the fact that the authority given to them in truth is not recognized. The illusion of prescribed action is all that is necessary to shore up and strengthen the foundations of hope. As long as hope is made available the human condition for self-preservation will continue to seek a positive outcome. Thus the invalid spent thirty-eight years clinging to the hope presented. Where there is deception truth is diluted and in the dilute solution a weakening of power is advanced. Honesty is the mortar that builds a monolith of faith, and in this structure there is found stability in whatever condition we may find ourselves inhabiting. Sadly the Sheep Gate pool did not offer honesty, but relied upon the trigger of hope to make manifest the desires of those who could find no release from their condition of hopelessness. Thus it was a scam with its underpinnings deeply rooted in the religious rulers of the day. Their ambitions and desire to remain in control of the populace outweighed the cries of the beaten broken battered and bruised, not only within the physical illnesses of the day but the mental anguish only fathomed by the outcasts of society. A healing given to the hopeless ignites a cascading river of love and faith in the receiver of such mercy. ***"Pick up your mat and walk,"*** are the very words spoken to us at the lowest moments of our former lives without Christ. When we remember where we were and how far we have drifted from our initial acknowledgement of truth, we then can return to the faith that was initially established throughout the totality of our being; the very moment of rebirth.

The authority we claim is the Word of God (Jesus), and in his authority we can move forward in the freedom God desires for us. It really makes sense for us to have a self-directing ability in all aspects of life. This is free will at its optimum. It is the ability to return to the beginning of creation wherein we had no barriers, save for the directive given by God. Just as we were empowered by God in the beginning so it is we receive again the ability to direct our lives through the truth present in faith. When there is no doubt that God will grant and give to us the righteous desires of our lives, this pure trust transforms the mustard seed of faith into the explosive force needed to move mountains. There is then no need for healing pools or charlatan preachers for we have come to God in the innocence of love.

Healing

Into the mist of cloud filled skies
The heart descends and spirit cries
Tremors race to temple's brace
Purchase heavy whispers, "Break."
Defense born at marrow's gate
Enter still the crashing waves of yesterday.
A shade a shroud a coffin pall
Ending day in westward fall
Wisp of cloud bows above
Through it all love remains the healer of souls.

With truth comes sweet surrender
To walk on water in the storm
To holdfast hope we have known
To see the fruit upon the vine
With leaves of green in sunlight reign
Etched into each the precious name
Of all God has saved.

John 15:5-7 "I am the vine and you are the branches. Whoever remains in me, and I in him, will bear much fruit; for you can do nothing without me. Whoever does not remain in me is thrown out like a branch and dries up; such branches are gathered up and thrown into the fire, where they are burned. If you remain in me and my words remain in you, then you will ask for anything you wish and you shall have it."

Scam Shame

❦

Beware of those fancy suits
Their hard sell of worldly pursuits
They'll invite you to purchase
A prayer cloth that's worthless
Or shares in an earthly campaign
It bolsters their image-theatrical visage
Rewarding with mansions and things
They are not serving the King!

❦

2 Corinthians 2:17 "Unlike so many, we do not peddle the word of God for profit. On the contrary, in Christ we speak before God with sincerity, like men sent from God."

Name It And Claim It

The electronic church of today brings pictures of worldly success.
The doctrine proclaimed is always the same: "Claim to your heart's
content."
We have witnessed television preachers dragged off to prison in tears
Not of repentance but lamenting the sentence deserving the doctrine they
claimed.
There was he who gave a deadline to congregations present and home
Proclaiming, "Funds must be raised or God will cut short my days."
Still, another displayed great emotion in forums of public devotion
His doctrine failing the test of desires presented to flesh.
Don't be misled by this poem not all TV preachers are wrong.

God never promised material worth not kingdoms or riches on earth.
But for those who believe him enough to receive him
Lay claim to new life in rebirth.

**Luke 12:15 Then he said to them, "Watch out! Be on your guard
against all kinds of greed; a man's life does not consist in the
abundance of his possessions."**

IT'S VERY LATE

Only in man is recognition of mortality suppressed and reluctance to do God's will found. Everything in life has an appointed time to become what is ordained to be. Everything has its built in timing. In man there is unwillingness to heed God's intent to become all he desires for us. There is an unwritten comfort zone that man embraces and like the setting of the sun it sends to him a conditioned signal to cease work. Man is not a part of the clockwork mechanisms set into motion by God, we do not have to rise with the sun or retire at its setting. Enter Jesus, and the time clocks of custom are reset to the compassionate rhythm of God.

Mark 6:34-36 When Jesus got out of the boat, he saw a large crowd, and his heart was filled with pity for them, because they were like sheep without a shepherd. So he began to teach them many things. When it was getting late, his disciples came to him and said, "It is already late, and this is a lonely place. Send the people away, and let them go to the nearby farms and villages in order to buy themselves something to eat," "You yourselves give them something to eat," Jesus answered.

He had compassion on them because they were like sheep without a shepherd. He had sympathy for their suffering because they were without someone to care for them. Earlier in the day Jesus left the crowd by boat and when he had reached shore he found the people waiting for him. They were like little children seeking the attention of a busy parent. They rushed after Jesus because they were hungry for the food that would not perish. The food sought by the hearts of men is the nourishment that satisfies the inner desire for God. They desired to be as sheep with a shepherd who is worthy to follow. They were seeking a shepherd who would lay down his life for his sheep, who would not abandon them to the hardships of the lost. They wanted one who would lead them to springs of life giving water and rest, derived from being loved.

Like foremen of factory operations the disciples call it a day and alert the owner of the business to pull the plug; it is getting very late and the time has come to shutdown production. Like older children the disciples interrupt the parent attending the younger siblings. They give instruction to Jesus that they believe is perfectly sound advice: **"It is already late, and this a lonely place. Send the people away, and let them go to the nearby farms and villages in order to buy themselves something to eat."** Jesus doesn't say to them what they expected to hear. Their expectation was one that might include, *"Yes you are right it is getting late and we have to find shelter and there is wood to gather and a fire to build and dinner to cook and lastly a lesson to be learned."* Instead, he tells them to feed the crowd and in that declaration reality hits home in the minds of the disciples. I wish I could have seen the incredulous look upon their faces when Jesus told them to feed the people. We know their response had to be one of dumbfounded disbelief. Jesus told them to feed five thousand people! With perplexed verbalizing they say, **"Do you want us to go and spend two hundred silver coins on bread in order to feed them?"** They couldn't even suggest a simple meal. It's apparent they needed to understand that man, **"does not live by bread alone."** There's no doubt a huge number relating to cost was tossed up into the air to emphasize the enormity of the task Jesus had placed upon them, not to mention the logistic problems that were not addressed. It was not as if they had a supermarket down the road, or a local fast food restaurant that delivers. Surely they could not carry all of the necessary food even if they could find it before nightfall. In the minds of the disciples they were doing what they had always done. That is, at the end of the day they reported to Jesus and settled in for a teaching and shared meal. The disciples had five loaves of bread and two fish. It was hardly enough for the disciples but this does not deter Jesus. He instructs them to have the people sit down on the green grass in groups of fifty and groups of a hundred. An awesome display of the provision of God is about to take place. Jesus takes the five loaves and two fish, looks up to heaven and gives thanks to God. He divides the food and tells the disciples to feed the people. They feed all of the people and still have twelve baskets of food leftover. More than enough for the twelve grumbling bellies forced to work overtime. Sure they had more than enough valid reasons for calling it a day. But in service to others it is God who provides the means for the servant to accomplish. The disciples had to be taught that it is God who provides even when there is no perception of possibility within the vision of man to do so. The irony of course is that Jesus is clearly visible. What we may think is our normal time for rest may not always be the agenda for the one we serve. Jesus had said, *John 5:17 "My Father is always at work, to this very day, and I, too, am working."* Therein we understand the meaning of the word follower. The disciples responded to the instruction of Jesus like so many of us when the time of day or the environment does not correspond to our way of thinking. It is no wonder Paul urges us to have the mind of Christ, *Philippians 2:5 "Your attitude should be the same as that of Christ Jesus."* All too often it seems we place our wants and needs ahead of others and fail to recognize the priorities of God. To follow instructions and keep our focus upon the one who leads is the purpose of sheep. The shepherd is always in command of the flock, no matter how close to the shepherd some sheep may be.

Jesus was not going to send the disciples shopping. He was leading them into an exercise of faith and recognition that nothing is impossible for God and everything is possible for the one who believes. They were set in their ways, tuned into the frequency of their lives, wherein routine expectation and perceived reality followed an order of reasoning that needed to be shattered by the reality of God. They had no idea concerning the harvest of faith that awaited them. Great is the reward of the obedient servant as evidenced by the twelve baskets of abundance remaining. The disciples had looked into the face of the impossible and had acted accordingly. Like so many of us we become convinced that with many voices, wrong can become right. It's like saying, "It's not just *me* but *we* have a problem with this situation." As if that were enough to justify our lack of recognition in God's abilities. Neither did they understand that a shepherd does not have a nine-to-five job. There are no time clocks in service to others. They did not recognize that compassion for others gives us strength to go beyond perception of personal ability. It brings us clearly into the realm of, *"all things are possible with God."*

As soon as Jesus instructs the disciples to feed the people, he is confronted by the negative response of incredulous disbelief. Say what? Jesus was going to feed the sheep with more than bread and fish. The main course would be their understanding of the presence of God. Jesus will not only provide food for the belly, but nourishment for the spirit as well. The people had followed Jesus because in all of their lives no one had cared enough to explain to them the truth of God, and that they were worth much more than they could ever imagine. Jesus shatters the bubble of limitation and injects the reality of God, by teaching and exhibiting tangible evidence of his wanting to care for and protect his flock against all adversity. This complete physical and spiritual care for the multitude was a display of the powerful compassion of God, never before witnessed in the lifetime of those present. God had never been up front and personal for the people to see or hear. There is also little doubt that the excitement generated was as contagious as a smile or laughter. It was truth they had come to hear, and Jesus did not disappoint them. He also showed to them the abundance of God's provision.

Jesus the bread of life

John 6:26-27 Jesus answered, "I tell you the truth, you are looking for me, not because you saw miraculous signs but because you ate the loaves and had your fill. Do not work for food that spoils, but for food that endures to eternal life, which the Son of Man will give you. On him God the Father has placed his seal of approval.

The day after the miracle of Jesus feeding five thousand people, the people searched for him. It is then that Jesus speaks to them with the emphasis upon spiritual food. Jesus says that he is this spiritual food that came down from heaven. Unlike the food their ancestors ate in the desert, which God had provided for their physical needs, so it is that God is providing again for the people through the awakening of their awareness of the God that loves them. The reality of this love is made manifest in both the person of Jesus and the miraculous signs he demonstrates. He is free of mankind's ambition as well as being the pure and holy intent of God toward his people. Jesus says to them that he is the true bread that has come down from heaven, and announces that anyone who eats his flesh and drinks his blood will have eternal life. It is at this time many of his disciples left him because they could not understand the spiritual implication of this presentation of truth. The comparison to the bread eaten by the children of Israel as they wandered in the desert, and the true bread of life (in the flesh) standing before them was too difficult for many to grasp. The idea of spiritual food presented by Jesus as a tangible substance that must be eaten (taken into the mind and stored in the heart) in order to have eternal life was a concept foreign to many in his day. Only when truth is embraced and taken into the heart of man will that individual begin to grasp and ultimately understand the excellent manner of teaching presented by our Lord. His teaching is purposely geared and aimed at those he knows will understand, while others are kept blinded to the truth by the evil god of this world. In many respects Jesus is a one-man covert operation.

Plans

"Ah, rest and relaxation.
At last the evening shadows chase away the day
And speak of rest deserving, the ministry, I pray.
Go away it's late!
The doors have all been locked, the sign is very clear
At this time of day, I'm not here."
Life is not set like a clock upon the wall
Neither is its rhythm without fault.
The servant sets the table for the master to arrive
The life for which we're chosen is never nine-to-five.

Isaiah 55:8-9 "My thoughts," Says the Lord, "are not like yours, and my ways are different from yours. As high as the heavens are above the earth, so high are my ways and thoughts above yours."

WHO'S THAT?

Here we find the disciples learning a vital truth concerning the kingdom of God. They had thought in a proprietary mindset exclusive to their little group. They had failed understanding of the infinite reach of God to permit good to be accomplished by whosoever found it in their heart to do so. This far reaching, all encompassing embracement of others who perform good in the name of the Lord for the glory of God, opens for us a window of truth, clarifying difference between man's thinking and the ways of God. It solidifies our understanding of justice and judgment within the thoughts of God. It is not theology that binds us together, rather, it is good deeds and righteous desires that show to others the choices we make emulate the good works of Christ. In this, God shows no partiality, for the man who walks upright and acts justly is acceptable to him.

Mark 9:38-40 John said to him, "Teacher, we saw a man who was driving out demons in your name, and we told him to stop, because he does not belong to our group." "Do not try to stop him," Jesus said to them, "because no one who performs a miracle in my name will be able soon afterward to say evil things about me. For whoever is not against us is for us."

It appears the disciples are swept into a proprietary mindset, one in which should not exist within the arena of doing good. We must be diligent in safeguarding our motivation to do good or else jealously and pride will mug humility at will. The disciples not only observed the man performing a miracle through the power present in the name of Jesus, but they rebuked him for doing it. Jesus is saying that his flock is so much more than the internal number of disciples, and anyone wanting to do good, is acceptable to him. Jesus is not distinguishing between who is for the advancement of the kingdom, based upon membership within the little group of disciples, to do so, would be to approve of the exclusive mindset proliferated by the religious of the day. Jesus is all about inclusiveness emphasized by faith present in the individual to do the will of God, absent fanfare of applause or worldly recognition. *Joel 2:32 "Everyone who calls upon the name of the Lord will be saved."* The apostle Peter says it a little differently, it takes him a little while, but he finally connects the dots. *Acts 10:34 Then Peter began to speak: "I now realize how true it is that God does not show favoritism but accepts men from every nation who fear him and do what is right."* It's obvious to us that this outsider not only stepped forward in faith and the power of God, but he did so in a spirit of humility and compassion, not expecting anything but the joy of knowing good had been done. Just as the outsider named Paul had sought only the approval of God, so too, this outsider whose name we do not know. Perhaps it is better to not know his name? In not knowing he can then represent for us the body of Christ apart from the established church of man; in so doing we find hope for everyone who places doing good above the recognition of the world. Doing good produces positive ripples of joy for everyone associated with the deed. Both the giver and the receiver find blessing. Good displays God's intent for hope, charity, compassion and love that most people want to dispense or be a recipient of. If we have a desire to do good things for others God will give us the means to accomplish. He will satisfy our desire. Doing good is mostly accomplished in small acts, but seeds are also small, before their actual fruition is revealed and true value is finally recognized.

It may be just a smile, or an advance of sound advice, but perpetuation of the deed is not always revealed. The one who sows is not always the one who reaps. However, we know that even the smallest good will remain in continuance forever. As a boulder is tossed into a lake the rippling outgrowth is felt for great distances. Just as good deeds and actions elicit a positive response in others, it must be recognized that doing bad or failing to do good will promote negatives that will also travel great distances. We never know what it is that may break or strengthen at the point of fracture thus we must understand that all of our actions will produce either blessing or consequences we cannot fully see or imagine. Failing to do good when called upon may be looked upon as a failure of responsibility for us who are soldiers in the army of the Lord. We may want to consider every good deed we do for others or is done for us as a miracle originating from the hand of God.

We don't know this man who performed the miracle of freeing those held in the grip of evil, but it is safe to assume that he had some contact with Jesus. Perhaps he heard him speak, or saw him perform a miracle? No matter, we have to realize that this could not be done without the man seeking to glorify God. There's no place for pride in the working of miracles, and there is also *no doubt* his motives for emulating Jesus were right with God. Not so with the majority of religious rulers of the day, they wore self-righteousness upon their outer garments, while inwardly they were deaf and uncaring toward the true plight of the people. They had the keys to the kingdom, they would not enter, neither would they allow anyone else to enter for fear the power of truth would set free those imprisoned by the exclusiveness of religiosity. Had these Pharisees and teachers of the law truly relied upon God (had not been corrupted) they too could have alleviated much of the suffering the people had experienced.

I can imagine how the rebuking of the man may have sounded, *"Hey! Who are you, and what the heck do you think you are doing? Who authorized you to use the name of Jesus? I don't remember seeing you with the Teacher."* Somebody failed to remember that the important thing was to do good and set free all who were caught in the grip of evil. Some of us long for the power of God to strongly rebuke the evil in this world, so much so that it doesn't take much encouragement to heed the call of God and do his will. To accomplish God's will requires focus and determination found only in a soul set free. The natural inclination for any of us who have received healing freedom is to give the knowledge of this freedom to others. No one lights a lamp and puts it under a bowl, but many have lamps that they refuse to light. Many know truth but they think of it as some personal treasure that permits a higher visibility affording greater privilege in this life. Good requires sacrifice for others, not the self-centered motivations that have no connection to God.

This man was performing miracles in the name of Jesus. His faith was awakened and set loose upon the tyranny that dominates the hearts of men and precludes focus upon God. He began immediately to aid in the hardships burdening people as one given a lamp in a land of darkness and gloom. He was given the light of Christ and he let it shine! A declaration of freedom cannot be silenced. The production of joy makes a wonderful sound. Hope realized is like lightning striking confidence into the heart of despair. The words of Jesus: *"Do not try to stop him,"* is an understatement by our Lord, for whoever has received cannot remain silent. No one who has heard the call of God within his heart can shortly thereafter deny the desire to do the good things we know to be right and pleasing to God. Once faith is ignited the good news consumes faster than a wildfire and is as contagious. Attempting to stop people from doing good things is never a prudent course of action. To do so is contrary to the will of God and impossible for those attempting to halt its forward intent. A miracle performed is the power of God in action. *"Do not try to stop him,"* is also a warning to not attempt to make war in an area you cannot possibly win. A house divided cannot stand and neither can a man who positions himself against God.

Bickering

A source of annoyance an irritable itch
It brings out the words surrounded by verbs
Unleashed from beneath the cover of pride.
A tantrum of movement portrayed in the eyes
Inscribed on the face by the tension of lies.

Ephesians 4:31-32 Get rid of all bitterness, rage and anger, brawling and slander, along with every form of malice. Be kind to one another, forgiving each other, just as in Christ, God forgives you.

Poison grows

‿‿‿

Ivy oak and sumac
Just to name a few
Of the varying varieties
That spread poison dew.
A danger to the wanderer
Who ventures wilder grove
Into the field unknowing
Where the poison grows.

‿‿‿

2 Peter 3:17 Therefore, dear friends, since you already know this, be on your guard so that you may not be carried away by error of lawless men and fall from your secure position. But grow in the grace and knowledge of our Lord and Savior Jesus Christ. To him be glory both now and forever! Amen.

Other lights

Today's diversity within Christianity is amazing. There are so many banners and everyone claiming allegiance to the banner of the cross. Within this segmentation there is the natural inclination toward competition to grow in numbers. This competition to put people in the pews and ultimately it is hoped will generate full-fledged membership can result in an "end justifies the means mindset" on the part of church leadership. Distinctive theological differences have promoted a constant among the flock that either ends in the frustration of a homeless sheep or the continuous movement of sheep throughout the various encampments within a given area. Some of these sheep have found homes in other denominations and others may find that the light they carry is not welcome within the lamp stand of authority, that will not recognize another's Christian's gifts, out of a desire to maintain a status quo within church leadership or lay ministries.

Continuance of the ministry's avowed purposes (at all cost) even if it means abusing the name of Jesus (as in prosperity or name it and claim it churches) has never been the mission of Christ. A prosperity doctrine is a golden thread extracted from scripture and made to apply to today's theology. Tithing for example is one instance in which the sheep are fleeced. Some religious organizations have adopted a government approach to doing good, they tax the lifeblood out of its citizens in the name of charity or redistribution, all the while placing the responsibility to increase one's wealth upon promise from either God or the policies they (the church) enact. This is an underhanded and misdirecting intention of scripture. The churches will not tell us to sell everything we own give the money to the poor and then follow them because it would then be the responsibility of the church to support us. But bringing an ancient tithing practice of the Hebrew people into today's theology does more than deceive the sheep into thinking commitment satisfied. *It establishes a limit upon the generosity of those, whose God knows no end to giving.*

It is clear that the motive behind such policy is clearly to increase the wealth of ministry or the position of those in political power. It gets very difficult to distinguish the genuine from the counterfeit church community of shepherds. As such we establish constant movement within the Christian community that was never intended. Entrance and exiting of sheep from various flocks cause disturbances for both the shepherd and the sheep. Most genuine sheep are looking for honesty within the word of God and are really not too concerned with a charismatic preacher or choir. The competition to maintain established positions within the church may be so competitive that should a little light venture into the church, fire alarms might be sounded in order to extinguish and diminish its attracting quality.

Matthew 24:26 "So if anyone tells you, 'There he is, out in the desert,' do not go out; or, 'here he is, in the inner rooms,' do not believe it. For as the lightning comes from the east and flashes to the west, so will be the coming of the Son of Man.

The above scripture quote is a warning for us to recognize not only false messiahs or false teachings presented by those who have been given a voice to preach and/or platform to elevate; it's a declaration to us to not rely upon anyone or anything pointing to what we are hoping for, but to rely totally upon the word of God. Finding a church without error is like attempting to find perfection in humanity; some have been so infiltrated by the personalities of leadership and membership that it becomes too hard to recognize the Christianity within them. When it becomes too difficult to understand the sheep leave. *"My church is much more spiritual and alive compared to those others. My pastor is wonderful he is so Spirit-filled and entertaining. Our music ministry is the best and the choir really rocks the house. The revival across town is the place to be if you really want to feel the Spirit."* What is going on in the body of Christ? Some churches emphasize a gift of the Spirit (speaking in tongues) as outward evidence of spiritual maturity. Others, it seems are obsessed with healing ministry or the outward display of being slain in the Spirit, as recognition of a pastor's anointing favor from God. Still there are those that have a laundry list of, "must be" or "must do" before being given a voice in the congregation, usually played out in the arena of the, "most spiritual contest." Others are drawn to the big tent in order to witness miraculous healing from God. These outward signs within the churches may result in the individual seeking the signs but failing to see truth. *We search for the water of life in a desert of want and wonder why it is we are continually thirsty.* We travel over mountains and roads of great heights and sometimes find ourselves in a valley of cooled emotions, thinking that these emotions are indicators of a healthy or unhealthy condition relevant to our connection to God. In so doing we fail to see the clear water enriching the valley dwellers provided by his hand. In the process of elated heights and valleys of emotional absence we lose our direction through trusting in feelings that more often than not lead us astray. Add to this mix of confusion those who purposely attempt to mislead and disguise truth for self-gain and we have a condition of designed dependency that fails to allow growth from within and neither will it give voice to those who would enter. **"For whoever is not against us is for us."** The church has so many enemies outside of Christianity, where do we ever find time to bicker and argue among ourselves?

POSSESSED DESPERATE AND DEAD

There are situations in life from which there appears to be no help. Hopelessness can be pervasive or it can be contained within the heart of just one person. Desperation can cause us to seek an end to life rather than to suffer. Yes, we can find ourselves not only contemplating, but actually doing harm to our self, as was the case of the man described in the possession narrative of Mark. The man would cry out in anguish and cut himself with stones, no matter how he was arrested he managed to free himself and continue his demon-possessed madness. Also within this chapter we find a woman with an incurable illness and she is at her point of desperation. She follows her heart straight to Jesus. Lastly we find a father whose worst fear has materialized, his child has died, and from this anguish Jesus restores his family. In every instance of healing we find the power of God willingly given directly from our Lord, and in the case of the woman seeking a cure, it is her faith that allows her to draw healing power from our Lord without a direct request.

Mark 5:1-4 "They went across the lake to the region of the Gerasenes. When Jesus got out of the boat, a man with an evil spirit came from the tombs to meet him. This man lived in the tombs, and no one could bind him any more, not even with a chain. For he had often been chained hand and foot, but he tore the chains apart and broke the irons at his feet. No one was strong enough to subdue him. Night and day among the tombs and in the hills he would cry out and cut himself with stones."

House cleaning

A day for the possessed desperate and dead begins with Jesus entering the region of Gerasa by boat (an area near the Sea of Galilee). In the gospel of Mark we are told Jesus encounters a man possessed by an evil spirit. The man lived in a graveyard replete with tombs, stones and bones. He roamed the hills crying out and cutting his self with stones. The cutting may very well be an attempt to drive out the evil spirits who had invaded the sanctuary of his mind/spirit. The people had attempted to restrain him, perhaps in an effort to keep him from inflicting harm to both his self and others. As soon as Jesus gets out of the boat the man rushed out of the burial caves. He is a victim of slavery in the worst form. A heralding of the freedom of God is about to take place. The limitations of man are about to be introduced to the power of God. This was not an insignificant demonic possession. Rather, it was one in which the man was inhabited by the self descriptive name of, **"Legion or Mob." "There are so many of us!"** It is bad enough to have a possession that in some way is specific and singular, as in, the demon tossed him into the fire, or caused a speech impediment. However, this man was possessed by an uncountable number of demonic beings, so much so the behavior exhibited terrorized everyone to the point they wouldn't travel the road close to his habitat. One has to ask, why would all of these inhabit just one man? Perhaps, just as within the natural realm wherein some criminal elements act in concert as a, *"mob"* and others as lone wolves, so too it may be true within the spiritual realm as well. When God is not in residence (within the life of a man) it becomes easy to overpower the rightful inhabitant, (the spirit of man) and then subjugate the freedoms he enjoyed. Their intent is to dominate and ultimately destroy. The ensuing deleterious behaviors are a direct reflection of the number of influences within the man, each vying for control. These possessions are not to be confused with the labeling of human weaknesses or dependencies metaphorically referred to as, *"The demon of alcohol, drugs or gambling."*

They must be understood as demonic individual entities of pure spiritual existence, whose intent is the demise of man. That this man had been the recipient of a housebreaking gang, speaks to the degree in which we are to acknowledge the depravity of evil. Whether it is singular or multiple the results are the same, except that the *"mob"* will fight amongst itself in order to leverage control over its victim. But this was about to change. Upon seeing Jesus the man runs out from the graveyard, falls at his feet and asks, ***"What do you want with me, Jesus, Son of the Most High God? Swear to God that you will not torture me!"*** What's interesting is the evil spirits had no mercy for the man's life (if it can be called that) his life was a living hell of torturous domination. What could possibly make the evil spirits think they could receive mercy? Why would the ***"mob"*** refer to their collective existence within the singular context of, ***"me?"*** Perhaps within the prospect of being, ***"tortured"*** they instantly found the collective unity of one voice? Somewhere from within the confines of the man we hear legalism declare, ***"It is not as yet our time for judgment, send us out into the pigs."*** The evil spirits are fearful for the crimes of demonic possession and rebellion against God. The purpose of Christ is to set as many free as will accept truth. Demonic possession was one of the earliest forms of rebellion against the will of God, as is represented in the Book of Genesis. ***Genesis 6:2 "The sons of God saw that the daughters of men were beautiful, and they married any of them they chose."*** A footnote in the New International Version indicates the Hebrew translation for angels is, ***"sons of God."*** However it is not the collective understanding that we would assign to such a term, since God never called any of his angels son.

The evil spirits begged Jesus not to send them out of the area. This may be a request to not be driven out of the man. They were content to be in possession of the man. One has to wonder why and what is the attraction for these occurrences? Perhaps it is the sin nature of man that attracts the rebellious? Maybe it is the ability of the body to find expression through the senses that makes possession desirable, or else it is just an avenue through which evil can manifest and destroy what God has placed value upon? No matter the motivation for possession, evil will always attempt to dominate and destroy through force and strength. Knowing they had to comply with the command to depart from the man, they beg to be sent into a nearby herd of pigs. How fitting it was that the unclean spirits should request to be sent into a herd of animals deemed by Jewish law to be unclean. Maybe it is the confinement within flesh and bone that attracts and offers a sense of darkness and security against the light of truth, ever present in the world of pure spiritual existence? The demons enter the pigs and all of them run into a lake and perish. What then was the fate of those evil spirits? We know that when an evil spirit is cast out, he goes into the desert (this desert is one of continually searching) for a while, he then returns to his former place of residence with some others. If nobody's home (if God is not filling the space reserved for him alone) the man would be worse off than before the initial evil had been cast out. It is paramount for us to always have God in residence, for we are made to be the temple of God. As for those demons who went into the pigs, one can only apply conjecture, they were perhaps, again loose to roam and seek another to possess, for the set time of judgment had not as yet come.

Let us take a moment to look at the difference between being possessed by an evil spirit and being the possessor of one. The two are different. In the one there is a takeover of the will of an individual, and in the other the evil is the individual. Clearly within depictions of possessions in biblical accounts, there is the pronouncement of an unauthorized habitation of the human being. God will not force himself upon us and make us bend to his will, and neither does he permit others to commit this offense. We understand, a home can be invaded through external force, or else someone willingly opens the door from within. Jesus had said, ***"I stand at the door and knock,"*** this statement signifies respect for an individual not shown by those who would enter unannounced and unwanted. Since we recognize *only* God is perfect and in this uniqueness, his knowledge of all things is heralded as an *all-encompassing* aspect of perfection, we can conclude *all others* have limitations and are subject to a learning process. Having said this, it is logical to assume the enemy has developed various forms of tactical strategies aimed at finding residence within the human condition and ever changing methodology designed to corrupt and destroy. As tactics change, presentations within snapshots of reality will shape perceptions of the world, all geared toward eventual erasure of the characteristics distinguishing right from wrong. What was clearly understood in earlier days of modern times, was the sinful, the unwanted, and the denounced behaviors that in today's setting not only finds acceptance but is encouraged by many holding positions of power and wealth. Let us always be mindful of the fact that as children all of us were innocent in the eyes of our Lord. Jesus had taught his disciples that they must be like little children, who, in their innocence have possession of the Kingdom of God. Something happened along the road of life that caused us to lose the key we formerly had in our possession. We lost the innocence of trust that is found to be in great abundance in a child, due to the gradual disappointment found within the corrupting influences of the world. When Jesus was tested in the desert he was offered position, power and wealth, the kingdom of materialism in exchange for his soul. ***"What does it profit a man to gain the whole world but lose his soul?"*** With the advent of Christ and his gift of defense against ever changing housebreaking techniques, the enemy has been forced to seek those who willingly permit entrance into the place reserved for God, effectively defiling the creation of God. Position power and wealth are offered to a man who will sell his soul to gain world offerings, and in the end forfeit his life. This was the temptation offered to Jesus during his testing in the desert; there could be no forced entry within the fortress of our Lord, as such, worldly enticements were laid at his feet. This says to us the Devil really did not know to whom he was addressing. He (Satan) saw a man and in the knowledge of mankind he attempted to appeal to human nature, known to be corrupt. After all, *"everything and everyone has its price"* is perhaps a saying as old as sin itself. Jesus did not fall into the temptation and still he lost his life to a corrupt system; within his resurrection we see our great hope of eternal life.

With the advent of Christ demonic possessions have either become a rarity (certainly they are less) or else, have been misdiagnosed by those dealing with insane, deviant abnormal behavior. This missed diagnosis, placing everything upon the platform of insanity allows for evil to evade and continue its existence under the guise of, *"cause unknown"*. In fact, in today's corrupt evasion of truth evil itself has been politically corrected to the point that those with a voice in the public arena go far out of their way to actually not use the word, *"evil."* Our enemies who are known to live where Satan himself has set up residence have no problem in calling us, *"The evil empire."* Seems to me that evil is permitted to disparage America while in the land of free speech we are finding increasingly more sacrosanct word usages. When we cannot find a sure cause for a particular behavior we then must apply conjecture, incorporating environment, or else, attributing said abnormal behavior to the nature of man as evil. Since there is a profound dislike in the world to denounce evil, for evil's sake, it may in many instances become indistinguishable between being possessed and being the possessor of an evil spirit. There is no shortage of those who will willingly unlock the door and permit evil residence. When this happens, the enemy gains a new recruit, an additional outpost or residence for the activity of evil is established, and lastly, the willing victim faces ultimate destruction, as was the plan from the beginning. We can believe demonic possession to mean an invasion by an evil entity, without the second guessing of superimposed behavioral science within today's definitions of insanity, simply because, it is the bible making the diagnosis. To read another definition into the biblical accounts is to allow the fallibility of man to sit in judgment of the infallible word of God. Simply put, Jesus' description of demonic possession was either correct or he was unaware of the naturally insane and otherwise unacceptable behavior that may occur without a need to create a generic label of demonic possession to catch and explain all aberrant behaviors.

An evil spirit does not seek forgiveness, because it is known that none is available. The rebellious do not know when judgment will arrive but they know it is coming. As with most questions, if we search the scriptures we can find an answer that hits the satisfaction sought. ***Jude 1:6 "And the angels who did not keep their positions of authority but abandoned their own home—these he kept in darkness, bound with everlasting chains for judgment on the great Day."*** These are the ones spoken of in Genesis as the sons of God. And so we may infer from the writing of Jude, some evil spirits are in chains, others are indeed homeless, and still, others are masquerading as the insane! Within the underlying reasons for possession is an attempt to regain a semblance of the permanence a home provides. Even offerings within graveyard ambience appear attractive, so long as the journey of unknown distance, absent hope, appears to find abatement. The chains and shackles employed by men in an attempt to subdue the demon possessed man are quite different from the chains holding those rebellious angels in darkness, for they are forged by the Word of God, and are fixed and immovable. As for those evil spirits still permitted to wreak havoc and destroy the homes of men, their time is coming and only God knows when.

Within the fabric of man (this body) is contained the infinite expanse of the spiritual realm, our true home, the residence of our God. Every so often God allows us to find a pearl of wisdom, or he urges us in a direction of something he knows will stir up hope and ignite joy, to the point of song and praise echoing off the temple walls, that is, this earthly tent we inhabit, as a warning to all who would dare enter where the King is in residence. To have joy and praise within us for our great God is to not just wear the entire armor of God, but it is to be the very fabric of the impenetrable, woven from God's gift to man, Jesus.

Wake up, O sleeper

Mark 5:21-24 When Jesus had again crossed over by boat to the other side of the lake, a large crowd gathered around him. While he was by the lake one of the synagogue rulers, named Jarius, came there. Seeing Jesus, he fell at his feet and pleaded earnestly with him, "My little daughter is dying. Please come and put your hands on her so that she will be healed and live." So Jesus went with him.

Jesus continues this day and from the midst of a large crowd comes one who is in grave need. It is Jarius, a synagogue ruler. He falls at the feet of Jesus and begs our Lord to heal his daughter who is at home dying. While he was with Jesus some men arrive and report that his daughter has died, and so, **"Why bother the teacher any longer?"** Jesus ignores the report of the child's death and says, **"Don't be afraid just believe."** He then selects a few of his disciples to accompany them to the little girl's home, he does not allow any others to follow. By not allowing the others to come along, Jesus shows compassion. The little girl's father has heard news that turns a parent's heart to fragments of meaningless disarray and fear. He had already begun the mourning process. Jesus would not allow the dignity of grief to be turned into a spectacle of wonder. He would not have a crowd following and asking, "What can Jesus do? The little girl is dead; case closed. Say some kind words and leave it alone." Most important is the need to separate Jarius from the unbelief that would surely surround them as they walked back to his home. Those who brought the news of the little girl's death did so with the finality that death has always imposed upon mortal man. It is important to the event about to take place that hope and faith in the power and compassion of God is present. It was desperation that sparked hope and stretched forth the flame of faith leading Jarius to the feet of Christ, and Jesus will not have this hope dissipated by the negative anticipations of a crowd. Upon arrival at the home of Jarius reality again reports in the form of crying and wailing. Undaunted by the sounds of death Jesus says to the mourners, *"Why all the commotion and wailing? The little girl is not dead but asleep."* With that statement by our Lord the mourners are transformed into mockers, whose laughter is an unwanted guest in the hearts of the little girl's parents. It is this very same laughter that will cause these mockers to deny what will take place next. Jesus plants into the hearts of those who would ridicule and deny the power of God the very instrument that will not allow them to see truth. They had mocked the statement that the little girl was not dead but asleep, and they will focus upon this and not be allowed to recognize the resurrecting power of God. What they had mocked will then become their truth! What then shall we say? Was the little girl dead or asleep? Within the words of Jesus we hear what appears to be contradictory to the reality seemingly conflicting with common sense and truth. The laughter is reaction to the paradox. Yes the little girl was dead, but the words of Christ are nevertheless true, since he is the author of life. *John 5:21 "For just as the Father raises the dead and gives them life, even so the Son gives life to whom he is pleased to give it."* Again, *John 5:25 "I tell you the truth, a time is coming, and has now come when the dead will hear the voice of the Son of God and those who hear will live."* Upon her awakening from the land of the deep sleep Jesus is focused upon the little girl's wellbeing. He says to the parents, *"Give her something to eat."* How many of us have awakened from a deep sleep hungry? Jesus knew the little girl would be hungry, and so, he instructs the parents to satisfy this immediate need; it may also be a confirmation for the parents that says, "Here is your child, cease mourning and resume parenting."

Can we imagine the state of awe present in the parents? What must have been going on in their hearts had to be great joy and jubilation over the awesome display of mercy, shown to them by the Lord of Mercy. We don't know how long the little girl was dead, but we might surmise, it was for a considerable length of time. Just by looking at the events that had to take place prior to the arrival of Jesus at the little girl's bedside, we can imagine at least a good portion of the day had transpired. When Jesus arrives the mourners are already in place; not only did Jarius have to find Jesus, but the messenger with the bad news had to find the father to make his report. Sometime after the father ventures forth to find Jesus, the little girl dies. I must ask myself this question, when the little girl dies, does she lose all conscious awareness of herself, or does her *"spirit return to God who gave it"* as it is written in Ecclesiastes? I'm reminded of the words of Jesus who told the disciples, little children are possessors of the Kingdom of God. I do believe this one statement by Jesus pronounces a continuation of the thinking faculty/spirit, not only for the innocence of a child but all who are saved. Of course, Jesus had not gone to the cross as yet, and so salvation through his death and resurrection was not as yet available, perhaps only, for the declared innocence of little children? What might have been the little girl's memories of the journey home to her Father's house? These thoughts ignite mystery, along with a desire to examine the truth contained in scripture. With respect to Jesus saying, *the dead will hear the voice of the Son of God and those who hear will live"* Jesus is not only speaking of those who have passed away, but he is also referring to those who are animated, are actually walking dead, having no life within them. Absent the truth of Jesus there is no real life in us, just a myriad of presentations offered by worldly reasoning absent the knowledge of God or his truth.

Healing touch

Mark 5:24-28 So Jesus went with him. A large crowd followed and pressed around him. And a woman was there who had been subject to bleeding for twelve years. She had suffered a great deal under the care of many doctors and had spent all she had, yet instead of getting better she got worse. When she heard about Jesus, she came up behind him in the crowd and touched his cloak, because she thought, "If I just touch his clothes, I will be healed." Lastly, we find a woman who has been healed by her faith. She is at the feet of Jesus, trembling and fearful, but no less focused upon the healing she knew was available to her in Christ; all who had come to Jesus had placed themselves at his feet, the possessed the desperate and the afflicted. She had been suffering with an illness for many years. The illness had caused her great suffering, the loss of her finances, and it was not getting better. From the very same desperation and faith that found Jarius at the feet of Jesus, she also finds within herself a voice that says, ***"If I could only touch the hem of his garment I will be healed."*** She approaches Jesus and touches his cloak and Jesus immediately says, ***"Who touched me?"*** The question is not understood for there is a great crowd and much close contact. But the woman understands the question and she understands that she has been healed. She knows that Jesus is looking for her. She then falls at his feet and tells our Lord the whole truth of what had happened. Jesus then confirms what the woman had already suspected. He says to her, ***"Daughter, your faith has healed you. Go in peace and be free of suffering."*** By usage of the word ***"daughter,"*** Jesus reveals the truth about himself as spoken by the prophet Isaiah. ***Isaiah 9:6 "And he will be called Wonderful Counselor, Mighty God, Everlasting Father, Prince of Peace."*** In every instance all who had come to Jesus were restored and those who had placed their faith in him were rewarded. ***John 6:37 "All that the Father gives me will come to me, and whoever comes to me I will never drive away."***

Faith

It's everywhere.
Darkest night sunshine bright
Deepest hole, heaven's heights
Mother's hand and children's eyes
It's everywhere.
Food court vendor used car fellow
Airline tickets cool wine cellar
Smiling faces unknown land
Hidden thoughts in outstretched hand
It's everywhere.
Judges lawyers doctors kings
Movie stars and playground swings
Ancient ruins bones and sand
Stake a flag in hearts of men.
It's everywhere.
Yes, we are a faith filled people in a world of rising din
But sometimes fail the whisper of the voice of God within.

Mark 11:22 Have faith in God Jesus answered.

THEY KNEW

The height of arrogance is never so pronounced as when denial of truth is blatant and uncaring. This was the condition of the ruling religious at the time of Christ. Power in hands unwilling to remain humble and focused upon the needs of mankind is power unworthy to be praised and sustained. There are so many parallels between the past and present that at times is becomes difficult to separate. Times and seasons change but the heart of man remains fixed and unyielding from generation to generation. Only within the individual can hope for change find rest. Rarely do we see this change on a direct level as it pertains to others, but in the case of Nicodemus what we find is a divulgence, or sharing of secret information with Jesus for the purpose of aiding the goodness he recognized standing before him. As with many a situation where it is we who think we are bringing a blessing, we find that it is we who are blessed. We may minister to the poor only to find that the richness they have is greater than the poverty we perceived. Such is the case where a religious Pharisee finds blessing from the Lord of All.

John 3:1-2 Now there was a man of the Pharisees named Nicodemus, a member of the Jewish ruling council. He came to Jesus at night and said, "Rabbi, we know that you are a teacher who has come from God. For no one could perform the miraculous signs you are doing if God were not with him." Arrogance, self-importance, contempt and disrespect for Jesus grew more intense with every day he revealed truth concerning God. With every miraculous deed freeing those held tightly by the grip of evil jealously among the leaders of the faith grew, for fear they would be exposed. As his popularity spread, concern and consternation became more complex of meaning, and like cornered rats the religious saw their movements monitored closely by those who awaited confirmation of the truth made clearly visible to the common man. Good old Nicodemus, he's actually a follower of Jesus and he comes to him covertly at night. Perhaps he is fearful of retribution over breaking ranks with his brothers who adamantly deny the truth that he Nicodemus just revealed. They knew Jesus was a man sent by God, but their disregard for the people and their fear of losing their grip upon power and wealth demanded they not recognize authority greater than themselves. This denial of truth is expected and understandable if it was a position taken by the godless, but these were the religious elite. These rulers were not only denying the truth of God, but they were misrepresenting him. What was their true purpose for being if not to point to truth and adhere to it as well? They failed by substituting truth, replacing it with a *most spiritual contest* labeling everyone except themselves as sinners. In time Jesus exposes them as hypocrites who knew the truth. He exposed them for their failure to enter the kingdom of God with the keys of truth and condemned them for their conscious effort to prevent others from also entering. They knew the truth that in the person of Christ, God had come to man, but they rejected him in favor of their own self-importance.

Wolves

Wolves in shepherd's garb never fooled real sheep, but for those aspiring to make it to the top, in the most spiritual contest, to win the prize of notoriety, they had to overlook the toothy smile of contest judges as a prerequisite of the game. The commandments of God and the laws of Moses had become just so much carryover from the past. Like the laws of today, everyone pretends to understand the letter and spirit of the law, everyone pretends expertise, but just like the days of old, the law has become just so many stones to hurl. Their relevance was a matter of interpretative discourse that dissected truth to the point it was unrecognizable, and unpalatable for consumption by the spirit of man seeking freedom and the ability to exercise prudence of the heart. The race for eternal life was a death sentence to those who thought they could be worthy to approach God based upon the approval of experts in the law. Everyone became wolves seeking the food of truth, unavailable upon the table of the religious. They ran with the pack and dined upon the bitterness of unfulfilled existence. Such was the hollowness of those who offered sacrifices to God but failed to be the living sacrifice he required. The age of innocence had passed and deep were the wounds inflicted upon the trusting. Thank God, deception can no longer hide within the tailored suit of hypocrisy.

Human desire begets corruption of truth

A willful corruption of the shepherd's code existed in the hearts of religious rulers. Protection of the sheep was not foremost in their plans to remain shepherds. These were the very same Pharisees who Jesus rebuked as children of their father, the Devil. He denounced them for speaking their father's natural language, the language of lies. These men had stone hearts that could pronounce a death sentence upon transgressors of the law, but they lived outside of the consequences they imposed upon others. They believed they were the law, and they failed to remember the God who gave the law to them. Oh sure, God was constantly upon their lips but the sound made was unintelligible to the heart within. These were the same religious who murdered the prophets and then built monuments of remembrance to them. Now it was God's turn to be made into mere monument status. Did they think God could be made into the symbolism of man? Could be a commemorative statue? What's going on? Was there a total lack of faith within the religious community? Were these celebrities of the time so taken in by their narcissistic enamoring that they had forgotten there really is a God? Could they, in their legalistic minds actually find a loophole that would allow them to know the truth and still deny the God who is its author? The answer to these questions is simple: The eye is most clear when truth is present and the lie is never so pronounced as when darkness rules. Evil intention will always produce destruction and the ways of man are filled with lies.

The desire to dominate others was greater than their fear of God. They had taken on an attitude that saw themselves as gods. They were high and lifted up in the eyes of the common man and they loved to be spotlighted. They were the stars of both the religious and secular forums. No waiting in line for good seats or reservations. They were ushered into the very best things of life and wallowed in the accolades heaped upon them. Yes indeed, they knew Jesus and in their hearts of stone rejected the truth of their origins, in favor of pride, that lit the flames of their destiny. Jesus said of the religious,

Matthew 23:6-7 "They love the best places at feasts and the reserved seats at synagogues; they love to be greeted with respect in the market places and to have people call them 'Teacher.'" It appears there's lots of competition today for those best seating arrangements. People love to appear special in the eye of the masses; they love the adoration and special treatment rarely afforded others; they love to be called stars and role models. Perhaps these role models and Pharisees of old have failed to recognize truth concerning the mortality of man and reality of God, because they have covered themselves in so much of worldly glitter? Usually it is not the wrapping but the content of the package that determines worth.

Glitter

~‿‿‿⟩

The flower of pride blooms
And takes on a color
That captures the scene.
Its fragrance, apart from the earth
Neither wholesome or strength filled like honesty of dirt.
Its roots seek depth and command, binding and holding the posture of
man.
Denial of truth, primping vision projected, clear are motives attached for
the ride
The end is not cared for or left with goodbye only the present is thought to
survive.
Outside it glitters and plastic the smiles self-centered with purpose that's
seen for miles.
Designed to endear, external beauty belies, the content beneath the
falsehood of pride.
Shined shoes pressed pants and hat whose top is sky-high
Stands out in the rain naked and plain with truth the beacon that shines.
Awards from the masses congrats from kings celebrity status and all of it
brings
Not a day older or peace for the mind, glitter of pride is commanded,
"You too must die."
In the order of things lofty and high lowly and weak all is accepted absent
pride
An ocean's volume and depth is unknown, can only be fathomed by the
Master of Storms.
The sun and the moon the universe wide were all made without the
glitter of pride.

⟨‿‿‿⟩

James 1:26-27 If anyone considers himself religious and does
not keep a tight reign on his tongue, he deceives himself and his
religion is worthless. Religion that God our Father considers pure
and faultless is this: to look after orphans and widows in their
distress and to keep ones self from being polluted by the world.

Peter F. Serra

Unwilling ears calcified hearts

John 3:9-11 "How can this be?" Nicodemus asked. "You are Israel's teacher" said Jesus, "and you do not understand these things? I tell you the truth, we speak of what we know and testify to what we have seen, but still you people do not accept our testimony." As the conversation continues between Jesus and the covert follower called Nicodemus, what we expect to hear from Jesus, we don't. One might expect to hear, "Well really, they actually _know_ that I am sent from God?" Jesus replies to Nicodemus' unveiling of truth with the first order of the shepherd's code, which is to secure and protect the sheep. Jesus points Nicodemus to salvation by revealing to him truth concerning the change of attitude and change of heart necessary, to not only see but to enter the kingdom of God. Jesus is aware of the hypocrisy of the powerful and politically connected religious, but he is not concerned with what they know or do not know. He is concerned with Nicodemus, and for all who will cherish truth and share it with those who are seeking the knowledge to admit-one into the reality that is God. There was much consternation among the rulers of the people and while they spoke readily about the advent of Messiah and prophesy associated with alerting them to his coming, they really did not expect to meet him! Their expectations were written in the books, proclaimed by the prophets, and finally, when Jesus shows up there is a concerted effort to not only deny but to kill him. So many of us today have failed to bring Jesus into the present, to look forward with assurance for the second coming of Christ. We have reached a point that rejects the reality of modern signs and ardent voices crying out in the wilderness. We have become so exhausted by the demands of the world that we fail to look to the heavens for our great hope. Poor Pharisees, they were taken unaware and by the time they realized the true status of Jesus it was too late for them. They were already in favor of a tombstone's pronouncement of life rather than to become alive in Christ. They had chosen to serve their own self-interests and failed to understand that salvation will never be found by looking inward to our own evaluation. It is looking outward that we find God ready to forgive our errant ways. Calling upon God is an outward expression that recognizes authority above us. When we assume authority or power through force or deception it cannot last.

146

Who can take what belongs to God? ***Acts 2:20-21 "The sun will be turned to darkness and the moon to blood before the coming of the great and glorious day of the Lord. And everyone who calls on the name of the Lord will be saved.***" Again, calling upon the name of the Lord is the ultimate of outward expression. Fear has its uses and if it promotes recognition of God then great! I suspect that when the signs of undeniable wonder appear and Jesus' imminent arrival is at hand there will still be some who miss it. But then, all of nature gently speaks to the wonders of God and many refuse to recognize its orchestra of constant praise. Powerful also was the signaling arrival of the birth of Christ, not only was there a stellar event, but just a few decades later appears John the Baptist heralding the coming of Messiah they had so longingly awaited. They kill John and they begin the character assassination of Jesus, eventually handing him over to worldly power. Arrogance cares not for truth and finds need only in lies designed to obscure and deceive. God's ways and his laws are not so complex for us to understand. Unfortunately many will not seek the freedom contained in scriptural truth for fear they will uncover restriction. From our point of view such fear of restriction seems incredible, especially from those who are already confined within the worldly caskets of finite existence.

Reflection

❦

The moon was illuminated in reflective radiance.
The old man had a full face that looked like he was smiling.
The stars spoke with a determination attempting to breach eternity.
Surely he thought, "Someone must have created all of this."
He had heard the villagers speak of this someone.
He wondered, "Did this someone need help in creating all of this?"
Smiling at the night he concluded, "The one who made the grape doesn't
need help."
His smile started to vanish when he realized
He did not know what this someone might require of him.
He decided to do only what this someone might find pleasing.
Thinking this to be wonderful he finished his evening wine.

❦

Genesis1:16 "God made two great lights—the greater light to
govern the day and the lesser light to govern the night. He also
made the stars.

God shows no favoritism, he is the impartial judge of man. In the above poem we find a man who has come to the truth concerning the existence of God. He does not know Jesus and in truth he does not know God, but he understands God must exist. In his conclusion he determines that he will live a life he believes will be pleasing to this God he does not know. Indirectly he has come to Christ because Jesus is Truth. Everyone who comes to Jesus he will in no way refuse them. The ways of God are not so complicated after all. Praise God!

Two Worlds

Creation bares itself in homage to the Lord
The tree in all its glory declares to us his hand
The fruit upon the branches the depth of love his plan
The roots beneath the ground serving notice to man
Reap his bounty of visions deep and near
Truth within the cycle of life and death is clear
Ever giving and rebuilding is our Father in our home
Until rest in time the season for trees flesh and bone
Then shall be revealed outside the circle neat
By the one we call Brother from a world we could not see
With resonating thunder his voice for us shall speak
"Father, here for your glory is my sheep."

John 10:27-30 My sheep listen to my voice; I know them and they follow me. I give them eternal life, and they shall never die. No one can snatch them away from me. What my Father has given me is greater than everything, and no one can snatch them away from the Father's care. The Father and I are one.

TIMING

The universe, indeed all of creation is like a giant clock ticking ever onward towards its appointed time of fulfillment. Everything in creation must comply with the appointed time and purpose assigned by God. Man defines the universe with the understanding of a given reference between two points of light. In terms of God's universe it is assigned the mystery of infinity. God lives outside of his appointed times. It is he who built into existence the clockwork order of creation.

John 2:3-4 When the wine was gone, Jesus' mother said to him, "They have no more wine." "Dear woman, why do you involve me?" Jesus replied, "My time has not yet come." The wedding feast of *"Cana"* exemplifies the involvement of God in our daily lives. The wedding feast reveals the glory of our Lord through the performance of his first miracle. Changing water into wine. God's schedule always takes into account the needs of his people. That it is a wedding feast and Jesus is an invited guest displays both the humanity and divinity of Jesus. His humanity is represented by the respect he shows by attending and his divinity provides richness where otherwise the poverty of **"no more wine"** would have been long remembered over the happiness of this special day. It is an embarrassing situation for the bride, the groom, guests and servants and also for the master of the banquet who obviously underestimated the amount of wine that would be necessary. Because Jesus was in attendance it meant that no poverty could be present. So while it was not as yet the time for the glory of Christ to be revealed to the world, it was a time to provide. Jesus would say that his Father is always working and that he must do the same, as such Jesus is constantly working for all things good. God is always providing for our needs and Jesus would not refuse the request to change the potential for negative talk (concerning a wedding he had attended) into a positive experience long to be remembered for the excellence of the wine served last. The best wine being served at the end of the feast may allude to the end of time where again the best wine will be served at the wedding feast of the Lamb.

At the last supper

Matthew 26:29 "I tell you, I will not drink of this fruit of the vine from now on until that day when I drink it anew with you in my Father's kingdom."

At the cross

Matthew 27: 33-34 They came to a place called Golgotha, which means, "The Place of the Skull." There they offered Jesus wine mixed with a bitter substance; but after tasting it, he would not drink it.

While on the cross

John 19:28-30 Jesus knew that by now everything had been completed; and in order to make the scripture come true he said, 'I am thirsty.' A bowl was there, full of cheap wine; so a sponge was soaked in the wine, put on a stalk of hyssop and lifted up to his lips. Jesus drank the wine and said, 'It is finished!' Then he bowed his head and died.
Psalm 22:18 "They divide my garments among them and cast lots for my clothing." Psalm 69:21 "They put gall in my food and gave me vinegar for my thirst." Gall is poisonous liver bile and this is what they attempted to give to Jesus when he was in route to the cross. The wine vinegar (cheap wine) that Jesus drank just before dying was taken by Jesus to complete what had been foretold. At the last supper Jesus said he would, *"not drink of this fruit of the vine from now on until the day when I drink it anew with you in my Father's kingdom."* The wine vinegar that Jesus drank just before his death

does not qualify as the ***"fruit of the vine"*** spoken of by Jesus at the last supper.

An interesting thought is the introduction of the hyssop stalk at the cross. It is hyssop that was used to mark the lintels and doorposts with the blood of an unblemished lamb (or goat) during the first Passover as a sign for the Angel of Death to Passover (not kill) the children of God residing within the homes so marked. Now about that goat, if we look into the book of Leviticus we can see a parallel between Jesus and the requirement for a sin offering that included two goats, one for sacrifice to the Lord and the other to be set free into the desert. Therein is the parallel occurrence of Jesus being brought before Pilate along with Barabbas. Jesus is the sacrifice for our sins and Barabbas is the one who escapes punishment; he is the initial scapegoat representing all of us, who, like Barabbas is deserving of punishment. ***Leviticus 16:6-10 "Aaron is to offer the bull for his own sin offering to make atonement for himself and his household. Then he is to take the two goats and present them before the Lord at the entrance to the Tent of Meeting. He is to cast lots for the two goats—one lot for the Lord and the other for the scapegoat. Aaron shall bring the goat whose lot falls to the Lord and sacrifice it for a sin offering. But the goat chosen by lot as the scapegoat shall be presented alive before the Lord to be used for making atonement by sending it into the desert as a scapegoat."***

Back to the wedding

The jars used to carry the water that was to be transformed into wine were empty. They were full at the beginning and as the guests arrived the water used for ritualistic washing had been depleted. Anyone arriving at the feast at a later time (after the water had been changed to wine) to them, Jesus is saying, tradition and ritual is always placed into a secondary position in favor of good being accomplished, without any sacrifice of tradition or custom. Good trumps all. There were six jars each having the capacity to hold from twenty to thirty gallons of liquid. As such the minimum quantity of wine produced was one hundred and twenty gallons of the best wine ever! The miracle producing the wine causes us to think that it was a holy vintage but in reality all that God produces for us is holy and good. As such we always receive God's provision in a spirit of reverence. As for the actual miracle of transforming water into wine, who knew it had taken place? The servants at the feast, it was they who had filled the jars with water. The work of God is not hidden from his servants. Wine making at the time of Jesus was prolific and everyone knew a good vintage when tasted. In fact wine was preferred over water because of the poor quality of water inherent in the surrounding area. ***"Cana"*** means, *"Place of reeds"* and from that description we may infer a poorer quality of water available. Jesus instructs the servants to bring some of the new wine to the master of the banquet (no doubt an expert consumer of wine) and so impressed is he with the vintage that he compliments the groom for saving the best for last. Jesus is not taking any bows, he allows the groom to gain in the eyes of all.

In the expected order of things the best wine was usually served first and later on when the guests are feeling no pain the cheaper wine is served. With the provision of God we can expect the best quality all of the time. Of course we can imagine the inability of the servants to contain their joy at the revealing of Christ's glory through the miracle, and neither can we as we witness the transformation and renewal of our lives in Christ. Like the empty jars we have been filled with the very best of the water of life. As the empty jars gained meaningful purpose by containing that which is holy we also have gained purpose and are filled with the holiness of God. As the disciples witnessed the first miracle performed by Jesus they placed their faith in him, in the same way we who received the miracle of rebirth have also invested in him our trust. Just as the depletion of wine had signaled a low point in the feast, we also at the realization of the emptiness in our lives are filled anew with both life and purpose. As the new wine filled the empty cups at the feast so too the cup of redemption brings new life to all who call upon the name of the Lord.

Simon the Pharisee and a woman's faith

Luke 7:37-38 *"When the woman who had lived a sinful life in that town learned that Jesus was eating at the Pharisee's house, she brought an alabaster jar of perfume, and as she stood behind at his feet weeping, she began to wet his feet with her tears. Then she wiped them with her hair, kissed them and poured perfume on them."*

Again we see our Lord as an invited guest. This time it is at the home of a Pharisee named Simon. The motives of Simon for inviting Jesus are clear. Simon is a part of the religious rulers in Israel and he invites Jesus in the manner that one would summon someone to court, but it is done covertly under pretext. Inwardly Simon looks upon Jesus as someone who is beneath the status that he (Simon) enjoys. But our Lord will receive the respect he deserves, even in the homes of those who will not advance the common traditional greeting or the ritual requirements of the religious. The Pharisee failed to greet Jesus with the customary kiss and failed to provide for him the water necessary for ritual cleansing. In his mind Simon would have no part of offering the product of the religious, which he may have thought could keep Jesus at a disadvantage or at a level below himself. But God provided the water of repentance in the tears of the sinful woman. It is interesting that the woman had no difficulty entering the home of Simon. She knew Simon and knew where he lived and by his own admission Simon knew her; the type of woman she was. That she was successful at what she had done is evident by the expensive perfume she brought with her to bestow upon our Lord. It follows that only the rich could afford her services and Simon fits that part of the equation as well. The Pharisee failed to give Jesus the customary kiss but this woman never ceased kissing his feet out of the love for forgiveness. Sometimes we can be so beat down by the world that we begin to believe that there really is no forgiveness for us, but when we finally understand that God loves us and will forgive us there is an explosion of gratitude accompanied by tears of joy.

Simon had thought to himself, *"If this man were really a prophet he would know the type of woman that is touching him."* Jesus asks of Simon, *"Who is it that loves more, he who is forgiven a lot or a little?"* Simon responds by saying, I suppose it is the one who is forgiven more. But Jesus, within his question to Simon, turns Simon's self-righteous thoughts right back at him. Simon believes himself to be one not in need of forgiveness and Jesus is tacitly saying to Simon, if you were as righteous as you pretend you would be able to recognize one who is sent by God through the love of righteousness alone. Jesus does not say to the woman, "Why do you involve me?" Or why are you carrying on in this outward display of emotional gratitude? Not at all, for the time for the woman had come to find redemption for her sins, and Jesus accepts her repentance and discards the judgment of the self-righteous. The woman who adopted the role of servant in the presence of the Lord knew that she was free of the life that kept her bound in sin. As the servants at the wedding feast recognized the glory of Christ, so it was with the woman who rushed to his feet for her miracle.

Who was this woman?

John 11:1-3 *"A man named Lazarus, who lived in Bethany, became sick. Bethany was the town where Mary and her sister Martha lived. (This Mary was the one who poured the perfume on the Lord's feet and wiped them with her hair; it was her brother Lazarus who was sick.) The sisters sent Jesus a message: "Lord, your dear friend is sick."*

Zacchaeus the mighty

LUKE 19:1-7 *Jesus entered Jericho and was passing through. A man was there by the name of Zacchaeus; he was a chief tax collector and wealthy. He wanted to see who Jesus was, but being a short man he could not, because of the crowd. So he ran ahead and climbed a sycamore-fig tree to see him, since Jesus was coming that way. When Jesus reached the spot, he looked up and said to him, "Zacchaeus, come down immediately, I must stay at your house today." So he came down at once and welcomed him gladly. All the people saw this and began to mutter, "He has gone to be a guest of a sinner."* Sometimes Jesus is an invited guest and then sometimes it appears that he invites himself. The chief tax collector was wrestling with a number of problems and Jesus knows it. He stops, looks up into the tree to find Zacchaeus who is hoping to get a look at the man whose reputation has preceded him like a wildfire. A good reputation always takes a forward position while a bad reputation is a constant burden and must be dragged along like an unruly child. Zacchhaeus was for all intent and purpose desiring to invite Jesus to his home, but he knew that he was labeled a sinner by those whose exterior posture is judgmental; he was content to get a look at Jesus from a vantage point (tree top) apart from the ground level obscurity that would surely accompany chance. Besides, he had lived a life where people looked down to him in every aspect of conceptual thought. What was true then is true today, it is we who must invite Jesus into our home whether it is done in public or in the privacy of the heart. Additionally there are times Jesus will invite himself into our lives when we are at our lowest point. Zacchaeus sounds like he could have qualified for leper status. Tax collectors were loved then as much as they are today. He was not only a tax collector but he was one advanced in the art of collecting. That is, he was a chief among them. That's got to be like a tribal leader of cannibals. Outsiders can find nothing that would attract or promote a meaningful relationship with either tax collectors or cannibals. To be an outcast even when one is wealthy promotes a desire to belong. Jesus is passing through Jericho and he draws a crowd. It is Jesus who understands that the time of salvation had come to the home of Zacchaeus. The last thing people expected of Jesus was that he would associate with a sinner of the proportions reserved for tax collectors. Zacchaeus is so happy for the acceptance by our Lord, he promises to make restitution to all he cheated and to give half of all of his possessions to the poor. Zacchaeus was hit with a threesome of repulsions. Not only is he a castoff because of his wealth and position he is also short in stature which invites comment. I can imagine the conversation as Zaccaheus went about his daily duties and rounds.

"Hey! Look, it's Zaccaheus the mighty, all who gaze upon his imposing form tremble in fear." Outcasts can usually be found at the punch line of derision. This must have endeared the people in the eyes of Zaccaheus. The faith of Zaccaheus in Jesus to not pass judgment upon him is displayed in his eagerness to just catch a glancing look upon our Lord. Not only does Zaccaheus get to look upon the Lord but he is honored above all of the self-righteous by having Jesus as a guest in his home. All of this is done in the perfect timing of God, who, by publicly accepting the sinner promotes jealously in the hearts of the self-righteous, so they also can recognize their need and be saved.

Perfect Timing

Never was I so blessed
As the day of heaven's reach
That entered inmost halls
And brought to life real peace.
It was the right time
And place for maximum grace.
Amen.

2 Corinthians 6:1-2 As God's fellow workers we urge you not to receive God's grace in vain. For he says, "In the time of my favor I heard you, and in the day of salvation I helped you." I tell you now is the time of God's favor, now is the time of salvation.

THOUGHTS AND DEEDS

The mind is a complex aspect of our existence. So much so that absent thought we can be declared dead. "Cogito ergo sum." (I think therefore I am), is a well-known and truthful saying. It is the basis for proving life in a manner a common man can understand. The quality of life is contingent upon the way we think and verbalization of our thoughts displays for all the inner-man inhabiting the earthly tents of flesh and bone.

Romans 7:14-20 "We know that the Law is spiritual; but I am a mortal man, sold as a slave to sin. I do not understand what I do; for I don't do what I would like to do, but instead I do what I hate. Since what I do is what I don't want to do, this shows that the Law is right. So I am not really the one who does this thing; rather it is the sin that lives in me—that is, in my human nature. For even though the desire to do the good is in me, I am not able to do it. I don't do the good I want to do; instead, I do the evil that I don't want to do. If I do what I don't want to do, this means that I am no longer the one who does it; instead, it is the sin that lives in me."

"We know that the Law is spiritual;" What is Paul saying to us? Let's look at the meaning of the word *spiritual* in order to find the beginning of what is meant. *Spiritual: "Affecting the human spirit or soul as opposed to material things."* We recognize the spirit is the thinking faculty of not only mankind but also God, who is Spirit. Paul goes on to say, **"but I am a mortal man sold as a slave to sin."** In this statement what we find is the pronouncement that the Law or the thinking of God is perfect. As such our knowledge of what is right has no bearing on what we do, since we have been conscripted into slavery.

Our recognition of what is right and our desire to no longer do what is wrong proves to us the thinking of God is correct. As a slave there is almost never the opportunity to say no to the one or thing that holds us in bondage. And so Paul realizes that what he does is not his fault! The spiritual aspect (our thinking) of our human condition is bound into slavery by the sin-nature we are born with. And so we know what is right and what we should do but we cannot do it because we are slaves to sin. This realization by Paul and his lamentation, culminating in the understanding that he is not a man without hope, rather, he is one who has been saved from the bondage of being forced to do the things he does not want to do. I would add that Paul also has no control over the unwanted thoughts generated by the nature of sin. Perhaps this is why Paul urges us to, **"pray constantly."** That is to say we should constantly be cognizant of the presence of God in our lives. **Romans: 7:24-25 "What an unhappy man I am! Who will rescue me from this body that is taking me to my death?" Thanks be to God, who does this through our Lord Jesus Christ! This then, is my condition: on my own I can serve God's Law only with my mind, while my human nature serves the law of sin."**

There are times when we wonder, "Where did that thought come from?" Often they are disturbing and unwanted but we have no control of their bubbling-up into the consciousness that is our focus. I find mostly it is the unwanted thoughts that appear as specters of the past, as if haunting and condemning me for youthful transgressions. This is perhaps the root cause for, *"If I only knew then what I know now."* It is the lamentation of the ages that haunts everyone, but once we understand the wisdom contained in the words of the apostle Paul, the mocking voice of yesteryear loses a good part of its volume. There are also those unwanted thoughts that come to us through stimulation presented through our senses. Such temptations are as magnets to our carnal/sinful nature. We cannot prevent their origination and ultimate presentation to our consciousness, but we no longer have to act upon the desire, whatever it may be.

Bad habits such as smoking or drugs and the more base forms of slavery can and are overcome in the knowledge that all things are possible with God. Again, most of our unwanted thoughts come to us through stimulation. Therefore it is important for us to steer clear or remove ourselves from such temptations as they are presented externally. When generated from within we must find refuge in both the knowledge that God is with us and also that through prayer the nagging cries of a defeated enemy are told to be quiet. A prisoner may be locked away for his crimes but he is always thinking of a way to again gain freedom. So it is with our nature. We are a complexity even to ourselves, constantly urged to focus upon a certain person, place, object or thing, past present or future through our senses. (I'm sure the physiologists will have a field day with this piece of revelation). There is so much baggage within us that only redemption can ward-off the mocking mistakes of our youth. Still we must be vigilant and recognize we cannot do it (remain holy and fixed upon the prize), if the prize of eternal life is not placed into the forefront. Even with redemption we cannot forget our past. We think our deeds are buried and forgotten but like the unexpected arrival of a Jack-in-the-box clown the mocking smile brings a sometimes tear. If we are blest we may get the opportunity to live in a manner that is pleasing to God. No matter what age we may come to the truth of the condition of man, God restores us to the innocence stolen and makes us aware of the future that is eternity.

Early in our lives, (and this means everyone), we are invited urged or tempted to acquire (via credit offerings or through compensation for labor, and yes, in extreme cases through criminal acts) the things of this world. We are young and believe there is a lifetime to pay for what is desired and acquired. This projected "lifetime" to pay for what is desired today, is somewhat of an illusion since no one is guaranteed tomorrow. Again, this urging for instant gratification always discounts reality and obscures the presence of God; as well as the consequence for failure. Unfortunately we never realize just how steep a price we are forced to pay when once we do what we know to be wrong. In most instances the temptations are colored by what are the excepted norms; people fall prey and are entrapped, as would the unawareness of an animal lured into a cage seeking the food on display. All of this forceful enticement whose promise is aimed at quelling the true desire to be free, is met with the ultimate recognition of society's (worldly) harmful overtures at a point when we are reduced to our weakest and are entrapped sufficiently by the tentacles of desire's mandates. Not only are we to fend-off the designs of both internal and external urges, constantly telling us we are not far from fulfilling worldly satisfaction, (read as freedom) but once realized that it is an empty pursuit it leaves us in ruin; which is the true intent of sin. Inasmuch as the acquisition of such motivation to acquire lasts for a bit and then a greater quest must be found, therein we find the frustration of a revolving door that will never permit us exit. The lamentations of the alcoholic or drug addict, resounding in the early morning, "Never again!" speaks to us the words of Paul, *"What an unhappy man I am!"* Regarding addictions, what we find is a reinforcement of the prison bars erected in order to keep the slave from escaping or even thinking escape is possible. Therein the reinforcement is a blend of emphasizing not only the spiritual capture but the physical as well. *"What an unhappy man I am!"* It is at these weakest moments in our lives that God's power for us is greatest. Perhaps this is because when we are down *so far* there is only one way we can possibly look, and that is the direction of up! The very direction we had discounted and/or had been denied by the, *"evil god of this world." Proverbs 27:20 Human desires are like the world of the dead-there is always room for more."* Sinful desires generated by the human condition cannot find satisfaction. There will always be room for more, or, there will always be a compelling and nagging persistence to return to a like (sinful) body of influence, akin to the sinful nature of man. Having said this, we must be on our guard against such thoughts that lead us away from the good we know we ought to do. Another way of expressing the above proverb is to call into mind another quote from wisdom, *Proverbs 27:22 Even if you beat a fool half to death, you still can't beat his foolishness out of him."* Some things do not change. The nature of man (the body that seeks gratification on many levels, both necessary and foolish) cannot be placed into a state of compliance; it will always seek to gravitate to its nature, which is sin. We must breathe and eat in order to live, breathing is automatic and hunger reminds us of our need to eat. These physical needs we cannot do without. They fall into the order of life sustaining and absolutely necessary. However, of the many things that man does the greatest majority are not connected to such absolutes, but fall into the category of self-gratification through acquisition. All of us have the knowledge of right and wrong and most will find remorse for thinking and then acting upon such thoughts after the fact. Still, there are those who appear unfazed and disconnected from acts of even the most heinous imaginations. These are evil personified and made to show to us the truth. Where there is the understanding of evil so too there is the recognition that there must be a good. The pinnacle of evil is understood to be the Evil One and conversely God is Love. Therein we find the reality of truth an aphorism or forceful expression of undeniable truth. The reality of God and evil can no longer be denied.

Wind

The internal wind carries us to places we would not go.
We are driven like a leaf in its downward fall.
Lifted high into the sky just to fall again
What is this force within me from which I can't defend?

How long will you live as the wind
Not knowing where you're going or caring where you've been?
Racing round in circles downward spiral's end
Torn by constant movement alone in troubled times
Captured held in bondage by blindfolds of the mind.

Denied within your core the truth of sunshine's breath
Will you keep on racing until this life does end?

Fire and rain flakes and frost cannot hold the wind
It travels hither yon knowing not a friend.
We are like the wind when we do not have a home
Where thoughts of coming danger are given to the strong.
When will you hush the wind and live life's intent from God?

Hosea 8:7 "When they sow the wind they will reap a storm!"

Well there we have it again, a forceful biblical truth making it impossible to deny the existence of good and evil. Not too many of us dwell upon the supernatural laws of God. Mostly people are concerned with both the natural and/or manmade laws. Unfortunately for many (I dare say the majority for the road is indeed narrow) the Laws of God will not cease for us when death arrives. Just as we can understand what may be fatal for the physical has no impact upon that which is spiritual, so long as we are in Christ, so too we must understand the poisons of this life can have a lasting impact upon the afterlife. It is difficult to breath in a windstorm and even more difficult to live a meaningful life in the conflicts that force us to go where we would not go. They toss us about, spit us out, and when we are no longer dizzy they do it all again! How long will we keep racing? As long as we deny the truth of God we will never find the peace that calms the storms of life. Our thoughts and deeds comprise the quality of our lives, and to a great extent the quality of life for those we love. Those nightmares that come to us at anytime of the day are but things that have been. They may have a residual impact but are no longer the fearful specters of their first appearance. Life in the Spirit of God has made all things possible for us. ***Romans 8:1-3 "There is no condemnation now for those who live in union with Christ Jesus. For the Law of the Spirit, which brings us life in union with Christ Jesus has set me free from the law of sin and death."***

Hurricane

❧

The hurricane breathing strong
Captures wistful wind of souls.
Desire soaring captured by the storm
Beat and battered by debris
Within the forceful flight
Tumbling ever downward
No end of depth in sight.
Contact with the world
Crash of flesh and bone
Scattered fragments faulty sight
Caustic visions haunting nights
Echo loudly grief and strife.
Mercy's mission healing touch upon marrow's moan
Cradled hope in forward steps seizes strength unknown.
Truth of life ingrained complete freedom's breath sustained
By drinking deeply water pure that calms the hurricane.
Taste the goodness of the Lord.
Praise his holy name!
Sing to him a joyful song
O redeemed from hurricanes!

❧

Mark 6:51 "Then he got into the boat with them and the wind died down."

Victory

The call to battles lost lingers in the mind.
It shouts defeat in crystal tones at all attempts toward change.
Confident of victories past says, "No escape remains!"
Trouble near within the heart despair the lot of man
Crushing laughter shouts, "No end!"
Hope sees not a friend.

Stone upon stone the sentry hushed by rumors in the bones.
Foundations quake and boulders break at the sound of love.
The knowing look of lies rebuked take flight from temple cleansed.
Silence sweet silence, peace at last.

Change proclaimed to captive man soaring spirit sighs.
At last deception is dragged into the light!
Truth is the key to freedom sought.
"Love!" is the victory cry!

1 John 5:5 "Who is it that overcomes the world? Only he who believes that Jesus is the Son of God."

No Surrender

~~~⌒~~~

There's a battle every day and with confidence to win
I call upon the Lord who strengthens and defends.
I can feel the struggle can taste it in my teeth
The pulsing of desires raging at their peak.
They promise respite from the conflict yes and no.
Lies designed for bondage to the things that hold and bind
Ball and chain submission to where we would not go
"No surrender!" is the answer says body mind and soul.

~~~⌒~~~

Philippians 4:13 I can do everything through him who gives me strength.

Shake-Shake

Shake-shake shudder a twinge within the pit
Fingers cold as tombstone frost
Laid upon my spine
Touching past transgressions hiding in my mind.
Shake-shake shudder unexpected come the waves
Washed upon the shore of forgotten yesterdays.
Shake-shake shudder a bowstring drawn to breath
Armed with piercing arrows dipped in poisons of regret.
Shake-shake shudder O the permanence of scars
Mocking spirit-body until we cry aloud for God.
Shake-shake shudder shouts, "Save me!" from within, to the Lord of
Glory
"Wash away my sins."

Psalm 25:17-18 The troubles of my heart have multiplied; free me from my anguish. Look upon my afflictions and distress and take away all of my sins.

DRUG ADDICTION A BRICKS
WITHOUT STRAW AFFLICTION

Many of us seek to find a measure of peace within a world of war. We will always have war in one of its many forms. Countries will make war against one another as well as internally. Consumers will search to find a bargain that has not overtly attacked and taken advantage of their finances, and physical desires are constantly in a warlike setting produced by influences presented on a daily basis. Some of these desires appeal to both the physical and spiritual characteristics of man. When man is captured on both of these levels he is lost. When saved, his objective is to not be overcome by the formerly formidable enemy of sin. Entire countries live in the tyranny imposed by a few, and those finding a measure of physical freedom must be constantly vigilant against the erosion of freedoms enjoyed. It is no different with those of us who have received God's grace; vigilance is required. In addition to tyrannical schemes, addictive behavior is designed to dominate actions and thoughts of man. There is the internal conflict that strives to capture and control, as would dictatorial lords, striving to subjugate the desire for freedom within the slave. It is to this reality the apostle Paul warns us against fruitless deeds of darkness, needing to be exposed by the light of Christ. Paul is also telling us to be true to our self and to recognize the condition of falling asleep for increasingly longer periods of time, until we are lulled into an existence that is in total denial of truth. Captive again. There are good deeds and bad, perhaps the first bad fruit originated in the garden of paradise. From that infraction came all manner of fruitless existence. Troubles in

life mostly come to us from our unwillingness to recognize and heed the pronouncements of God. Substance abuse becomes the dictatorial lord of our life in place of God. All parents look forward to the day their children can become independent, but parents never want to hear they are no longer needed. God is no different in this respect because he knows for us to assume independence in all things is to find the cold edge of reality poised to come crashing down upon us.

Ephesians 5:11-14 Have nothing to do with the fruitless deeds of darkness, but rather expose them. For it is shameful even to mention what the disobedient do in secret. But everything exposed by the light becomes visible, for it is light that makes everything visible. This is why it is said: "Wake up, O sleeper, rise from the dead, and Christ will shine on you."

Have nothing to do with deeds that will not bring forth fruit. What does not bring forth fruit is dead. Deeds of darkness are those that we would be ashamed to have revealed. Even if one does not feel ashamed for the deeds done in secret, we still would not want them to be exposed. Light doesn't allow discretionary revelation, whether or not we permit exposure. Without notice light instantly transforms what was hidden into revelation. The light of truth illuminates in a way all can see what is contained in darkness. It uncovers hidden things within us that even we are not aware of. It exposes uncovers discovers and forces recognition through bathing in its presence. It shouts a wake up call for us to realize that nothing can be hidden from the light of God. Truth brings sight, and in the gaining of sight all things are transformed in its light. Truth is light. What was secret is no longer hidden, and what is right and pleasing to God is illuminated and highlighted, for all to see, as it contrasts with things that are wrong and evil in the pronouncements of God. Jesus is the light of the world.

In this life we have often found ourselves in trouble. If we are not promoting problems for ourselves there is always someone eager to lead us into the so-called jackpot. A rock and hard place predicament, affording no hope for reversal, until the intervention of light points the way to freedom. **Ephesians 1:18 I pray also that the eyes of your heart may be enlightened in order that you may know the hope to which he has called you, the riches of his glorious inheritance in the saints.** A good example of externally imposed slavery may be viewed within the captivity of the ancient Hebrew people, held tenaciously within the grip of their Egyptian rulers. The Hebrew slaves in ancient Egypt were faced with a no win situation. They were forced to make bricks without the straw normally provided by their captors. This meant they were to not only make the bricks required, but also glean the straw from the fields in their off hours. ***Exodus 5:6-9 That same day Pharaoh gave this order to the slave drivers and foreman in charge of the people: "You are no longer to supply the people with straw for making bricks; let them go and gather their own straw. But require them to make the same number of bricks as before; don't reduce the quota. They are lazy; that is why they are crying out, 'Let us go and sacrifice to our God.' Make the work harder for the men so that they keep working and pay no attention to lies."*** Many a slave is kept working to fulfill the desires generated within, by our nature, and in the case of the Hebrew slaves, they were forced to endure because of the evil that held them against their will. In both cases of slavery, internal or externally imposed, there is desire for freedom and a longing to find and offer (sacrifice) one's self to God. The thirst for freedom is unrelenting and will seek even illusory measures in efforts to quell the reality of a slave condition. Within the pretense of freedom, physical bondage still exists; it is just made more bearable through an illusion of escape through the usage of drugs and alcohol. A meaningless life appears to gain direction through escape routes within pockets of the mind; the only place left for retreat.

Yes, the people saw hope in Moses, but the darkness of Pharaoh fought back with tenacity to keep the people in bondage. Pharaoh called the message of God's truth, ***"lies"*** but the people saw hope. They believed in the message that God was concerned for them and the initial breaking of chains began in their hearts. From that point on it was just a matter of bending the back of Pharaoh with heavy burdens the Lord God would place upon him. Hope then is the switch that turns on the light that sets free all who are kept in darkness and denied freedom. Freedom calls to all who will hear and believe the message that God cares for us. The problems that we may find ourselves confronted with may be similar to a make bricks without straw condition, imposed by not only others but in large measure ourselves. The problems created, as was the edict ascribed by Pharaoh, (They are lazy), are really traps designed to keep us in bondage. The fear and feelings of utter hopelessness are as real as the shackles placed upon our feet to prevent us from running from our situation. Gambling drug addiction immorality and a host of other chains are traps designed to keep us in bondage, and in service to others for their enrichment. The enslavers (unknowingly) are no better off than the brick makers, until recognition and acceptance of God shines into their hearts as well. All of us are trapped by the reality of sin taking us to our death. Those of us who recognize the light are afforded salvation present within its freedom bearing illumination. Some people have unwittingly rejected the reality of sin, because darkness and deception keeps them ignorant of the good news of Christ. Some knowingly deny obvious prohibitions of wrong in order to pursue an agenda positioned against the will of God. These are the people whose deeds are fruitless and shameful, and must be exposed for they have sunk deep into the quagmire of evil. They declare their self to be a god (just as Pharaoh) in order to assume the mantle of lord and master over thoughts and actions. When we adore our self we may arrive at the doorstep of divinity declaring our self to be a god. Perhaps the evil one was the very first narcissist? Perhaps it is he who established the new age religions of today? They may have different names and the packaging may be different but at its root lives a belief in the divinity of man, never intended to inhabit his creation. The purpose of false religion is the denial of truth always intended for us to see. It was the lie that buried us, and it is truth that puts an end to the grave. It used to be only a Caesar or Pharaoh would be exposed to sufficient pride to accept this demigod notion. Today it is offered to anyone who finds it attractive or allows himself to venture into lands clearly marked as off-limits and dangerous. Celebrities are made to shine as stars high above us in the heavens. Unlike the wise men following a star provided by God, the bright lights and stars of this world are meant to lead us away from the reality that is God, and the truth he provides. The stars of this world are presented to us as having no prohibitions limitations or responsibility imposed upon their actions, because their manmade godlike status precludes worldly justice. When a star is found flawed (only when there is no escaping truth), he or she is immediately rehabbed and restored to their place of brilliance, in order to guide us into the perception that all things are good and can be explained away without accepting responsibility. The star is actually applauded and adored even more, by bowing to restorative measures. We have teen idols, screen and print projections of what is declared as perfection, stars that are given as role models to emulate and recognize as free and uninhibited by the hardships afflicting common man. Truly it is the blind leading the blind. Restoration is done skillfully by spin-doctors who used to be called liars. These masters of the lie speak a language of duplicitous ambiguity that never allows or permits an answer without back door plausibility, designed to mislead and deny truth. They purposely refuse a response of *"yes"* or *"no"* to probing questions, the equivalent of drawing blinds to disallow light's entrance. As long as the world denies truth it matters not how bright the light may shine. If we continually attempt to conceal the things we know to be lies it promotes a self serving agenda. There are those who clean pigeon droppings from park statues and this also is a form of restoration, but the statues are as dead as those who deny truth. By resisting having our deeds brought into the light for fear wrong will be exposed is of itself condemnation igniting the war within—the conflict in man spoken of by the apostle Paul.

Prisons of concrete and bone

Laws are enacted to protect society (in general) from those who would take a new age philosophy to the extreme. That is, those who would use any means possible in order to both satisfy human desires and quell the repeated uproars contained within the prison of conscience. Who can accept the lie that man is good and there is no wrong? Accepting this lie is to remain in a bricks without straw condition of slavery, to the sin that rules in us. If there is no wrong in the minds of some then it is plausible to assume the creativity to achieve the dictates of the flesh, have no boundaries to prevent harm to others or our self. Thus external prisons of brick are constructed to confine those who are already enslaved within the darkness of their own hearts. We don't help ourselves by heralding new age religions that deny the existence of wrong, and in the same breath declare humanity to be gods with the ability to do whatever pleases, providing we do not impose our self determinations, beliefs and desires upon other godly realms. Thus street language incorporates the phrase young people unwittingly express to each other, *"It's all good!"* By announcing what a god calls good and another does not is a contradiction of the core belief that wrong does not exist. Wrong puts a dent in the star of repeated rehab. Since there is this belief that wrong does not exist, the confusion generated begets a greater need to embrace darkness affording shelter and the comfort of ignorance. This absurdity takes us deeper into slavery. If the core of man is declared to be good and unflawed by sin then not only a deeper corruption of man is sought after (through bathing deeply in the waters of vain pursuits), but a denunciation of biblical truth is the underlying goal. If sin does not exist it follows everything is indeed good and the bible is wrong by stating that there are none who are righteous. So insidious are the attempts to once again bring to the fore the dark days of ignorance that permeated the hearts of men. God's truth conquers worldly lies and leads to freedom so desperately desired. This is a constant thorn in the heart of evil, for as the good news of biblical truth forces darkness deeper into obscurity the more deliberate are the attacks upon the most helpless of creation appear. As such, the dual objectives of good and evil are racing to a point in time of God's choosing, and in this meeting God's Word will completely destroy all deception. In the restoration of all things God will erase sin from even the memory of man. We are so desperately in need of recognizing our dependency upon God. Unfortunately for those who accept the pronouncement of man's divinity and independence, along with the belief that one can be free from the condemnations of conscience, what is soon found is a profound dislike for one's self, that may foster a seriously eroded self esteem begetting self loathing. The root cause for belief in the non-existence of wrong is the inability to say no. If a god is powerless to say no, another set of problems sprouts forth to tarnish the new age thought. It's the condition of the walking dead. We can declare that all things we do are good and permitted. We may undergo all kinds of erasure therapy, to denounce conscience, and we can band together in an attempt to be free of the condemnations of truth, but all that is accomplished is a deeper enslavement to the sin nature that rules our lives. Within the downward spiral into the limitless dictates of a slave's existence we also acquire a profound stubbornness that adamantly refuses internal change. We may try to run away from the reality of our lives, but no matter how we try and what we may ingest to aid in the attempt to deny our condition, we cannot achieve the peace that only accompanies freedom. We cannot run away from ourselves but we can give ourselves to God, who has the ability to set us free from the condition of slavery whether self imposed or forced upon us.

The world's pull is the hope for change

The pull of the world promises peace from the condemnations of conscience and hope for freedom from a slave's existence; it is a lie manifesting itself in the temporary disconnects of addiction. These send us off into altered states of consciousness that tell us, *"It's all good!"* With tones of mocking captivity that bite into the fabric of marrow and bones, as chains would wear upon flesh, the spirit endures, as does the flesh captured by the allurement of the world. Substance abuse is not the cure for the life of a slave; it is deception designed to keep us enslaved by promising relief from pains inflicted by the war within. These remedies do not cure. Rather, they aid in prolonging the agony of a slave, and make deeper the darkness of those who may otherwise see. Instability within our lives is caused in part by our nature dictating itself against the knowledge of what is right, by our desire to break free from a condition that we are not in control of, and by the cumulative impact of this duality that adds rapidity to our increasing descent into darkness. Instability turns us upside down, headlong into deeper solitude manufactured by darkness that denies us an upward view, having ability to set us free. Instability increases the speed in which we experience life and increases our chances for missing critical signs of danger. When we first taste the goodness of the Lord our hearts are penetrated by the light of truth and the chains that rendered us impotent are broken. We are then permitted to exercise the ability to say *"no"* to the things that held us captive. This is joyful, and cause to celebrate, but it does not end there. The light of truth and the healing warmth it affords radiates outward throughout our entire being and begins to construct the foundation that brings stability to our new life in Christ. Stability in our life begins with biblical truth. It is truth that arrests and places the dictates of a slave condition, into a used-to-be way of life. For those who are seeking a way out of slavery, other than by truth, what is found does not come without a cost. Embracing a world-view placing mankind at the godhead of existence is not baggage free. One such responsibility that clings to the *independence from sin philosophy* is to find contentment through a value oriented rating of success. *"Your life is a success when you can shape your identity through your possessions. Life becomes a rock of stability when your possessions declare independence from the hardships of life."* When the outward person is dishonest and expresses an inner condition of peace, where there is none, it is easy to conclude by those wishing to break free that materialism solves all problems, both internal and external in nature. We know this to be a false premise because human desires can never be satisfied. They must be put to death through the receipt of a new spirit in man. Our true worth is expressed in the sacrifice of Christ upon the cross. There will always be another carrot that promises to arrest the hunger in man. A drug addict may be sitting on a mountain of drugs and still there is the desire for more. And so it was with the ancient Hebrew people freed from slavery, there was a price to pay. They needed to recognize and believe God. They needed to deny their desires to go in differing directions and adopt a desire to follow in God's ways. Embracing a world-view of *anything goes* denies dependency upon God for it has already declared itself to be a god.

People who cannot admit dependency will certainly find it difficult to seek God, for they have embraced an independent and prideful position that declares their existence free from all things having an absolute label attached. Those who will not admit to substance abuse are destined to continue seeking spiritual and physical freedom for the remainder of their days. Of course the world-view accepts death as an absolute and therein lives the contradiction generating encapsulation. The war within that leads to *battle fatigue* is an emotional disturbance within the heart and mind of man. Acceptance of truth concerning God requires us to recognize our need for God. Again, we must admit that God is right and we are not. A stable and successful life is dependent upon our ability to recognize God and our decision to choose to do what God requires of us. When we exist in a slave's reality what we are really saying is, *"I don't want to do it."* This is a denouncement of, ***"Thy will be done."*** When we are in rebellion against the rightful authority of God, in pursuit of our own desires and dictates, it then is condensed into the *"me-myself and I"* syndrome, that encapsulates and makes central the sole purpose of our existence. There are perhaps many reasons for some to build or allow a wall to be built around the heart, but the windows and doors are always locked from within. Therein the isolation of captivity deepens and impacts negatively upon all aspects of our lives. Spiritual and physical infirmities must always accompany the life of a slave. *A fly trapped in a bag makes an undeniable plea, rushing and buzzing upward and down, unmistakable is the sound, seeking freedom.* We can all see the condition of slavery and somehow we fail to recognize the cause to be plain old-fashioned sin. It's no wonder the world denies sin exists. It is the chief enslaver! We all have experienced the war within. We recognize what is right and our inability to do it, and still we are deluded into thinking it is just another speed bump upon the road of life. Even a muffled cry from within an encapsulated heart will bring the light of truth into the darkness of captivity.

Concrete Soldiers

Warmed over graves zombies walking
Eyeballs bulging sockets depressed
Heartbeats shouting, "Race for the quest!"
Stone soldiers seeking rest for the head
Mark time in movement silent as death.
Gather in doorways
And subways at night
Avoiding light.
Cash in hand hope in a spoon
The bayonet hungers searching for food.
A nickel a dime a compromise
Brings rest for the body and sleep for the eyes.
Reveille stings a monotone call
"Rise up with the masses and sing the same song."
The body is passing slowly away
The concrete soldier doesn't notice the fade.
Daytime awakens the dead
Like thunder and lighting inside the head
Demanding compliance surrender of dreams
When the mess kit is empty the body shakes
The mind screams, "Please!"
They won't gain trust or parades.
They won't come back as monuments.
The concrete soldier has numbered his days.

**Isaiah 61: 13 The Spirit of the Sovereign Lord is on me, because
the Lord has anointed me to preach good news to the poor. He has
sent me to bind up the brokenhearted, to proclaim freedom to the
captives and release for the prisoners, to proclaim the year of the
Lord's favor and the day of vengeance of our God, to comfort all who
mourn, and provide for all who grieve in Zion—to bestow on them
the crown of beauty instead of ashes, the oil of gladness instead of
mourning, and a garment of praise instead of a spirit of despair.**

Just as Pharaoh needed to be beaten down before he grudgingly had to recognize that there was someone greater than him, we also are beaten down in our pursuit of failed worldly remedies that eventually cause us to look outside of ourselves for the freedom God wants to bestow. Lifting up our hands in frustration incorporates recognition of someone above us. Within the frustration we may also find anger over our inability to gain freedom from the things that hold us captive. This also is recognition of intuitive knowledge that tells us we know that freedom is available, but we do not know where it can be obtained. Frustration and anger invites a downpour of ashes (ruin) that erases gladness and brings forth a steady state of mourning, inviting a spirit of despair. We mourn for our animated self that understands the death within us, and this manifests itself in a spirit of despair, a spirit of defeat. When we raise our hands up into the air in frustration and anger it is also a language that all can understand. It is a universal language that says, *"I surrender. I give up. I'm done. Cease hostilities. I seek peace."* When hand raising is done in a time of war the one who surrenders willingly gives himself over to the enemy, knowing that captivity is certain. But hope is born, instead of the certain death we know will occur without surrender. We can surrender into the hands of our enemies and still have hope for survival, how much more will our hope be rewarded when we surrender to God who wants to set us free? Jesus is our ***"great hope"*** and no matter how bleak the landscape of our life appears he is always with us. He is always seeking our surrender to him so that we can be restored to a life filled with joy, to focus upon the things that build up, as opposed to those that destroy.

Prism

❧

The nature of light reveals.
In darkness all is concealed.
A forest of night a room without light
A candle of wax absent wick
Inhibited movement caution advised
What good is beauty without light?
Corrective lens high wattage bulb
Movement captured by the timing of strobe
Fly to the paper moth to the flame
The nature of man does the same.
Within the rainbow nothing's concealed
In the spectrum of light all is revealed.
All must be tested
And where there is darkness
Its movement arrested.

❧

1 John 4:1 Dear friends, do not believe every spirit, but test the spirits to see if they are from God, because many false prophets have gone out into the world.

In the travels of the apostle Paul he visited Berea, and there he found willing ears to listen but they also had the wisdom to recognize that all that is presented as truth must be tested and verified by the Holy Scriptures. Thus they searched the scriptures to see if what Paul was telling them was true. Biblical truth is the only basis for us to test all that is presented to us. There is much deception and clever argument presented by those whose foundation does not rest upon biblical truth. Therein these arguments can be shaped into something that is attractive to the sin nature of man, but not ever silencing the conscience that gnaws upon the unhealthy food, unwittingly allowed to be ingested. God's word is alerting us to the fact that there are many who claim to be sent by God, but their message is tainted by their motives. They are adept in the art of deception and cunning in the ways of the world. As such we are kept focused by the warning contained in scripture to test everything in the light of truth. Truth sets us free and keeps us free!

Cause And Cure

Compulsions of the flesh are thought of in the main
To be caused by a missing chemical that shouts, "do wrong" to the brain.
Others teach the theory a "defective gene" is the cause
Confusing our thinking and making us, "choose wrong."

Worldly street physicians have exploited human need
By selling drugs they call, "The cure" satisfying greed.
Alcohol and drug abuse are not the cure proclaimed
They aggravate the symptoms but the cause remains the same.

The world is in denial of where it all begins
Because it fails to recognize plain-old-fashioned sin!
When we know the cause we may then approach the cure.
Jesus.

Romans 3:10-11 As it is written: There is no one righteous, not even one; no one who understands no one who seeks God.

Daylight Saving

Supporting cast is ready with labels bathed in light
For us to choose our company in this the falling night
Heightened pews where elbows come to rest
Lend solitary respite from worldly cares and stress
Somber figures passing within the lifted glass
Touch the deep recesses of future present past
Conversation flowing to cadence of refill
Ever dim bulbs glowing within the hallowed zone
Emotions searching troubled homes of bone
Within each daylight morning that whispers saving grace
Like liquid crystal pouring through night's veil for us to gain
The hope that is renewal's bliss to wash away the pain
That kept life passing quickly down through open drains.

Psalm 18:28-29 You, O Lord, keep my lamp burning; my God turns my darkness into light. With your help I can advance against a troop. With my God I can scale a wall.

Overdose

❧

Hombre, Night Train, Twister, and words of kindred zest
Were popular with children of contemporary quests.
Rheingold, Schlitz, and Pabst, were playmates on the roof
That lifted comprehension to words with higher proofs.
Southern Comfort and Crème de Menthe were words that did their level best
Putting "Hair of the dog that bit you" firmly to the test.
Ambassador and Dewar's were words we learned in bars
That bid us, "Please do enter," with your I.D. cards.
A plant called Marijuana made, "mellow" a household word
And Cocaine ran the fastest of all the words we heard.
LSD and Speed were words that came from labs
To satisfy the greed that laid children out on slabs.
Heroine was an old word
That made O.D. a byword for those who went to sleep
It too was a bad word far away to keep.
Crack served in plastic
In one word: "Fantastic."
In its ability to shake
And tear apart the fabric of all within its wake.
If only we had known the good words
With their ability to lift away the fog
We could have declared to all those bad words:
"You can't overdose on God!"

❧

Matthew 18:6-7 But if anyone causes one of these little ones who believe in me to sin, it would be better for him to have a large millstone hung around his neck and be drowned in the depths of the sea, then for him to cause one of these little ones to fall.

Problems

They vary in appearance and not always are alone
These troublesome predicaments upset our happy homes.
They have a lot of friends with names like grief and strife
And always are imagined to be larger than life.

Designed as fun they have an awful habit
Of showing up after the fun is done.
The biggest break our night
And fill our waking hours with non-descriptive fright.

Most problems wait in storage as jars upon a shelf
They wait for us to come along and pick them up ourselves.

The truth concerning problems is they can be overcome
Not by being downcast by limits we perceive
Rather, it's by knowing, everything is possible for us who will believe.

Psalm 5:2-3 Give ear to my words, O Lord, consider my sighing. Listen to my cry for help, my King and my God, for to you I pray. Morning by morning, O Lord, you hear my voice. Morning by morning, I lay my requests before you and wait in expectation.

Compulsion

❧

To go where we do not want and do what we should not do
Compelled by an inner voice that has not time for life
Its purpose is to satisfy that which cannot be eased
Cannot be told to rest awhile or to get some sleep.
Cannot be put into a box or stored upon a shelf
Or buried deep within the grave or made to go away
By hiding in a darkened room as man within a cage
And all this time he's wondering, "How to quell this rage?"
Pacing this way that always in confusion
He cannot understand what is truth and what's illusion.
He cannot hear freedom calling just outside his ear.
To quench the thirst within
He's bowing to compulsion to gather up the straw
To make the bricks of passion placed at deception's door.

❧

Romans 8:6-8 The mind of the sinful man is death, but the mind controlled by the Spirit is life and peace; the sinful mind is hostile to God. It does not submit to God's law, nor can it do so. Those controlled by the sinful nature cannot please God.

<u>Bricks of condemnation</u>

Self-condemnation has the ability to slow spiritual growth. This spiritual growth aspect has to do with developing confidence in the grace of God, and reliance upon him in the face of all adversity, even when our past transgressions shake us to the bone.

We sometimes look back upon the ocean of time and many things are visible upon the surface of the water, much has been buried in the deep places of memories forgotten. These are the heavy elements that over time sink to the bottom where darkness attempts to hide them away. Unfortunately, these heavy elements are like storms appearing without notice, bringing fears and threats of danger. They sometimes wake us in the middle of the night and disallow sleep. When they appear it's like an accusing finger pointing directly at our heart. There is the underlining and highlighted accusation of unworthiness, prompting us to flee from the surety of grace. It doesn't matter that we are saved and clothed in the righteousness of Christ, the flashback brings us to a time regrettable, and mocks our present day with what is dead and buried. It is at these times we should remind ourselves that God loves us. We cannot forget, but we must learn to recognize the truth concerning compulsion; what we were forced to do as slaves is not our fault. A slave does not have a choice he must comply with the demands of his master. We were ruled by the sin that lives in us. What we should also recognize is the full impact of sin in our lives, as long as we are housed in this body sin will make demands and attempt to have a dominate impact once again. Now that we have been freed, we must choose to follow along the path of righteousness. Just as the Hebrew people had to fix their sights upon the Lord, so must we. This recognition serves as a liberating force empowering us to withstand the voice of accusation, by adding desire to *no longer* create bottom dwelling debris. We should not dwell upon buried memories except as learning tools, for they are dead in the eyes of Christ.

Understanding bends back the finger of accusation and points it to the originator of corrupt behavior. Since we are no longer slaves we are free to rejoice in the present and not dwell in the condemnations of the past. We know that to look back is to lose focus upon the prize awaiting. All of us have had moments in our lives where we said, *"If I only knew then what I know now, I would do things differently."* We have already been given the prize of life through the victory of Christ, and we sometimes forget just how big a prize it is. We sometimes forget that we are recipients at all. We allow past guilt to label us as losers. We should notice that there is a distinct difference between what is lasting and what is not. ***Matthew 16:26 "What good is it for a man if he gains the whole world, yet forfeits his soul?"*** This life that we live is filled with heavy elements that cause us pain due to the weight it brings to bear upon the totality of our being. Jesus asks us to give to him all of our burdens and he will give us rest for body and mind. Jesus also tells us not to worry or be concerned for the everyday needs of life. Keep our eyes on the prize and we will have food to sustain us that the world does not know exists. It is the nourishment that renews and encourages joy through the knowledge of God. Renewal is something that is taking place constantly within all of creation. Everything in nature has a building up and tearing down process. Along with the words of Jesus who tells us not to worry over things we cannot change, we must recognize the things set into motion by God and include ourselves within the master plan, which translates into eternal life. We cannot forget our past in the context of sin, but remembrance of the cross of Christ sends those memories back to the deep place of darkness.

Within God's truth one job done well buries a multitude of mistakes. As such, when the bottom dwellers present themselves as blasts from the past, with expectation of causing us to turn inward, remember Jesus and send the bad memory packing.

Conscience Replay

Who can stand this weight upon the soul?
I would do all that I could to undo the dye cast.
I would do all I could.
But who can resurrect the past?
Like the dead who can repay them?
All that I possess is nothing compared to the pain of regret.
Regret that sneaks up like a thief in the night.

Who can count my youthful transgressions?
They assault me without notice.
Like daggers close in upon my soul.
As the grave remains cold even in summer's day
So too the inner recesses of my life.

O Lord, allow me to forgive myself.
Even the knowledge of you, at times runs away from me.
It is not that I scorn your forgiveness, Lord,
But how can I forget and forgive myself?
How can I stop replaying the past?
Renew my joy and trust,
That I may declare with strength to the shroud
Surrounding my heart:
God loves me depart!

Philippians 3:13-14 Brothers, I do not consider myself yet to have taken hold of it. But one thing I do: Forgetting what is behind and straining toward what is ahead.

HUMILITY AND TRUTH

The festival of tabernacles is a feast wherein the people looked back to the time when they spent forty-years in the desert fully aware that God was among them caring for and providing for all of their needs. It is fitting that we now see Jesus attending the feast and preaching among the people within the temple courts. He also is caring for their needs. While his disciples went openly to the festival he did so secretly because the Jewish authorities were looking to arrest him. Of course when he began to preach there was no longer the undercover Jesus who had entered the city covertly. There was much whispering about his performing good acts and miracles but still the people did not speak of him openly for fear of the Jewish authorities. The people had asked one another, "Is he the Messiah?" "Isn't he the man the authorities are trying to kill?" In addition, many believed him to be the Messiah for they had asked each other, "When the Messiah comes will he perform more miracles than this man has?" After much speculation concerning Jesus they find him in the temple courts speaking to them in a loud voice,

John: 7:28-30 "Do you really know me and know where I am from? I have not come on my own authority he who sent me however, is truthful. You do not know him, but I know him, because I came from him and he sent me." Then they tried to seize him, but no one laid a hand on him because his hour had not yet come. So much for the undercover work, it is now within the confines of the temple with the people hungering for his teaching that he appears, knowing the Jewish authorities were looking for him. Actually the guards sent to arrest Jesus were so enthralled by his teaching that they forgot *about their mission and permitted themselves the experience of learning firsthand. The rumors are still flying today, but most are attempting to malign and otherwise reduce Jesus to common man status; a sinner just like the rest of us. Even the Muslim community has contemplated the impact Jesus has had upon humanity, and they have come to the conclusion that he is a great prophet of God. Of course we then have to ask of them, why do you not believe his message? Perhaps it is the pride that says, "This is our truth and we are unwilling to recognize what others say, even if it is from a, "great prophet."*

1 Corinthians 1:26-29 "Now remember what you were, my friends, when God called you. From the human point of view few of you were wise or powerful or of high social standing. God purposely chose what the world considers nonsense in order to shame the wise, and he chose what the world considers weak in order to shame the powerful. He chose what the world looks down on and despises and thinks is nothing, in order to destroy what the world thinks is important. This means that no one can boast in God's presence."

Whenever we see in Scripture someone who has become confused by words of wisdom, we rejoice in the knowledge that God's very own wisdom was used to confuse the so-called wise and in turn illuminate the unlearned or common man. God confuses the wise for two reasons. First, he does so in order for to them to recognize they are not the wealth of knowledge they suppose others should account to them, because of their schooling or training. Secondly, God wants them to understand there is so much more outside of their cloistered or otherwise confined existence that cries out to them as well. God confuses the wise so that they who have constructed a high tower of worldly pride can see there is something more to amaze outside of their own intellect.

In simple terms, it is God who wishes none to be destroyed, (even the so-called wise) and so it is we find Jesus teaching in the temple courts even when he knows the authorities are looking for him. A man known to have no formal rabbinical training within the halls of higher religious learning, is teaching in a manner never before heard from any of the known accredited teachers of the Law, says to those who have the desire to choose God's will as their way of life, as their lamp stand of righteousness and illumination, ***"Whoever is willing*** *to do what God wants will know whether what I teach comes from God,"* by God's wisdom which is always accompanied by humility, absent the worldly expressions wrapped and packaged in pride. As a boy Jesus was among the teachers of the Law and they were amazed by the wealth of wisdom's understanding he had displayed. On the day of Pentecost all of those who heard the apostles proclaim the wonders of God accomplished in the man called Jesus, ask of themselves the same question concerning the apostles, *Acts 2:7 In amazement and wonder they exclaimed, "These people who are talking like this are Galileans! How is it, that all of us hear them speaking in our own native language?"* This is basically the same question those hearing Jesus at this time in the temple courts ask of themselves, *"How did this man get such learning?"* The answer is that wisdom comes from God alone; it originates as it issues forth from his mouth. Jesus says to the people, *"My teaching is not my own."* In speaking in this manner he is giving honor to God. Jesus challenges those listening by saying, *John 7:17-18 Whoever is willing to do what God wants will know whether what I teach comes from God or whether I speak on my own authority. Those who speak on their own authority are trying to gain glory for themselves. But he who wants glory for the one who sent him is honest, and there is nothing false in him.* The challenge is the willingness to do God's will.

Well there we have it folks, the one who speaks the words of he who sent him is honest and there is nothing false in him. Wow! This statement must have made all of the teachers of the Law run for the armory. By Jesus speaking in this manner, giving glory to God, he is not only appealing to the intellect of man but he is speaking to the truthfulness that all men know resides within their very own hearts. Speaking to us in this manner awakens in us the understanding that it is God speaking directly to us, one to one, and not within the context of shotgun statements that are either hit or miss. Those speaking in a manner absent humility (perhaps unknowing) do so not only under a cloud of suspicion that must accompany pride, but their spoken words have the tendency to close ears rather than to open hearts through the connection with honesty. Let's face it no one is attracted to self-aggrandizing hot air. More than not we will be repelled by the dishonesty presented by pride even if what is spoken appears to makes sense. When man is amazed by the words of wisdom never contemplated within his inner core, and from one who has not had the opportunities of the learned, he then must ask himself, ***"How can this be?"*** By asking himself this question he has embarked upon the road leading to God. Within the overall teaching of Jesus, his parables and also in straightforward speech we find the emphasis upon truthful humility. He speaks to his disciples in this manner,

Matthew 23:11-12 "But he that is greatest among you shall be your servant. And whosoever shall exalt himself shall be abased, and he that shall humble himself shall be exalted." In another scripture reference we hear, *Luke 14:8-9 "When someone invites you to a wedding feast, do not sit down in the best place. It could happen that someone more important than you has been invited, and your host, who invited both of you, would have to come and say to you, 'Let him have this place.' Then you would be embarrassed and have to sit in the lowest place."* This marriage between humility and truth is as lasting as eternity, and in this understanding we can see that where humility is absent, especially noteworthy within the context of the world stage, we can be assured of the absence of truth. Here then is the humility of wisdom speaking truth: *Our worth originates in Christ, and in Christ, God finds us acceptable and important.* When mankind heaps upon himself accolades, seeks glory, sets himself above others, (others can also include God) he then may begin to believe his existence and self worth comes from his ability to remain independent and above the thoughts and hardships of common man. *Within this self assured reasoning the flower of pride blooms, and from its root corruption finds avenue to destroy the rightful place God desires for us to reside.* This self-important attitude will cause others to look upon us as simply glory seekers. Glory seekers filled with a message we proclaim to be our own, thus rendering it simply of not much importance, because there is so much pride within the world not many are paying attention to those who seek glory for their own gain. It's as if saying, "We have heard it all before!" About as much interest will be shown as would accompany a summer rerun from the era of silent movies. All of the teachings of Jesus are pointedly meant for us to take a step-back attitude in the knowledge of the greatness of God. When we place God first (his rightful place), we are then removed from the worldly race for greatness, which can translate into pride, position and power, along with their sister greed from which all will find the emptiness of worldly illusion as a worthless commodity. In all honesty, absent these worldly pursuits we become reliant upon God in just the same manner as the feast of tabernacles had represented to the ancient Hebrew people. We recognize that God provides for us even in the wilderness and the unforgiving desert of want.

Humility

Step up with open arms and in modesty's respect
Make way for he alone is reserved the highest place.
Serve God with all that he bestows
Deep within the heart and mind and deeper still the soul.
Allow his healing touch to make a flower grow
Glory and praise are the things that must be given
They must be earned through proof of sacrifice
Never to be taken as a thief in stealth of night.
Put pride behind and keep it in the rear
Listen to the voice of God whisper truth foremost
Hear the chorus in the heart sung as heaven's host
"Doing what is right and good is what God loves the most."
Choose the ways of God and welcome knowing bliss
Entering the heart and mind with strength of humbleness.
O God of Holiness, in you, we find our rightful place.
And at the Wedding Feast of Christ all will live in peace.
United then forever under banners truth and love
Humbleness is true strength that needs not primp about.

Proverbs 16:18 Pride goes before destruction, a haughty spirit before a fall.

Crowns

❧

Kings and queens of royalty
Of pride and vanity displayed
Of countless ventures high atop
The common man arrayed
Will come to naught
When life is brought
Gentle to the grave.
Knowledge of our rightful place
Says, "Take these things away."
Humility transforms
And calms the rush of worldly ways.
May all the crowns
Kiss the ground
At the feet of Lord and King
He who holds head held high
Be humbled by God's grace
And enter into paradise
To receive a rightful place

❧

**Revelation 4:9-11 The four living creatures give glory, honor
and thanks to him who sits on the throne and who lives forever
and ever, the twenty-four elders fall down before him who lives
forever and ever. They lay their crowns before the throne and say:
"You are worthy, our Lord and God, to receive glory and honor
and power, for you created all things, and by your will they were
created and have their being.**

THE STREAM

All of us find it necessary to utilize judgment. The apostle Paul is making a judgment concerning those who have not portrayed the good news of Christ accurately. Paul had always built a foundation wherein corruption would not find an easy entrance into the church. Now he finds a few infiltrators attempting to create cracks in the foundation he had so arduously constructed. They are attempting to dismantle not only the foundation he constructed, but his reputation as well. His approach to the problem is one that can be likened to the discipline a parent may have to dispense; he is stern but he never has his love for the church sidetracked. Neither will he have his convictions put aside in order to win approval of men. The problems facing the early church have not really gone away; new packaging of ancient maladies will not change the content of a boastful heart, and the most spiritual contests still are widespread within many celebrated super apostles of our day.

2 Corinthians 12:2** "I know a man in Christ who fourteen years ago was caught up to the third heaven. Whether it was in the body or out of the body I do not know—God knows. And I know that this man—whether in the body or apart from the body I do not know, but God knows was caught up to paradise."* The deep places of streams are not always evident to the one attempting a crossing. The flow appears to be known from the relative safety of the bank but the underlying eddy is not always revealed at the surface. Life is in some ways like a stream. We don't always know when we will be caught up into a moment of necessity. Paul is finding it necessary to both defend his apostleship and denounce so-called ***"super apostles"

and he does so by way of boasting. His boasting is a mocking of those whose spiritual competitiveness and talents of persuasion mislead the church in Corinth by superficial appearance designed to deceive. Paul is angry and he is taking off on a tangent tempered by love and correction of those so easily led into the vain pursuits of others, whose outward character hides a muddied and incorrect teaching of the gospel. As long as there is self-pride there will always be a potential for widespread deception seeking spotlight attention at the expense of truth. Man will always have a penchant for wanting to be something more in the eyes of others. For those weak or new in the faith, emulation of others of self-proclaimed spiritual adulthood, can easily lead into a belief in exterior pronouncements and/or behavior that is contrary to truth. Paul finds himself in the position of having to reestablish his initial groundwork and foundational structure because of the infiltration of those who would be great in the eyes of new converts to Christ. Sheep have a tendency to follow the shepherd. They have a tendency to emulate the leader, but it is not always a good characteristic as evidenced by many a fallen leader past and present.

Years ago, (the 1980's) during the so-called, "Charismatic movement" a widespread appearance of the gift of tongues captured many into thinking that without such a gift one lacked the outward sign of spiritual maturity. Whole assemblies were led to emulate core members speaking the language of clanging bells. Paul says that these people (then and now) are not really the children of God, but like Satan their talent lies in the appearance of truth and in reality is a corrosive blend of poison. The topping of the cake may be sweet but sometimes the inside is filled with stuff not to our liking. There may be a consequence for taking an unknowing bite. If only we could view the inside before committing ourselves to purchase. With Jesus, what we see is what we get. The outside is the same as the inside. The exterior of super apostles may be innocuous at first glance, as may be the calm surface of a stream, but the underlying motives like unseen currents may be deadly to the one who ventures into the trusting care of a lie. What motives? The Scriptures clearly tell us that some preach the gospel for *"profit."* Paul is willing to act as if boasting in order to refocus those so enamored by the boastings of those who would be great in the eyes of men and care not for the glory of God. He is attempting to alert the church to the collective flow of hidden agendas not in anyway related to the message of Christ-crucified. Moreover, he is exposing the hypocrisy of those who would be great in the eyes of others. The apostles had asked Jesus, "*Who among them would be the greatest in the kingdom?*" The answer was simply that for those who would be great they must serve others. For some, **"*profit*"** is not always a need to acquire worldly riches but a desire for power that translates into control over others. We see this in the political world all of the time, only the very rich can afford to wage a political campaign.

Serving others without desiring the applause and accolades of adoring fans and followers is a selfless and Christ like attitude. After all, what then could be our real motive within the context of leadership, if not for Christ's gain? Pride always holds the potential for flash flooding. The impurity of hypocrisy pollutes and attempts to deceive through self-aggrandizement. We must always recognize boasting for what it is or more specifically for what it is not. It is not humility and therein we recognize a most important quality that must accompany the man or woman of God. The one chosen by God with the purpose of leadership within a given church, or as witness to others will find trepidation. Perhaps this is why some ministers of the gospel wear long robes? The robe denies the sight of knees knocking together. Responsibility in this area is a humbling experience. The spirituality of man carries us into the reality of infinite perception. Truth is the beacon that illuminates the lives of men and points us toward the humility of Christ. Truth encourages us to be humble and recognizes the absence of humility within others. This absence is in stark contrast with must be present in the one who is associated with Christ. Who can be in the presence of Jesus and carry with him one ounce of pride? So it is that Paul boasts in this manner by stating he knows of a man, and not that he is the man. Paul states that this man was taken up to the third heaven; was taken up to paradise. No doubt the experience of being swept into the reality of the formerly unknown was cause to declare exposure to paradise. The third heaven as it relates to Paul's descriptive is defined by some as the, "mesosphere," a part of the earth's atmosphere located some fifty-three miles above the earth. The logic offered in this assumption is that man did not have the knowledge of science that we have today and neither did man know of the separating layers in the atmosphere, thus the designation of all things above the earth as heaven(s) was the only way Paul could recall his account of what had happened.

This logic is flawed, not because it is not the mesosphere (it doesn't matter), rather, because it attempts to remove the input of God as author of the text (however subtle the attempt may be). When man superimposes his understanding of science above the knowledge of God (all Scripture is inspired by the Holy Spirit, and therein, is not dependent upon man's scientific knowledge or understanding), he then jumps to the conclusion that it must be the mesosphere or third heaven. Again, the failure in this assumption is that one discounts the knowledge of God. By doing so a veiled deception is created and designed to replace the infallibility of the bible with the fallibility of man.

For many years the world was considered to be flat, but if we look into the book of Isaiah we find science a long way behind the knowledge of Scripture. ***Isaiah 40:22 "He sits enthroned above the circle of the earth, and its people are like grasshoppers."*** Well there you go, when last I looked a circle is round. The book of Isaiah was written long before circumnavigation of the planet. Long before horizon and the curvature of the earth are understood, God understood everything. What had taken place or just where Paul was taken in his account is not what is important. What is important is the contrast between truth and deception, between the man of God and those who clearly are not. While walking closely with Jesus we can expect to be given the vision and the understanding of our Lord. Not as a special occurrence, but as a matter of flow within the stream. I mention this mesosphere presentation because in today's world Christians are looked upon as people who do not accept science, specifically the science of global warming, and it is we (mankind) who must save the planet. Another way of expression is, *"We must save our self."* If we could save the planet and ourselves we would have no need for Jesus. *News flash:* God will make everything new, which actually means that all things will pass away. *News flash:* God is always is control. *News flash:* We cannot make one hair upon our head turn gray. What makes us think we can change the order of creation? Of course when mankind adopts an attitude that he is a god, his pride and need to have it continually fed is kept blind to the truth. When man continually attempts to remove God and place himself into the pinnacle of existence, deception is not far from capturing the so-called gods or super apostles, as well as those who would blindly follow. In worldly matters we are continually going against the currents, but in the water of life we are invited to go with the flow. By being in accord with what God requires of us we are freed from the daily cares of struggling against the dictates of opposing forces, and no longer forced to go along with the flow of unwanted and overpowering waves.

With Christ we are taken and caught up into the paradise of truth. Just as Jesus opened up the Scriptures to the disciples along the road to Emmaus, so it is with us. Our close proximity to Jesus will reveal to us the deep parts of the stream. *Joy comes with knowing the truth of Christ. Mystery allows us to understand that there are some things that cannot be fathomed.* While it is possible for us to understand many things concerning God, we don't have the capacity to plumb the complete depths of sacrifice, the total joy of paradise or the mystery of God's love for us. Paul is unsure of just how he arrived into the third heaven (in the body or not) but he knows paradise when he sees it. Paul is caught up like a moon shot eagerly embracing the freedom of flight and like the stone released from David's sling he is sure of his destination. What is revealed in the journey beyond the confines of this earthly tent heeds not natural laws, and opens an awareness of the infinite by imprinting truth upon the heart. Truth revealed cannot be ignored denied or misunderstood, for it is the intent of God for man to understand. Here we may find a deeper realization of the command, **"Let there be light."** As the heavens are captured and revealed through starlit windows allowing sight, so it is the light of understanding is glimpsed and held fast by the one whose flow of existence is in tune with humility. Surely one moment of clarity concerning the majesty of creation must cancel out all thoughts of self importance in the hearts of those blessed to see. Here then is the point of Paul as he repudiates the super apostles. Unlike the sponge that absorbs and fills itself with a surrounding liquid, humility removes what is unwanted and reinforces a true sense of importance. Humility reduces the man to the level of fallibility (all of us share) and reinforces the infallibility of God. If we look at Paul in another situation we see that he is completely opposite in his description of himself. His sense of humility allows him to place upon his head the mantle of **"worst sinner."** Paul is always attempting to focus us on the one who is worthy of accolades and applause. He is telling us that total freedom of flight exists within the faith that allows entrance (into paradise) and once there we will experience a baptism in the stream of God's infinite reality. This view of paradise is one that erases all doubt and all obstacles that hinder our faith, and can only be granted to us as one who is seeking and thirsting for God. In this instance we are the dry bones of the prophet Ezekiel's vision, seeking to be filled with the good things God has to offer. There is a great difference between pride puffing us up and God filling us with his very own character traits. A raindrop falls into a stream and instantly becomes one with the body of water. Like the raindrop it is we whose direction in life has been changed by the Spirit of God, convicting us of our sins and convincing us of the God who loves us. Being born again brings to us windows of clarity, removes the notion of pride, and replaces it with self worth established in the sacrifice of Christ. Paul is vociferous in his denouncements of those whose motives within the church are clearly seen by him as false. Paul has tasted the water of life and will not allow others to portray its purity in a diluted and false state. *John 7:3 "Whoever believes in me, as the Scripture has said, streams of living water will flow from within him."*

The Boast

~~~

"I make five hundred dollars a week!"
Said the man to the clerk in the convenience store.
"My friend," said a voice, "I made that today,
And tomorrow I'll make more."
"I build houses for a living and I sell them by the score."
Said a man to the men inside the store.

"My father owns a chain of these stores!"
Said the clerk to the men with a roar.
"My Father is King of the Universe."
Said a voice in the line at the rear of the store.
"If it's riches we must talk about then mine are stored with him.
He keeps a running tally of the things we do as men.
He delights in those who understand
True value on this earth comes from the mouth of God
Where wisdom saw her birth."

~~~

Proverbs 27: 1-2 Do not boast about tomorrow for you do not know what a day may bring forth. Let another praise you and not your own mouth someone else and not your own lips.

Passing

The Creator of all in nature's expanse
Set forth in motion all things to pass.
All creatures of breath lowly and high
Heavenly bodies:
Earth moon sky
Mountains and valleys of green forest lawn
Must submit to the passing as must the dawn
Night's gentle calling to light, "Withdraw."
Then there is time it too is passing
Movement of moments quickly unwind
Step to the beat of a chorus in line
Captured by the camera's flash
Never again the present to be
Movement of moments passing are we.
Nothing breaks the rhythm of time
Not pausing nor roadblocks or signaling signs
Not laughter sorrow anger or fear
Can silence the drumbeat steady and clear.
Passing as soldiers marching in rows
Sure as a heartbeat silenced and cold
Movement of moments so quickly grow old
But from within this home flesh and bone
Like thunder and lightning present in storms
Come reports of good news given to say:
"God's word is not passing.
God's word will stay.
Sure promise of life to the
Passing away."

1 John 5:13 I am writing this to you so that you may know that you have eternal life—you that believe in the Son of God.

JUMP

All things in life require proof. It's the understanding that without such proof there may be a consequence for not seeking. When it comes to the question of God there is among many the overwhelming desire to see proof in the form of a miracle. In fact there were those who demanded of Jesus a sign that would prove he is the Messiah. Jesus said to them, **"It is an evil generation that seeks a sign."** *However, to us Jesus says,* **"Ask seek and knock,"** *and God will give to us the desire of our heart. When mankind demands proof of reality the absence thereof brings about a lessening of his desire for it. The converse is also true: When mankind asks of God to convict and convince us of the existence of truth, we are then given an abundance of reality through the Holy Spirit's entry into our lives. The first demand for proof regarding the authenticity of Jesus came from the devil in the desert. The devil seeks a sign by covertly demanding,* **"If you are the Son of God,"** *he said,* **"throw yourself down from here."**

Is it a wonder why Jesus labels this kind of thought an evil generation? Within the setting of forty-days in the wilderness we find our Lord deprived and suffering not only from a lack of physical nourishment but also from exposure to the elements of the unforgiving desert. Upon emerging from the self-imposed exile he embarked upon his mission to proclaim the good news to mankind*: Isaiah 61: 1-3 "The Spirit of the Lord God is upon me, because the Lord has anointed me to bring glad tidings to the lowly, to heal the brokenhearted, to proclaim liberty to the captives and release the prisoners, to announce a year of favor from the Lord and a day of vindication by our God, to comfort all who mourn; to place on* *those who mourn in Zion a diadem instead of ashes, to give them oil of gladness in place of mourning, a glorious mantle instead of a listless spirit. They will be called oaks of justice, planted by the Lord to show his glory." NAB* Before Jesus could embark on his mission of good news and salvation he had to deal with the devil in the desert. The devil was testing him (just as he tests all of us). We too are put to the test and many times we fail because we do not act as if we are the sons and daughters of God. The devil wants Jesus to jump off a cliff, and he quotes scripture as reinforcement against the truth that all of us know: If we jump off a cliff we will have a quick meeting with the ground below! Don't worry, is the tacit implication in the invitation to jump, you know as well as I that, *"His angels will uphold you."* This demand from the devil is really an attempt to have Jesus bow to his wishes, and in turn Jesus will have exhibited a modicum amount of pride, a small crack, just enough to allow the devil's foot to enter into the mind of Christ; the pride that is so evident in the devil's makeup. In fact all of the temptations in the desert were designed by the devil to have Jesus abdicate his divinity (if Jesus had proven to the devil the truth concerning himself), or if Jesus had accepted the offerings packaged as, *"all the kingdoms of the world."*

One thing is clear, the devil and all of those religious and secular rulers were poised to kill anyone who would bring to the people the keys to the Kingdom of God. The keys of the kingdom were forged in the truth Jesus was about to proclaim, and from the moment he performed his first miracle evil began to plot against him. We know the devil was not satisfied with his failure to tempt and so he did not remove himself from the ultimate mission of evil, which is to destroy what God has created. The attempt by the devil upon our Lord's life was not the first. As long as there are men who are willing surrogates of evil there will always be attempts to destroy innocence. The first attempt to kill Jesus was made by Herod and later on during his ministry other attempts were made; they failed because it was not time for our Lord to die. Even when Jesus was hanging on the cross there were those who attempted to deter him from his purpose of salvation for mankind; again he heard the words, *"If you are the Son of God, come down from that cross."* Jump! Jump! Jump! There's no doubt there was present the flavor of mocking in those words, but the reminder to Jesus was still a temptation in the midst of suffering.

Jesus knew he could come down from the cross, but he would not, for the love that had taken him to the agony he was experiencing could not be denied. Everyone knew of the miracles Jesus performed and of his healing of those who were held tightly by the grip of the devil; for these it must have been very perplexing to have witnessed the performance of such feats, (not from the demands of man for a sign), but out of love for humanity evidenced by, *"God with us"* made manifest in the person of Christ. It must have been perplexing for those who saw the openly given good deeds and miracles that Jesus had done and still the religious refused to recognize what the common man had clearly witnessed.

The insecurity of those in power to rule over others was most evident in the time of Christ. Power over others is perhaps the most tempting of all to the human condition, made manifest in greater intensity by the perception of one's wealth that misleads one into thinking he can do all things a mortal man may conceive. There is not much difference today, save for a few exceptions; we no longer feed people to lions. But the craving for political power and accolades in the arena of worldly recognition are always with us when humility is trampled into the dust in favor of the offerings of the world. Many people know the truth of God but their voices are denied a podium. The individual cannot broadcast the good news from his front porch to the ears of the world, and if he should trust in others to do so for him, what he finds is disappointment as the message spoken by others appears to be tainted, by the desire to acquire as opposed to the message of the truth that sets men free.

Therein the disadvantage of voice leaves truth weakened, not much different from those who attempted to kill Jesus in an effort to suppress truth. Even in the secular world of politics truth is the enemy to those who would lord over others. The Christian today is constantly attacked for his beliefs and even the symbolism of such faith is continually finding irritation to those whose avowed belief is said to be in nothing. The main reason Christians suffer such attacks is rooted in the primary irritant to those who live in darkness: it is truth! Jesus had said, *"Foxes have holes and birds have nests but the Son of Man has no place to rest his head."* By this Jesus is referring to himself as Truth. He had referred to himself as the, *"Way the Truth and the Life,"* As such Christianity finds no rest from the onslaught of the evil intent of the world. What was true in the time of Christ is true today. Those who persecuted Christ knew that he had to be a man sent by God, *"because no one could do the things you are doing, without God."* Moreover it was good works miracles and truth that was ultimately shunned and mocked along with Jesus, simply because evil does not want to alleviate suffering on any level of existence. Without any reservations both then and now the world has placed itself upon a wartime setting against God. The world knows of the existence of God but it attempts to keep this knowledge secret through the corrupting influence of the devil. He (the devil) has managed to pull tightly the blindfolds over the eyes of the willing.

Persecution of other religious faiths in the manner forced upon the Christian is not evident, simply because absent within these others are the keys to the kingdom of God; the truth of Christ's sacrifice laid bare for all the world to accept or reject.

Remedy

❦

This worldly remedy and philosophy
Has been handed down through the ages:
"No man no problem no threat to ruling reign
When the breath of man has left our status remains."

They thought it was the end of love.
Something the rulers knew very little of.
"All will remain blind," and, "We shall be untouched."

The vision of the cross would soon confuse their lives.
In the span of three short days the world would be surprised.
"He is risen!" came the cry.
And still proof is demanded to satisfy their eyes.

Are men demanding proof today?
Sure they are, nothing's changed.
Some have put the question to bed,
"There is no God and Christ is dead!"
This then is the depth to which being lost takes a man.

Truth is self evident it stands alone.
Demanding proof is like saying, "Make bread from stone."
No matter, the stones have a better chance of praising God
Than those whose stone hearts mark the entrance to graveyards!

His eyes closed shut earth rumbled forth its ire
Tombs gave up their dead and the sky became a pyre.
Earthquakes parted ground and tremors rushed the source
And laid awaiting movement at the foot of the cross.
Heads lifted up into the sky angry clouds and feathered cries.
The dripping of his blood had now its turn to speak:
"It is finished.
Will you now believe?"

❦

***Matthew 27:24** When the centurion and those with him who were guarding Jesus saw the earthquake and all that had happened, they were terrified, and exclaimed, "Surely he was the Son of God."*

Proof

~~~

When demand for proof is made
The absence thereof lessens its desire.
A coin once spent has seen its hour
Where once it called us, "home," it seeks another to empower.
When we ask to be convicted of the crime of disbelief
All the proof is given for us to find God's peace.
Transcending all within to the heavens song is sent
Known only to the captive whose chains are torn and spent!
Absent is the coinage whose song is, "lend and gone"
Forever is the faith spoken to the heart.
Removing all the cobwebs obscuring light of truth
No longer left to wander upon highways hurt and pain
Abundance then is given from the Lord and Great I AM.

~~~

***Luke 4:9** "If you are the Son of God," he said, "throw yourself down from here"*

We must teach each succeeding generation the content of scripture in order to establish in them the truth necessary to live this life with the great hope of Christ. The word of God once embedded into a person forms the foundational strength to withstand the worldly sound bites seeking to distract and ensnare. Yes, to those whose existence is perceived to be finite we are nuisance troublemakers, simply because truth on the loose will set people free from the unending lies present in the world. By our making sure the truth of God is presented to our children we ensure for them the great hope of eternal life. The world wants so desperately to deny truth, simply because evil's intent has always been to destroy. *Let's always keep this truth in mind: What we permit defines us, what we ignore blinds us, truth gives us wings and wrong denies the King.*

One last thought on this subject of proof. Is it a wonder why little children gravitate to emulating superhero characters? They do so because they see clearly through the eyes of innocence. They understand the bad guy and the good guy and because they have not as yet been corrupted by the world they seek to right injustice, if only in their hearts and minds. Remember, Jesus said of the little children, ***"Suffer not the little children to come unto me, for to such as these belongs the kingdom of God."*** Jesus declared little children to be innocent. He also said of those who would harm these little ones this warning: ***"Things that cause people to sin are bound to come, but woe to him through whom they come. It would better for him to have a millstone tied around his neck and tossed into the depths of the sea, than for him to cause one of these little ones to fall. So watch yourselves."*** Jesus is speaking to the world, saying, *"Woe to you who would cloud the vision of the innocent and make them compromise the knowledge of right and wrong." Again, "Woe to the world that will not recognize the excellence of truth and the righteous manner in which to live, and deny to others the ability to do so!"*

JUDGMENT ON THE INSTALLMENT PLAN

I am struck by the words of the apostle John, especially the emphasis upon a new heaven and new earth. I am not an astronomer and have very little understanding of what is taking place within our solar system, and to a greater extent the galaxy. However, there is one thing that shouts out to me like an avalanche of provocative thought. All of the planets in our system appear to be devoid of life. On none of our immediate planets can we find even a hint of life. This leads me to ask myself why that should be? Certainly everything in nature has purpose. I suppose we can say the purpose of the heavenly bodies is to show to us the greatness of God's artistic talents. Perhaps there is unknown and yet to be discovered contributory aspects within the overall design of our system we do not understand? The operational details of a clock are kept hidden. The clockmaker understands its intricate movements, but most people are only interested with its accuracy and appearance. Certainly such intricacies within the solar system are present with purpose other than just the artistic handiwork of God. I suspect there is something much more, in the form of ominous warning presented in the absence of life apart from the planet earth. Can it be at one time these planets actually supported life, and did not appear as they do today? Could it be they were not only conducive to life but because of the presence of God and his providence they flourished with an abundance of life? What I am really hinting at is the probability that such planets were once inhabited, and with the decline of the resident populations morality they eventually faced judgment, leaving only the tombstone of former existence. God is holy and what he creates must eventually reflect his character. When God's creation ceases to reflect his

goodness the decline of life is rapid. Rapid insomuch as compared to what was intended for creation-to last forever. Again, when godliness ceases the decline of creation is rapid.

Vanished

Revelation 21:1-2 Then I saw a new heaven and a new earth. The first heaven and the first earth disappeared, and the sea vanished. If these planets were once conducive to life and in fact permitted life to flourish, what then could have happened? Perhaps the failure to live in accord with the desire of the Creator had found them in the same predicament that faces the earth in this the last and final age? They may have been judged to the point all life had been destroyed pretty much in the same way the city of Sodom met its fate. Except that the planets still stand as a warning to all who would dare to rebel against God. We know through biblical pronouncements that everything will disappear and be made new; everything will be destroyed and a new beginning for creation will come into being. "Everything," is an all-inclusive statement, which means the planets and the heavens as well. This is an awesome thought in both power and liberating recognition. Yes, just the idea of existence that no longer contains injustice and corruption is sufficient for us to shout for joy! Of course there may be other reasons for the absence of life apart from the hostile environments within such planets. Perhaps we on the planet earth have been given a replenishment source for necessary minerals as our own natural resources are depleted? Of course this would necessitate the ability of our sciences to travel not only from planet to planet but to also transport such resources in meaningful quantities to offset both need and cost. Actually I do believe that all things in nature replenish and/or have been incorporated to last until the end of the age. I certainly do not believe in the untimely exhaustion of so-called fossil fuels. Even more unbelievable is all such crude oil is believed a derivative from the decomposition of beasts formerly inhabiting the planet. Where did that idea come from? It is totally contrary to what we know of decomposition of flesh, *"dust to dust."*

What's coming?

Now, having taken a look at the possibilities of the planets within our solar system at one time being inhabited, and the obvious absence of such life today, the purpose of such planets remains unclear unless the former inhabitants faced an apocalyptic event. A progression of judgment is certainly not unimaginable. It shouts to the inhabitants of creation, "Repent or else find uninhabitable the garden given to you." Just as Sodom was an example to the people of the earth in the display of God's awesome power, so too it is plausible that the solar system, indeed all of creation, is given notice as well. It may be that we on earth are the last of the system's inhabitants to recognize or deny the coming inescapable wrath of God. Well at least some of us recognize the end is coming to sin's influence. An end is coming to injustice, to the mocking of God and all that is holy through God's inescapable judgment. That there is life apart from the earth is a certainty, for we have been given the testimony from biblical pronouncements as well as eyewitness accounts of alien sightings throughout mankind's history. However, it is not evident in the solar system we occupy, except for the reported visitations of either angelic-spiritual or corporeal beings. For the believer there is no doubt of the existence of angelic beings of either purely spiritual existence (beings of thought) and/or of corporeal design. We believe heaven occupies a place within the physical universe, simply because it is told to us, "the first heaven" will pass away or vanish. We understand Jesus was taken up to heaven in bodily form and his intended purpose in part, upon arrival there was to prepare a place for those who will follow. In this representation of Christ as the new Adam being taken back to his Father's house or place of residence, we find much unanswered as to just where heaven is and what exactly shall we become? But it is understood that once we too are resurrected we shall become like him.

The sun

Another mystery to me is the Sun. Like a great torch giving light and warmth to mankind we are told it is a continuously burning, erupting, and immeasurably powerful mass of combustible matter, for want of a better understanding, a ball of fire. I understand that in order for combustion to take place upon the earth there must be the ingredient called oxygen. Somehow this ingredient appears to be in short supply within the system and yet the sun continues to burn? The usage of the term, *"solar system"* simply means, *"Energy derived by the sun."* Our solar system remains operational due to the power derived by the sun. More to the point we remain in existence because God has so ordained us to live. The sun is classified as a star and just as all other things in creation there is limitation to its existence. Truly it takes great calculation to design such longevity. This appears to me to be a miracle of combustion unless there is a pocket of oxygen continually feeding the needs of the sun, not to mention what appears to be an inexhaustible supply of fuel. I don't know how a definitive explanation for such a magnificent display can be determined by science, simply because of the great distance between the sun and the earth. Ninety-three million miles away is no hop skip and jump. But in comparison to the overall majesty of the heavens eternal and infinite perception, it is just around the corner. Now having danced all around the universe with questions and its possibilities as to why such majesty contained in the presence of the planets is absent life today, I can only imagine the planets awaiting a new creation simply because if there was not a problem with their present existence why then would God make all things new? There must have been a falling away from their original purpose, thus leaving them devoid of life. I am reminded of the words of the apostle John at the end of his gospel, wherein he says to us that he supposes if all of the things Jesus did were to be written down into books the earth could not contain them. This is a gigantic statement of supposition immediately taking us into the realm of infinity. The concept of infinity is not shunned or placed into the catalog of disbelief, simply because it appears to us logical to assume such infinite continuance of space. We recognize the opposite of infinite to be finite and this is clearly represented within our structured unshakable truth existing in nature. For everything there is an opposite, life death, up and down truth and the lie, and so forth. All things in nature have a biotic and antibiotic cycle of existence. That is to say there is a building up and tearing down process. This applies to everything, most prominent is our lives. As such we must recognize the solar system as a part of nature and subject to the same forces of life and death clearly recognizable upon the earth.

Why would God want to create anew that which was never alive? I suppose there is an exhaustible lifespan for planetary existence as well as living things. However, be that as it may, the suspected purpose is to completely erase and renew all things in creation that had been touched and consequently infected by sin. Even the thought of sin will have been removed from creation. Therein we recognize the **"great void"** in the parable of the **"Rich Man and Lazarus."** It is this void that separates such new creation from that which was former. The place called hell will be the singular repository of such remembrance of sin. It is staggering to contemplate the progression of sin in the concept of encompassing contamination of the entire order of creation. What is even more mind boggling is the ability of God to not only make new all of his original design but to remove any trace of the cause for its decline.

We are not alone

I have come to the realization that we as a life form, created in the image and likeness of God (having his good characteristics), are not alone in the cosmos. Jesus said, **"My Father is always working and I must do the same."** It seems to me the work of creation is one aspect of God's work that is continually ongoing. It is only logical that other life forms would also reflect such good qualities endowed by the Creator of all things. And it is also logical that such others may very well have been corrupted by the infection of rebellious sin. Thus as such infection reaches epidemic proportions from planet to planet radical surgery is necessary for its removal. It is a snowball effect pronouncing judgment on both the small scale of individualism and the grand scale of engulfing an entire planet. As far as our solar system is concerned it may seem to be a very large place to traverse, but when traveling at the speed of thought it is a small junket. Moreover, I don't suppose the angelic host is reliant upon any vehicle for transportation. It may be that others outside of the supernatural realm have discovered how to travel great distances in the void of space, but that is still open to conjecture. Throughout all of this supposition remains truth contained in the knowledge that nothing lasts forever. Nothing can survive except for what God so decides will not pass away. This supposition of other life forms, particularly within the form of bodily creation, leaves open the question as to whether such outer worldly creation, if corrupted by sin, has such sin been paid in full by the sacrifice of Christ? We do know that for pure spiritual beings there is no salvation for they cannot understand the joy accompanying it. Basically there is no excuse for those within the supernatural realm. They have had complete understanding of the impact for rebelling against God and in this understanding they clearly made the choice to rebel, fully understanding a day of judgment for them will come to be. It is conceivable that God would create other humans apart from the planet earth and that they in turn would share in the sacrifice of Jesus.

Angels of light and a succession of fright

I remember a time as a sailor in the U.S. Navy, at sea gazing up into the sky, I saw a movement of lights (at least one half dozen) as if stars and they appeared as distant. As if in formation the lights moved in directions and speed that nothing on this earth could possibly accomplish. Truly the meaning of UFO was brought home to reality. Later on I came to the conclusion that such lights were angelic in nature. The bible speaks of angels of light and in this case I do believe it speaks to me in the literal sense. It is perhaps good for us to examine our surroundings with an open mind, recognizing we do not know everything. I don't say we should embrace our conclusions as if they are embedded in the word of God, but excursions into the possibility of such flights of fancy opens for us an avenue of excitement in the same way a child's imagination is ever exploring. One other thought that speaks to me from the subject verse is this: John tells us the first heaven and the first earth vanished, and almost as an afterthought he includes, *"and the sea vanished."* What is strikingly truthful in this comment is that we would expect the seas to disappear through evaporation should an entire planet be engulfed in flames. I don't know of any water being found on the planets in our system. Although there are signs that oceans may have existed at some point in the past. Throughout the Book of Revelation there is a steady flow of judgment that eventually culminates with the final victory of God. We see the seals that are opened and with each there is announced the impending catastrophic events that will be visited upon the earth. And then as if a drum-roll demanding silence, a seventh seal is broken and the wrath of God is thrown down to the earth in the form of earthquakes and fire. We then see another announcement given by trumpets, and each succeeding one bringing additional horror upon the earth's inhabitants. Again the culmination of these announcements is heralded in the seventh trumpet's call, proclaiming, ***"The power to rule over the world belongs now to our Lord and Messiah."*** It is now becoming obvious to us that judgment is pronounced in stages not the least of which is the plagues and the bowls of God's anger that follows the seals and trumpets. Having viewed this pattern of specific increasing horrors we can then assume such increments may very well have been exercised throughout creation's vast array of planets, where the inhabitants had increasingly fallen into greater sins until the patience and outrage of God had been exhausted and provoked. Such incremental judgment is meant to warn and alert people to change from their ways. We are told by John, even after all of the horrors inflicted upon the earth and its inhabitants mankind refused to turn away from their evil ways. ***Revelation 9:20-21 "The rest of mankind who had not been killed by these plagues, did not turn away from what they themselves had made. They did not stop worshiping demons, nor idols of gold, silver, bronze, stone, and wood, which cannot see, hear, or walk. Nor did they repent of their murders, their magic, their sexual immorality or their stealing."*** So it may also be that the planets stand as memorials to those who failed to turn away from their evil ways.

Second chances

God has always given warning of impending doom orchestrated by his own hand. To the people of Israel they were continually warned of their failure to heed the way of the Lord through the prophets, and even in the city of Sodom the inhabitants were given warning against attempting to corrupt the holy angels who had visited Lot. They (the inhabitants of Sodom) were struck blind when they attempted to take hold of the visitors. This should have been sufficient warning for those within the city to recognize something big was about to take place. Lot had even gone so far through appeasement as to offer to the people his own daughters in place of the holy visitors. This appeasement gesture alerts us to perhaps the willingness of his daughters to engage in such behavior. Certainly it would go against the grain of a father's natural instinct, which is to protect his family, and so we can safely conclude they had already found the lifestyle in Sodom to be to their liking. We recognize that Lot's wife failed to leave the lifestyle behind her by disobeying the warning to not look back upon the city as they departed. Everywhere in nature we see the provision of God offering to man a second chance. The one that shines for me is the understanding of human nature God has built into his creation. He understood the foolishness of youth and he built into our nature safeguards. The simplest form of second chance is baby teeth. Our baby teeth take the brunt of excess as well as hit and miss dental care. I suppose God figured that by the time the permanent teeth arrived the child would understand the need for brushing. ***Proverbs 22:6 Teach a child how he should live, and he will remember it all of his life.*** In this incorporation allowing for another set of teeth God may be saying to us, "*I will provide for all of your needs if you will but trust in me. If you will heed the warning of such loss attributed to the excess of uninformed youth all other ancillary support will not be necessary, for I have designed into my creation the longevity necessary for man to fulfill his purpose on an individual basis.*"

Additional purpose

Acts 2:19-21 "I will perform miracles in the sky above and wonders on the earth below. There will be blood, fire, and thick smoke; the sun will be darkened, and the moon will turn red as blood, before the great and glorious Day of the Lord comes. And then whoever calls out to the Lord for help will be saved." Within this declaration by the Apostle Peter we see additional purpose for the heavenly lights. It is an indirect form of communication from God to man meant for us to heed their meanings. For those who heed the signs their opportunity for salvation is made manifest. Additionally we have found other usages of the heavenly fixtures, for our good. Perhaps the greatest is the appearance of the star that led the wise men to the house where Jesus lived.

Matthew 2:7-11 So Herod called the visitors from the East to a secret meeting and found out from them the exact time the star had appeared. Then he sent them to Bethlehem with these

instructions: "Go and make a careful search for the child; and when you find him, let me know, so that I too may go and worship him." And so they left, and on their way they saw the same star they had seen in the East. When they saw it, how happy they were, what joy was theirs! It went ahead of them until it stopped over the place where the child was. They went into the house, and when they saw the child with his mother Mary, they knelt down and worshipped him. GNB Sometimes when we are traveling along a scriptural route we need to make a detour from the original intent of a thought in order to not leave open-ended fragments along the road. The question that naturally must follow the aforementioned wise men as they pursue the Christ child is this: Where did they ultimately find Jesus and when did this finding take place? What we find is Herod telling the wise men to look for the child *"and when you find him, let me know, so that I too may go and worship him."* The wise men don't return to Herod after they find Jesus and Herod realizes he was tricked. *Matthew 2:16-18 When Herod realized that the visitors from the East had tricked him, he was furious. He gave orders to kill all of the boys in Bethlehem and its neighborhood who were two years old-this was done in accordance with what he had learned from the visitors about the time the star had appeared.* Remember Herod had found out the exact time the star had appeared. Herod decides to kill every male child two years old or younger and so one can safely say the first time the visitors saw the star was two years prior to their inquiry of Herod. Herod was seeking to know when the Christ child was born, they already knew from scripture the place of the foretold birth. Why the holy family was still in Bethlehem at the time of the inquiry of Herod is open for conjecture, but it safe to say that traveling with an infant child was probably not the best of decisions to make. It is probably safe to say the holy family remained in Bethlehem for some time after the birth of Jesus. The wise men had seen the star for the first time while they were at home in the East in the place called Babylon. These wise men (astronomers) knew of this foretelling because they had the Hebrew scriptures from the time of the Babylonian captivity. These wise men (we are told) were actually magicians (Magi is a corruption of the word magician) and when they spotted the star it was because they had been looking for the sign in the heavens. Was it really a star? I don't know but it is safe to say it was certainly a heavenly celestial light that went ahead of the wise men to show the way. Was it an angel of light? In any event they were led to the Christ child the second time the star appeared. Led to *"the house"* where the holy family stayed. It was not the same place where the shepherds had gone to see Jesus. As such the wise men were probably not there at the time of the actual birth. I'm sure they did not buy tickets on the local airline and fly over to Bethlehem. It was more like arranging for a long trip, gathering provisions and necessary transportation (probably camels) and then heading off in the westerly direction. Upon arrival they meet with Herod and ask for directions as to where the one foretold was to be born. Of course tradition has painted a condensed picture of the birth of Jesus, depicting the wise men as present at the time of our Lord's birth, but it really is of no consequence except to understand that God has the ability to get his message across to those who are seeking to know.

Heralding

Warnings and heralding of importance are not whispers in the dark. God does not want anyone to miss the events that are announced simply because they are messages from God and are important! So we find a heralding through prophetic announcement materializing in the heavens, as either good news (the birth and the baptism of Jesus) or else we find warnings of impending judgment. In all aspects of prophetic fulfillment or warnings of impending judgment it is clear to us that God has not hidden his intention for mankind. There are no favorites in the plan of God for the salvation of humanity. It is written, **"Whoever calls out to the Lord for help will be saved."** It is written elsewhere, **Hebrews 3:15 "If you hear God's voice today, do not be stubborn as your ancestors were when they rebelled against God."** So many voices and signs and still the world is deaf and blind. What will it take to wake mankind up from his stupor? Has the wall of pride been built so high that even the heavenly majestic handiwork of God is cast off as just so much accidental occurrence? The scriptures tell us, **Hebrews 2:7-8 You made him for a little while lower than the angels; you crowned him with glory and honor, and made him ruler over all things."** This scripture quote is referring to mankind and it is also pointing out to us how powerless we have become. Man cannot even take control of himself let alone rule over all things. Let us heed the voices and signs of creation in order to live in freedom and gain eternal life. Amen.

Warning

〰️

I have to admit I don't hold all of the pieces to the puzzle.
Some things are kept hidden from my sight.
The sun the moon and spheres all appear so bright.
But why is there no life?
Could it be a long time back footprints dotted Mars?
Did Saturn spin a different way and roads were built for cars?
Could Jupiter be found with excavation lines?
Measured and surprised, did ships speed across its sky?
All within creation will find upward and then down
Some will find eternity and others wear a frown.
Disconnection from the one who made us all
Finds incremental judgment knocking on the door.
I see it plain and clear within solar system's light
The planets hang as globes
But absent is the laughter that comes from joyful life.
A giant jigsaw puzzle moving dot to dot
What was and is and is to come has definition not.
Conjecture is a trying thing like intended sport
It takes us up and down the field and sometimes truth is scored.
The mind of man was made for playful thoughts.
Imagine this or that and see where it leads and ends
A rabbit's hole mysterious filled with twists and bends.
It would be nice to understand why the planets seem to stare.
Stoic as a statue, saying, "There's nothing living here."

〰️

Revelation 11:1-3 I was given a stick that looked like a measuring-rod, and was told, "Go and measure the temple of God and the altar, and count those who are worshiping in the temple. But do not measure the outer courts, because they have been given to the heathen, who will trample on the Holy City for forty-two months. I will send two witnesses dressed in sackcloth, and they will proclaim God's message during those 1,260 days."

Now back to judgment on the installment plan.

Prince of this world

John 14:30-31 I will not speak with you much longer, for the prince of this world is coming. He has no hold on me, but the world must learn that I love the Father and that I do exactly what my Father has commanded me. This particular scripture quotation by our Lord, opens for us a wealth of understanding that otherwise would go unnoticed should we decide to give only cursory attention to the full implication of what is actually being related to the disciples. Let us see just what is contained in this passage and in so doing attempt to recognize the implications for us in this day and time. Jesus is speaking to his disciples in preparation for his departure from this world. He is preparing them for his arrest, crucifixion, death, resurrection and ascension back to his Father's house. He is also alerting them (and us) to the eventual appearance of, ***"the prince of this world."*** The New International Version in the above scripture quote uses terminology of, ***"prince"*** as opposed to both the Good News Bible and the New American Bible, wherein the word used for prince is, ***"ruler"*** to describe the advent of the one who is coming. The usage of the word prince is so much more revealing, because it points to the advent of the Antichrist. He will be embraced by the world because he will declare his own authority.

Jesus said that he would have also been accepted by the world had he done the same, (basically declared himself to be God). Because of the world's corruption it will only recognize that which is corrupt enough to declare himself possessing authority of inherently singular origin. One who is sent to present truth to a world of lies will always become outcast and denied by those whose agenda promotes and adores power and authority, especially when it is utilized in accord with the already established order of corruption. For those who currently rule over the nations the advent of the Antichrist must, out of necessity, insure to such leadership their continued roles of power, even if it is only an illusory belief, (man being deceived is nothing new).

Many evil people have sought to conquer and dominate humanity through brute force, to the point of slaughtering all who would dare to oppose such efforts. Of course it is instilled in mankind to be free from tyranny and the ugly suffocating demands that must accompany the evil of dictatorial domination. As with all of the plans of evil they are never discussed in the light of day, otherwise many would reject and resist such deceitful intention, (some people actually believe in government transparency). As such, the Antichrist will arrive with a wave of peace, as if to lull to sleep all of those who will seek to gain credit through association, and in so doing believe that they will then have reinforced their positions of authority, from the one whose authority is answerable to no one. By Jesus saying, *"He has no hold on me,"* he is really alluding to the fact that his mission as the, *"Son of God"* had not been compromised by sin, neither was it sold or otherwise in any danger of failure because of the love he has to be obedient to the Father. Let us remember, during his trial of temptations in the desert, the devil himself had offered to him all of the kingdoms of the world, if he would only deny his allegiance to God the Father and in turn worship him. Let us also remind ourselves that the devil is a liar, as such, this authority to give to Jesus all of the world's governments (kingdoms) was perhaps an offering that like all things in nature finds itself only temporarily bestowed. Besides, within this temptation of great wealth and power even we know there is always a price to pay. In this case it would be Jesus abdicating his authority of God. This begs the question, did the devil actually know he was tempting God incarnate? The devil does ask Jesus, *"If"* you are the *"Son of God,"* and just as we find the usage of the term, *"this world"* intriguing, we also must contemplate the limits to the devil's understanding of God's plan for the salvation of mankind with his usage of the word, *"If."*

Conquest of the world must be viewed in the context of what God will permit. Certainly, had Jesus succumbed to the devil's advances (any one of them) especially the offering of the world's governments, there would necessarily have to be worldwide war and unimaginable destruction, not the wave of peace that will be attempted by the Antichrist. *Remember, when the first of mankind fell it was done through deception, without the use of force. Later on we see Job the servant of God tormented by the devil absent the subtleties of the pure lie. There is every reason to believe that if the temptations of Jesus had succeeded, next on the agenda would have to be violence. Mankind will not give up its structured elitism without a fight. Not until the Antichrist arrives and announces* *authority of his own will the transformation to global government under the direction of one person will this take place without wars. This will take place simply because when people believe that all authority is vested in the one person, they will bow to such authority thinking that said person can and will ensure their own positions of authority, so long as they fall into line with the leader. It is not until the Antichrist declares himself to be God that conflict breaks out against the Jewish people. The Bible calls this triggering the, "**Abomination of desolation."***

Shifts in power between rulers of nations are an orchestration of God. We see this especially when God wants to punish those who know the truth but refuse to acknowledge it. Such was the case of the ancient Hebrew kings, at times they were overthrown and their people taken into captivity. One example of such captivity was the forty-years of rule under the Philistines. These were judgments by God and in these judgments there was and still is a very pertinent message for all of us today. Simply put, God is and will always be the ultimate authority no matter what may take place upon the earth or throughout the universe.

Now let us look at one very interesting aspect of what Jesus had said to his disciples. Jesus did not say that the *prince or ruler of the world is coming.* No, what he actually said was the, "***prince of this world***" is coming. By saying "***this world***" we can infer there are others. The usage of the word "***prince***" elevates our understanding to one of either a son of a king or the son of a ruler. Jesus as the "***Prince of Peace***" is recognized as the Son of God, the embodiment of, "*God with us*" in both the corporeal as well as the divine. As such, we must look at the "***prince of this world***" as the embodiment of evil, the joining together of both the natural and the supernatural in a completely evil state of being. This follows the same reasoning structure of parental lineage. Satan within the construct of human form; how this is accomplished is more interesting as to why? From the book of Genesis we know that the "***sons of God***" saw that the women of the earth were beautiful and mated with them. Again how a purely spiritual being accomplished such I cannot fathom (having offspring) but it is safe to say it is demonic possession. However, the assumption is that demonic possession does not have to be purely spiritual. There are devils in bodily form upon the earth and possibly not of this world? Remember, "***the prince of this world***" infers there are other inhabited worlds. So it may be the ultimate demonic appearance may be upon the horizon, and that may not be too far away, given the rapidity of the downward spiral that humanity, with almost total abandonment of common sense, has joined the outcry against the mention of God and/or Jesus. This movement toward prohibitions against the mention of God in the workplace, in the public schools and in the very hearts and minds of man, calls to our attention just how threatened the worldly powers really are. Of course this brings us to the question as to why other religions are not shunned in the same manner? The only reason possible is that contained in the teachings of Christ is the ability to set free all held in captivity. Truth is indeed the greatest and only weapon that needs no defense! It also tells us that the world recognizes there is only one truth that threatens their deceptions. As such all of the other religions, while there may be some truth contained therein, it is not the pure unadulterated truth of Christ. As with all deception the *"prince of this world"* is a counterfeit that will disguise his self as the true, *"Prince of Peace."* The Evil One, (Satan) whose name means the one who opposes man, could not find fault with Jesus and could not accuse him of misrepresentation of God's truth, as such, the only possible conclusion is a war against God and his people. This war has been ongoing since the rebellion of Satan and his followers, and from the inception of man's first sin. The culmination of the final conflict between good and evil will end in the obliteration of not only all those who act in a manner against God but also against truth. God's truth is universal it applies everywhere the hand of creation has touched.

Overflowing Cup

Enough is enough even in God's tolerance and patience
We've heard of his righteous destruction in the awesome flood
His patience pushed in the places of human denigration
And the world will see again the fall of evil's friends
When the Antichrist in bold and determined sin
Walks into the light and declares, "All must worship him."
O what a sight to see, when Israel steps back in time.
When she sees herself carried off to other lands within her mind.
The sin of idolatry once again says, "Take my hand!"
Demanding of her worship where God alone can stand.
She will say no! And the world will call for her end
Led by the Antichrist and all that call him friend.
The cup of indignation will then find its rim
Filled to overflowing and calling out to Him,
"O God, of righteousness rain down upon their heads
The flames of indignation that have built since time began.
Upon the heads of those who shunned and cursed your name
Send the flames of many voices and to them bring only shame!
Upon those who hate the truth and hide themselves in caves
Let them see your righteousness and unbridled strength
Let all of them but most of all, the Evil One feel pain
That built up through generations that tortured all of man.
Hallelujah!"

Matthew 24:15-16 "When you see the desolating abomination spoken of through Daniel the prophet standing in the holy place (let the reader understand) then those in Judea must flee to the mountains, a person on a rooftop must not go down to get things out of his house, a person in a field must not return to get his cloak. NAB

Jesus says, **"The world must learn that I love the Father"** and in this declaration we can see the intent of Jesus for us to learn and understand. We must follow the example of Christ and love the Father through our determination to do what is pleasing to him. This lesson of learning is perhaps paramount for us to comprehend. Jesus says, ***"You must love God with all of your mind, heart soul and strength,"*** this is the proof that we must have living in us. We must "learn" through the sacrifice he has made, and in turn must recognize just how much love had to be present in order for him to embrace the cross. Unless we are in love with everything he stands for, there is the possibility there may be something out in the world that can vie for our affection. So long as we remain in love with God we can be assured not to fail in our mission in this life. Yes, just as Jesus had his mission to accomplish, we also have been commissioned to obey and convey the message of truth that cost so much for us to be set free. All wars have cost and in the end even the victors find a need to lament those who have been lost. None of us want to find that we could have been influential in the life of someone had we only taken the time to do so. Had we taken the time to point the way to Christ, (the one who made our life complete and fulfilled in the knowledge of God's love) perhaps that person may have come to the realization of truth sooner?

Throughout the history of mankind we find direct intervention by the hand of God into the affairs of man when the situations reach outcry proportions. These can represent to us incremental judgments into the affairs of man. Ultimately the total destruction of the planet and the totality of creation will be made new. This is a previously determined fact pronounced by the word of God to man. In the same way the Lord said to himself that he would not hide from Abraham what he was about to do concerning Sodom and Gomorrah, so it is with the world. God does not hide his intentions to destroy evil and make new all things in creation. He has sent to us his Son (a personal intervention) to reveal to us all things that must come to be. It is up to us to listen to truth and heed the warnings of the coming storm.

Signs

~~~~~~~

So many signs and voices and still the world is blind.
It's an amazing thing even in today's light.
We have leaders speaking lies and scandals day and night
And still some people think their voices will not lie?
Woe to you for bowing to gods of gold and cash
Of idols made of stone and statues made of brass
For worship at the altar of murder, magic, lust,
Indeed your bones shall rot and no longer will you strut!

I suppose with the world's deceptive tactics it's easy to hide truth?
A cannon blast of truth will not turn a head
It will not make a path away from wrong or wickedness
If it's cold and dark and mind and heart are dead.
Even when the heavens bleed
And thick smoke fills the air
When the sun and moon are darkened
When fire spreads like flares
When the moon's blood soaked eye has a vacant stare
Still they will not listen to the signs and wonders clear.
"Turn away from wicked ways judgment day has come
In this the end of days there's no place to hide or run!

~~~~~~~

Revelation 13:1-4 "Then I saw a beast coming up out of the sea. It had ten horns and seven heads; each of its horns was a crown, and on each of its heads was a name that was insulting to God. The beast looked like a leopard, with feet like a bears feet and a mouth like a lion's mouth. The dragon gave the beast its own power, his throne, and his vast authority. One of the heads of the beast seemed to have been fatally wounded, but the wound had healed. The whole earth was amazed and followed the beast. Everyone worshipped the dragon because he had given his authority to the beast." GNB

227

Parallel offering with different outcome

I'm reminded of the temptations Jesus was presented during his time in the desert, just prior to the beginning of his ministry. He had refused all of the kingdoms of the world. But here in the book of revelations we see the dragon (Satan) giving the kingdoms of the world to the beast (the Antichrist accepts the offer Jesus would have nothing to do with) and in the giving we see that all of the inhabitants of the earth are *forced* (there's that anticipated violence or threat of violence spoken about earlier) to worship the first beast. ***Revelation 13:12 It forced the earth and all who live on it to worship the first beast.*** Well so much for freedom of choice! This power inflicted upon humanity and the earth itself (I'm trying to understand how the earth itself is forced to worship) has such a hold on people that there is no means of escaping, save for starvation and death. Can it be the power of evil is so gripping that even the earth itself will not yield its harvest unless it falls under the control of such evil? Yes, just as Sodom had proven to be totally debased and separated from any redeeming qualities, so it shall be for the inhabitants of the earth and even the earth itself. The earth itself will have been so defiled by corruption and wickedness that it too must be cleansed by the flames that also consumed the city of Sodom. Forcing the earth into submission, may very well be done by refusing to irrigate parched lands during times of draught, and in so doing the land will not bring forth a harvest. This would be one way of forcing the land to fail to yield its crops, because the Antichrist has taken control of all the water resources necessary for the crops to grow.

Let my people go

Let's take one last look at how God deals with evil within the setting of incremental judgment delivered by the hand of God against the ancient Egyptians. This example is perhaps the best known of all of God's actions on behalf of the captive people of Israel. The king of Egypt is reluctant to let the people go. In fact he is adamantly opposed to letting the people go and worship in the desert. And so he tightens the screws on the people by increasing their work load, thinking them to be lazy and in need of additional activity. But God has other plans for the people and so he begins to tighten the screws on the king through the insistence of Moses. God delivers plagues upon the Egyptians. He turns the Nile River to blood the fish die and the stink is really bad. But then the magicians of the king do the same thing and the king remains as stubborn as ever. Once again Moses goes to the king saying, *"Let my people go."* The king is told that his refusal will bring about a plague of frogs so much so that the Nile will be so full of frogs they will leave it and go into your palaces. Basically Moses tells him the frogs will be everywhere. Again those pesky magicians also make frogs come up out of the land, but the king wants the frogs gone so he calls for Moses. He requests of Moses to *"Pray to the Lord to take away these frogs, and I will let your people go, so that they can offer sacrifices to the Lord."* Moses tells the king he would be glad to pray for him and his officials, *"Just tell me the time when I am to pray for you and you will be rid of the frogs."* The king replies, *"Pray for me tomorrow."* Just as should be expected from liars and those with great power, once the frogs are dead the king again becomes stubborn. He refuses to let the people go. Well next comes the plague of gnats, followed by flies, death of the animals, boils, hail, locusts, darkness and the death of the first born of Egypt. About halfway through the plagues the king and his officials realize the country is ruined and so they decide to let the men of Israel go and worship the Lord.

They ask Moses, "Who will go to worship?" Moses answers, "Everyone, our women and children and cattle, everyone and everything will go to worship the Lord." This is what the king believes is the negotiation stage of his problem. Unfortunately for the king he does something strange. The king said, *"I swear by the Lord that I will never let you take your women and children! It is clear that you are plotting a revolt. No! Only the men may go and worship the Lord if that is what you want!"* The king then throws them out from his presence. He swears by the Lord? Well there seems to be a conversion on the horizon for the king. But in his case the realization that God is who he says he is will not bring about his salvation. For most of us when we come to the realization of the reality of God we change our lives and discontinue our former ways for several reasons, suffice to say truth permits us to walk in the way God wants us to go. However, for the Egyptians their pride and lust for power derived through the suffering of others was their downfall. This incremental execution of judgment clearly shows to us the mercy of God present even when he is administering justice. God is and always will be patient toward those who do wrong. But just as all things in life have limitation, so it also may be said of the patience of God toward evil. This king of Egypt who is steeped in magic and demonic worship had the nerve to swear in the name of the Lord. Basically he took an oath in the name of the Lord and then thumbed his nose at him. Not a very bright king. He had to realize he was refusing the Lord God Almighty, but then maybe not. Today's world leaders don't appear to be any brighter. They too are worshiping the demons of gold silver power and greed. How great then will their fall be?

Revelation 18:1-3 After this I saw another angel coming down out of heaven. He had great authority, and his splendor brightened the whole earth. He cried out in a loud voice: "She has fallen! Great Babylon has fallen! She is now haunted by demons and unclean spirits-all kinds of filthy and hateful birds live in her. For all the nations have drunk her wine-the strong wine of her immoral lust. The kings of the earth practiced sexual immorality with her, and the merchants of the world grew rich from her unrestrained lust." Then I heard another voice from heaven saying, "Come out, my people! Come out from her!" There's a great lesson to be learned in the practice of immorality. It seems it is always in the mix of humanity's troubles. From Sodom to the fall of Babylon the Great the end is delivered in one day. *"Because of this, in one day she will be struck with plagues-disease, grief and famine. And she will be burned with fire, because the Lord God, who judges her, is mighty."* Babylon the Great like Sodom are examples of cities given over to worldly desires and they are consumed by fire. The inhabitants had already been consumed and drunk with immorality, and in this it is only fitting to find their final consumption in the form of fire. This is only the first stage of the incremental judgment, for death is not the end, it is merely the beginning of the end. The fire continues to burn in the place called hell, for all who will not heed the voices, signs and wonders, displayed upon the earth and in the heavens. In the above passage we see that the kings of the earth practiced immorality in this city called Babylon. Also we see the merchants of the world lining their pockets from the unrestrained lust practiced there. Basically what we are looking at is the city of Sodom resurrected in the name of a place called Babylon and its influence has encompassed the whole world. We can see how an entire planet can be engulfed by the flames of insatiable greed, lust for power, and immorality, why then should it come as a surprise that such corrupt influence had not reached out into the planets? Yes, I do think there is an ominous warning to the inhabitants of the earth when we view the heavens and do not see life. History will repeat itself, just as God removed his people from the clutches of the ancient evil in Egypt, so too he will call to those who have not become a part of the world's practices: *"Come out, my people! Come out from her!"*

Just Words

~~~

Everywhere we look there are vacant words
Hollow as a shell empty as is dark
The wordage used by man is for profit and not love.
Speak a tingling phrase watch it run from ground to leg
Let it capture all whose lives are lost in these last days.
Minds seeking one with meaning for their ways
Hearts who know not God but are seeking one to praise
When that day arrives they will think themselves as blessed
And when the curtain falls the man behind is seen
Say goodbye to freedom and learn to yell and scream!

Deception finds a friend
In words that speak to wants and needs
But always there is kept a man upon his knees.
When he fails to know the truth of God's great plan
To rid the world of lies and deception's evilness
He's but a statistic on the wall of endless shame
Passing into nothingness absent even name.

We don't have to look very far or wide
We need not light a torch to find the face of pride.
We do not have to look underneath rocks or search in caves
To find the words enslaving the hearts and minds of men
We need only to be found at the feet of truthfulness
And all will be revealed to the one who will be blessed.

How clear it is to me
This vision we call sight.
When all that's placed within our view
Is seen in holy light.
How silly they appear these flatterers
Speaking empty words.

How evil is their hearts to deceive the weak?
How will they react when illusions are revealed?
Their nakedness displayed as truth in open fields.

～～～

Jude 16 "These people are complainers, disgruntled ones who live by their desires; their mouths utter bombast as they fawn over people to gain advantage."

THIRST

The commitment of the heart to seek God within the activity of life is paramount to finding him. We are solely responsible to respond to the cries of the spirit thirsting to be united with God. We are led to believe that once we come to Christ we have found God and therein our journey is over. In reality it has just begun. Our relationship with Jesus is one in which we are continually taught all things concerning God. Like finding a really good tasting drink that quenches we are easily persuaded to return to what had satisfied. So too it is with the teachings of Christ. We reach out our hand and God our Father does not allow us to grope in the dark. Reaching out from and within the confines of the darkness that is our human identity is both an admission of our need and a submission to the reality of someone greater than our self-awareness. It's a belief and hope in someone infinitely greater than the sum total of our existence, brought about through our thirst for truth. There is a point in life where we are forced to look outside of ourselves and seek answers and help. Some of us see and hear the reply while many others are so distracted by the cares of this life it appears to them the emptiness felt is never to be filled. It appears to all of us who have heard the voice of God that he has impeccable timing. God gets to us at the very moment when there is very little for us to take hold of in the downward spiral of our rebellion. The rebellion need not be a conscious one but it is there nonetheless. It is at this moment of revelation the thirst for God is most pronounced. This thirst or desire for God can be likened to the hunger contained within parched dry bones that have tasted the water of life and are eager to be filled. As we look back upon our

former beliefs that omitted the reality of God we can hardly understand how it is we could have not believed. It is as if we were mockers of truth.

The outside source

The Wright Brothers persisted and insisted man flight was possible but to the everyday person this was folly. Still, the Wright Brothers saw in nature what everyone else seemingly discounted. One look at the majesty of an eagle proved the reality of flight. All of nature proves the existence of God and we wonder what took us so long to come to this realization. *"Necessity is the mother of invention"* is a true saying, and recognizing our need is the first step or indicator that our lives are parched and thirsting for God. When we realize this truth we are no longer bound by our former way of thinking that encapsulated our thoughts with a belief in the independence of man. The reality of God breaks down all of the barriers of a grounded existence and allows us to soar with the eagle. Once we are set free in the truth that God provides for all of our needs we are no longer bound by the limitations of this natural world. However, we must be cautious in the knowledge that the activities of life with its high and low points have ability to distract and render secondary the place reserved for God alone. That is, with a belief in financial independence comes a false sense of security that refocuses our attention away from our true source of providence. Therein we can see the improbability of the rich gaining the kingdom of God, as expressed by Christ. The statement, ***"It would be easier to put a camel through the eye of a needle than for a rich man to enter the kingdom of God"*** is not a condemnation of worldly riches, but a directional finder that emphasizes the rightful place of adoration that God deserves. We ***"cannot serve both God and money."*** We will love one and hate the other. We cannot thirst after both the offerings of the world and the things of God. The two are incompatible.

When Jesus was on the cross he said, ***"I thirst,"*** which was instantly translated by those who were listening into a request to satisfy a physical need. On a deeper level Jesus was thirsting for God and those listening had no frame of reference for understanding. At the well with the Samaritan woman Jesus refers to the water of life that would satisfy her thirst forever. Drawing of water from a well, like the activities of life, have the ability to render to ashes the fire that must burn deep within the bones; have the ability to keep us drawing worldly water that does not satisfy the thirst for God. The desire to find a sense of fulfillment, to become complete and whole is derived from the spiritual aspect of man's existence. It is the spirit of man that seeks to find God who breathed life into the clay of the earth. Because there are obstacles (life's activities) that obscure the truth of creation (dependency of man upon God), the search to become whole finds error through our placing physical needs above the cries of the spirit. Therein the journey into futility begins. All of our attempts to silence the call of the spirit for God through self-gratification are destined for failure, and we are once again groping in the dark for the permanence of a peace filled heart. Theory upon theory and thought upon thought within the reasoning of man cannot recognize the spiritual aspect of our existence until we are renewed by truth and grace. As such, while the body is in a constant state of change brought about by the advent of sin, the spirit, estranged from God cannot be made whole and allowed to lead in the search for the only thing that can quench our thirst. With each failed attempt to satisfy the spirit, through mistakenly thinking we are thirsting for a material need, a greater sense of loss is found, and, the call of the spirit is reduced to muffled-cries obscuring the identity of who we really are. In its place are forged the chains of unhappiness in a soul thirsting to be set free.

Refreshed

Truth casts a healing balm
That reaches deep-set scars
It opens gates denied a quenching storm
Allows innocence of thought
Soaring with the eagle connecting hearts with God.

John 7:37-39 On the last and greatest day of the feast, Jesus stood and said in a loud voice, "If a man is thirsty, let him come to me and drink. Whoever believes in me, as the Scripture has said, streams of living water will flow from within him." By this he meant the Spirit, whom those who believed in him were later to receive. Up to that time the Spirit had not been given, since Jesus had not yet been glorified.

The spirit of man is handicapped. No matter how smart or how smart others may think we are we remain unknowingly wanting the knowledge of truth concerning God. Until our thinking is changed by the transformation made possible by the Holy Spirit we remain empty inside and like men in the darkness we are compelled to search for peace in the offerings of the world. The Holy Spirit (God) is the missing element in our lives that makes the blind man see. Our thoughts can never be completely correct until we know the reality of who we are in Christ. As such, we are incomplete and constantly seeking life, the living water of life. Maintaining our physical existence requires a constant infusion of water food and air, so too we must receive the Holy Spirit in order for us to be complete. The Holy Spirit is the down payment that strengthens us and makes possible the hope of eternal life. Without God touching and bringing us into the reality of truth we cannot see or hear the rushing waters of life. ***Psalm 63:1 O God, you are my God, and I long for you. My whole being desires you; like a dry, worn out land, my soul is thirsty for you.*** In this one verse the psalmist encapsulates tremendous depth of self—acknowledgement. It's an awareness of need for God in his life. The absence of God in our lives finds us continually desiring a downpour of God's presence, as would a dry parched land. It's interesting to reflect upon the words of the creation narrative: ***Genesis 2:7 Then the Lord God took some soil from the ground and formed a man out of it; he breathed life-giving breath into his nostrils and the man began to live.*** GNB This initial life-giving breath is the infusion of God into his creation. It is this same breath of life (presence of God) that when missing keeps us searching in a land of darkness until the light of truth shines in our heart, and with illumination, conviction and convincing, the Spirit of God once again takes up residence in our life, transforming us into the temple of God once again.

When man sinned there was a separation from God. Mankind was estranged from the life-giving breath that provided eternal life, the streams of living water. As long as sin existed (without Christ's sacrifice) mankind could not approach God to once again be united to the life giving water necessary, not only for eternal life but equally important for permitting life in the present existence of man. Without finding God in the here and now there will not be an ever after. This is exactly what the psalmist is asking of God. ***Psalm 63:2 Let me see you in the sanctuary; let me see how mighty and glorious you are.*** This is what we must be asking as well. We must ask God to take up residence in the sanctuary of our heart. Once this is done the reality of God continually is expanding our understanding, regarding the might and glory of God. When we speak of God's glory, we are speaking of his excellent reputation. The more he is revealed to us the greater is our understanding. Of course we cannot completely fathom such excellence and perfection because there is no way we can imagine an end to infinity. ***Matthew 6:22-23 "The eyes are like a lamp for the body. If your eyes are sound, your whole body will be full of light; but if your eyes are no good, your body will be in darkness. So if the light in you is darkness, how terribly dark it will be!"*** I can only imagine the longing of one who is denied light's entry into the body. However, I know of a man who is blind and in this physical blindness he has found joy in the knowledge of God. Where there is the knowledge of God, hope in all of its power to seek what is possible (for God) becomes a reality. So many people have placed their hope in the promise of change, only to find the promises of others empty and filled by the ambitions of self-serving motives. Hope is looked for in the oddest of places: the bottom of a bottle the sting of a syringe, a charismatic world leader or the bright lights of Hollywood, these are momentary distractions away from the darkness inside a man, when God is not in residence. Many are they who have placed their hope for peace and independence (for the one who is monetarily rich), misplaced and disappointing at the very least. They continue to seek the offerings of the world to quell the call of the spirit, (the call of the spirit is the intuitive knowledge that peace is available), but they do not know where it can be found.

The darkness that keeps people searching for a way out of a life of disappointment becomes impenetrable when we continually are led in the wrong direction! This misleading element is to be expected especially when the darkness inside a man is complete. A complete absence of the knowledge and belief in God is total darkness. A change in thinking will occur when light is shown into such darkness. Even if we are within our own home and suddenly the lights go out at night, we will not move about in the same manner of confidence when the home was lighted. The same is true when the darkness within a man is present. His thoughts are not filled with confidence or the peace that one should expect within his very own home-his heart and mind. As such a man is forced to seek such confidence and peace in the offerings of the world. Unfortunately this search is futile, for nowhere within the treasures of this life is to be found the sought after peace, which is brought to a man when the light of understanding shines into his heart. Again, a man must be born again by receiving a new spirit, the very Spirit that was breathed into his nostrils at the very beginning. This new spirit is actually the conscious awareness of God. It is his eyesight that is given to us-his light that makes confident our pathways. Not only will we know what road to take in this journey, additionally, our steps will be filled with the knowledge that we are not alone. Therein all of our limitations are confronted with the almighty power of God.

Acts 3:17-21 "And now my friends, I know that what you and your leaders did to Jesus was due to your ignorance. God announced long ago through all the prophets that his Messiah had to suffer; and he made it come true in this way. Repent, then, and turn to God, so that he will forgive your sins. If you do, times of spiritual strength will come from the Lord, and he will send Jesus, who is the Messiah he has already chosen for you. He must

remain in heaven until the time comes for all things to be made new, as God announced through his holy prophets long ago." GNB The apostle Peter is addressing the people within the temple courts and in part what he is saying to them is they are living in darkness and/or ignorance of God's salvation made available in Christ. Not only are they living life unaware but they really have no spiritual strength. That is, the thinking process of a man living in darkness is absent awareness that the light of truth is available to shine into his heart. All of life becomes a guessing game akin to the blind extending their hands hoping to find direction in a world absent sight. Now, at this time (when the apostles went out to preach) many **"miracles and wonders were being done by the apostles, and everyone was filled with awe."** It is one thing to witness a miracle and find what you see is so beyond our understanding that we are then focused on the belief in God's power made available to us. But for the one who receives the miracle the belief is transformed into knowing and in knowing the awe is transformed into love. The very same power of God is present in the one who is born again; transformed from a place of darkness into illumination not only of belief but into the solid foundation of knowing the reality and love of God. There are times when we need to find examples from life that express our intention with regard to attempting to find avenues of attraction that satisfy. I'm reminded of an old song by the singer, Dee Sharp titled, "Party Lights." *"I see the lights I see the party lights they're red and blue and green everybody in the crowd's there but you won't let me make a scene."*

The lights of the world are attractive for the young. The song goes on the say, *"Mama, can't you hear? Everybody in the crowd's there, but you won't let me make the scene."* Apparently Mama is aware of the pitfalls of *making the scene* and with effort is denying her daughter the opportunity to follow the crowd. We expect this from parents. It is no less true of God our Father, he does not want us to follow the crowd or be blinded by the party lights. We find colorful lights inherent in all attractions offered by the world's entertainment industry, or they are present within a myriad of innocuous celebratory events. I'm not saying that all colorful events are meant to attract and induce us into activities that inherently may cause us harm, rather, it is the lights themselves that are the attraction, simply because we do not know the true light needed for illumination within. It is the underlying search for satisfaction that keeps us not only attracted to the offerings of the world, but like a lure attracts and brings to an end the life of a fish, so it is with the life of a man if he should continue to seek what cannot be given by the world. All is but temporary gratification, after which the search for *more* continues, perhaps with greater intensity as the succession of failures mounts to unforeseen proportions. If we are blessed at the moment where there is no place to turn, beaten down by the unfilled promises of life we will then find truth through the intervention of God. He will not break down the doors and barriers we may have constructed; he will knock and ask to be invited in. It is at this time we can either accept or reject the intervention of truth. We don't know if the singer went to the party and consequently did not heed the direction of her mother. What we do know is for every truth contained within the light of God there is a distraction lending the appearance of being genuine.

Within human beings there is an entire science geared to deceive. From the simplest form of pretence involving actors whose physical features resemble the actual celebrity and those whose voices we have come to recognize through their celebrity status, the purpose is always geared toward gain for the commercial and at times a loss for the one so enamored into purchasing the product. The term, *"buyer-beware"* is a true saying. Unless we are aware of the tactics we may notice the similarities but on a subconscious level there is that pull designed for us to indulge. After all is said and done the genuine actor has been shown to be lifted up and has overcome the hardships plaguing ordinary mortals. If he or she says it is good then it must be so, right? Where is the fiber within a person that says to the one directing the charade, *I won't be a part of deception aimed at leading others away from truth.* I suppose when the person with the similar features or voice decides they too want to become famous and rich therein we find the same temptation offered to Jesus when he was in the desert of want. ***"If you will but worship me I will give you all of the kingdoms of the earth."*** Perhaps the fall of a man to the temptations offering fame and riches is not looked upon as reaching the same level of offense but a lie is a lie no matter how it is packaged. This little *"white lie"* sugarcoating has been designed to appear palatable to the spirit but in truth once ingested and then accepted there is a price to pay for the assault on conscience. It has been said that the journey of a thousand miles begins with the first step, and so it is true when we first take a bite from the fruit of the forbidden tree. All of us have taken that bite knowingly or because we are always wanting to believe in others. When we ingest something we believed to be truth spoken by another it settles into our vast array of storage ability called memory. The object of our belief will not rest if it is not completely true.

You see, it is written, *1 Corinthians 2:10-12 But it was to us that God made known his secret by means of his Spirit. The Spirit searches everything, even the hidden depths of God's purposes. It is only our own spirit within us that knows all about us; in the same way, only God's Spirit knows all about God. We have not received this world's spirit; instead, we have received the Spirit sent by God.* A common experience that we as Christians come across from time to time is this: someone tells us something and we take it into our heart and bestow on it belief status. After all the person telling us of the matter is trustworthy in our opinion. Sometime later perhaps while sleeping we are awakened by the knowledge that the person's divulgence is wrong. This then my friends is the Holy Spirit searching even the deep parts of our lives. Just as the party lights and the activities of life have been taken in and found acceptable, so it may come to be that such a grade of good will not hold up against the scrutiny of the Holy Spirit.

Beauty

Stepping out and stepping loud
Brand new kicks for neon crowd
Talking trash without a sound
What to do when it comes crashing down
Beauty.
With every step you bowed to vanity so proud
It got you what you wanted
Notice from the street
Deep within you felt the taunting
What to do when it comes it crashing down?
Beauty.
The hip-hop in the step is gone
It had a time to visit.
The mind recalls the shallow talk
Amazed through present eyes, surprise!
What to do when it dies?
Beauty.
Now the days of nothing praise
All is gone and muted
In its place you find the grace
That always seemed illusive
Beauty.

Ecclesiastes 1-2 "Meaningless! Meaningless!" says the teacher.
Utterly meaningless! Everything is meaningless."

HIDEAWAY

As a child the world appeared as a place of wonder. No matter where we were we could always find a hideaway, and imaginary friend was always willing to play. Day trips to the great parks within urban settings were opportunities to hideaway and explore the old trails, where legend had it once walked the Indians of yesteryear. The majesty of trees and grass open meadows and acres of new sights and sounds lent excitement to the hearts of young explorers. Leaving the sunshine and the meadow for the canopy of the trees touched upon different emotions of joy expertly blended with just a pinch of fear. "Keep a good lookout, and watch out for those overgrown tree roots raised high off of the ground." Alongside of these hideaway places we could see the hexagon shaped stone pavement of the park pathways, and the concrete and wood benches lined along the outer edges of the path. Adults were seemingly oblivious to our games, but old folks always watched for what mischief a kid would get into. Finding a path that led to the zoo (other than the one everyone knew) was a secret route and from the cover of the trees we could burst upon the activities and disappear at will. Yes, back into the trees to plan the next move and rest. The resting allowed our imaginations to enter areas that grownups can rarely find. The world of make believe has become a distant memory clouded by the pace of today's high-speed realities. With maturity the mysterious excitement of the long-ago hideaways have become shadowed, like phantoms that vanish as the days of youth.

Today we rarely seek a secret place or hideaway. Our brief time for vacation is spent with activities that leave us wanting to rest upon returning home. Most often rest is put aside in favor of rightful family priorities and life responsibilities, that can be read as interlaced with struggles. Still, the contemplative moments of prayer allow us access to God's secret place and therein we can hideaway in the presence of love. This secret hideaway has been established for us alone. Within the shade and the shadow of the Almighty we find renewal and strength. The hideaway that we should be spending much more time exploring is the Kingdom of God. The awareness of God has the ability to bring back to our conscious thoughts the reality that we are his children. We need to be as little children, because the innocence of youth is the key to finding what little children see clearly.

Playtime

She tossed off the pillows from couch
And lined up the soldiers for muster
Lumpy and Eeyore and dinosaur guy
Thumper and Elmo and others wide eyed.
Stacked up and lined up piled up as waves
These stuffed up and puffed up crowded to play,
With Isabella, and brother PJ.

Acorn Hunting

⌒⌒⌒

Squirrels could only watch in bemused wonder
A granddaughter age four with grandpa,
Little brother carried vertical with head facing rear
Searching for autumn's bounty.
"Grandpa, do bears eat acorns too?"
Isabella, I suppose bears will eat anything when hungry.
"Grandpa, I feel sad that we are taking the acorns away from the bears."
Isabella, who made the acorns?
"Grandpa, God made them."
Well then Isabella, he made enough for everyone
Including your school project.
"Thank you grandpa, I feel better now."

⌒⌒⌒

Matthew 18:3 I assure you that unless you change and become like little children, you will never enter the Kingdom of heaven.

GHOST OF GOD

What a sight! Just looking at her filled me with feelings of awe. Purple vestments arrayed in formal ship's dress. Not flashy, more like crushed velvet that conveyed majesty unique. I could not see the breath of her stature only her width and great superstructure were visible. Upon the hull of the fantail bore the name, **"Ghost Of God."** *There were other inscriptions beneath her name but these had no meaning for me. As I gazed upon this wonderful ship I could see a crewman and a passenger several decks below him. The crewman was having some trouble with the remaining portion of ship's dress and he indicated his need for help by pointing where the last portion of the royal velvet had grouped and was prevented from opening by an obstruction. The accommodation ladder had not as yet been lowered into place, and so, try as I may I could not assist him. No matter, for at my realization the remaining vestment came free. The passenger seemed thrilled to be in port. We spoke but I cannot remember our words. All preparations complete the ship was now ready for the official arrival pronouncement. I reclined on the pier and rested in the vision of this magnificent ship. Upon awakening the* **"Ghost Of God"** *filled me still.*

Bedtime

"Now I lay me down to sleep"
Aware of places deep
Reality the pillowed bed
Mindful places dark and dread
Conscious dwelling fixed as flint
Sealed within deep with strength
Nothing fancy straight and plain
Reside with me O, Holy Name!
Faith in grace steadfast shield
Humbling truth dispatch in haste
Evil from this place!
Spirit Sword knowledge swift
Steadfast love upon my lips
Readiness within my feet
Helmet fastened slumber sweet
"I pray the Lord my soul to keep."

John 7:37:39 On the last and greatest day of the feast, Jesus stood and said in a loud voice, "If a man is thirsty, let him come to me and drink. Whoever believes in me, as the Scripture has said, streams of living water will flow from within him." By this he meant the Spirit, whom those who believed in him were later to receive. Up to that time the Spirit had not been given, since Jesus had not yet been glorified.

FOLLOWERS FAKERS AND OUTRIGHT FRAUDS

There are those who lead and those who follow. In both there are many pretenders. It has happened only once in the history of mankind; only once has one led a perfect life and has led others perfectly by his example; this is (in part) the reason why Jesus is adored and followed by seekers of truth.

Matthew 8:21 A teacher of the Law came to him. "Teacher," he said, "I am ready to go with you wherever you go." Another man, who was a disciple, said, "Sir, first let me go back and bury my father." "Follow me." Jesus answered, "and let the dead bury their own dead." GNB Jesus followed his Father's example by expressing to all who will see and hear, truth concerning God. In this way he leads these same people to the place of God's original intent for humanity, which is eternal life. In the above scripture quotation we find one who declares his undying commitment to follow no matter where he (Jesus) may lead, and in the other we hear the excuse everyone recognizes as legitimate and permitting time away from the firsthand duties and responsibilities of life's demands. Such duties and responsibilities are immediately rendered secondary when responsibility to the dead comes knocking. Even in wartime allowances will be made for the soldier to return home, if at all possible. But in the war against deception the follower of Christ is told to remain steady and focused.

We may find this a bit out of character for Jesus, at first glance we may even find his denial for bereavement leave to be uncaring. In truth the would-be follower is told, "The deceased will take care of themselves." This of course is a referral to those who have passed away and also for those who do not have life in them. To those who do not have the truth of God and the presence of God living within them. In addition to this (let the dead bury their own), Jesus goes on to tell a teacher of the Law, who openly declared he would follow Jesus anywhere, that, ***"Foxes have holes, and birds have nests, but the Son of Man has no place to lie down and rest."*** In order for us to understand this statement we have to recognize it is *truth* Jesus is referring to. Truth will always find itself on the defensive and pursued for reasons attempting to insert the negative thought of doubt into the declarations of truth. Remember it was Jesus who said, ***"I am the way and the truth and the life."*** As such, there is no place for truth to rest. Truth is an outcast simply because it is not of this world. Truth belongs to the Kingdom of God. The world, from the inception of sin has rejected truth because its light uncovers the reality of deception. Let's not forget that those who cannot see the truth of God are kept blinded by the evil god of this world. Also present with the would-be followers is a gathering crowd. He orders his disciples to go to the other side of the lake. He *orders* them to separate themselves from the crowd. This is indicative of the motives brought into question regarding the crowds of people Jesus had been attracting. The news of Jesus healing not only the sick but healing those held tightly in the grip of the devil (the demon possessed) is spreading rapidly. His *Sermon on the Mount* and preaching, interlaced with parables is attracting not only the common man but also the elite rulers of society. Ordering his disciples to cross over to the other side of the lake is perhaps a measure aimed at protecting the disciples from the ruling powers of this world. Certainly within the crowd there were those whose only attraction is based upon the celebrity of Jesus. Not much has changed in today's seekers of celebrities who have the ability to attract through prosperity and a voice to influence. The leadership of Jesus is genuinely understood and affirmed as the pinnacle of truth. If this were not the case no one would follow. Understanding and affirmation of truth is brought to us not only through our own conscience, (inherent knowledge of right and wrong), more importantly through the actual intervention by the Holy Spirit of God. I have never met a man who has found Christ and then was able to say a bad thing about him.

Both the teacher of the Law and the other disciple are being exposed to both the discipline necessary to follow, and the sacrifices that must come with the cost of aligning one's self with truth. Increasingly in today's world we find the attacks upon truth (defined as Christianity), to be no longer hidden away in the darkness where plans and schemes to vilify are made in the dead of night; formerly the chosen home for deception. Indeed, the viciousness of today's deceivers with increasing boldness have moved their activities from such darkness into the brightness of day, as if there is no longer a penalty for such deception. For this reason we are made to recognize truth: so that we will not be misled by those who claim to be a part of the fold but are really wolves in sheep clothing.

Travelers

Narrow and straight
Crooked and wide
It's yours to decide.
Givers and takers fanatical fans
Leaders and fakers dependent and proud
Commoners kings neutrals unbowed
Pretenders show the outside of man
Under it all is ashes and dirt
The spirit inside determines his worth.
Heed the time when light comes to shine
Where dead men walk and burials peak
The time of day and the moment that speaks:
"This is your last breath and last chance to seek.
This is your life or judgment to reap.
Come out from the darkness and open your eyes
See the world of deception the mountain of lies.
Truth is impartial to all it will give
The clear and decisive moment to live."

Matthew 7:13-14 "Go in through the narrow gate, because the gate to hell is wide and the road that leads to it is easy, and there are many who travel it. But the gate to life is narrow and the way to it is hard, and there are few people who find it." GNB

It is apparently natural for people to be attracted to celebrities. Fans flock to their appearances, hoping to see and hear for themselves what it is they have to say and/or perform. There was no difference during the time of Christ's ministry. Jesus was a celebrity of colossal magnitude. Let's consider the fact that there wasn't instant communication or cable television, only the word-of-mouth that generated such excitement and interest in the appearances of our Lord. There were not police barriers along with intense security, protecting not only the celebrity of Jesus but also his disciples, what today might be called the celebrity's supporting cast and entourage. Not at all, in truth, while many were flocking to Jesus with intentions of pure interest absent any malice, there were those whose presence was not innocent. As such, Jesus sees the large crowd and orders the disciples to cross over to the other side of the lake. Herein we see Jesus obeying the Shepherd's cardinal rule, which is to protect the sheep at all cost. This is the complete opposite of today's celebrities, wherein it is *protect the celebrity at all cost.* Much later on we see the disciples and Jesus clearly confronted by a crowd of hostile people seeking to arrest him. What we see from Jesus is the same protectiveness of his disciples.

John 18:7-9 Again Jesus asked them, "Who is it you are looking for?" "Jesus of Nazareth," they said. "I have already told you that I am he," Jesus said. "If then, you are looking for me, let these others go." (He said this so that what he had said might come true: "Father, I have not lost even one of those you gave me.") GNB

When we look at the account of the arrest of Jesus in the gospel of Luke we hear the words of Jesus as expressed in the other accounts basically saying, *"I was with you in the Temple every day, and you did not try to arrest me. But this is your hour to act, when the power of darkness rules."* Within Luke's account we find an added smack in the face to those coming to arrest him, *But this is your hour to act, when the power of darkness rules."* Yes, they came to arrest Jesus under the cover of darkness but on a deeper level what we are hearing is simply that the hour for being handed over to the evil of the world had come. The hour of God's choosing had permitted evil to arrest our Lord. In this we not only see evil's proliferation in the world, having taken upon itself a character that can only be described as despotic wickedness at its most base level, within the rule of darkness, but it has the appearance of free reign. Increasingly over the past one-hundred-years, because of the speed within which communication has been able to travel we are bombarded with the evil acts of both private individuals and governments, heightening our awareness to the lawlessness perpetrated without the aid of deception. Pure boldness and in-your-face defiance to all that is righteous and holy, giving the appearance that nothing has really changed since the hour darkness was permitted to rule. The good that is done in this world is not given much attention by those whose voices are given a platform to be heard. The desired outcome of such communicative saturation is to make humanity so manifestly scarred and calloused as to not feel the outrage!

There are many today who have chosen to be a part of the evil and there are those who do not know there is a choice that they *must* make in order to live life abundantly. There are many today who follow and there is not the appearance of abundance. This is not a contradiction of the words of Jesus, not at all, for the ***"abundant life"*** he spoke of had to do with not only eternal life but life that includes truth, through which the wisdom to see clearly the lies of the world, brings to a man the stability of peace that eliminates or at least eases the unnecessary stress associated with the daily grind of today's living. All of this is summed up in the ***"Lord's Prayer"*** that not only reminds us of our status as sons and daughters of Almighty God, but additionally we are alerted to just how rich we really are. My brother once called me the, "richest poorest man he knows." I'm sure many followers of Jesus are not only poor, but, they live in poverty and persecution; still they are rich in the knowledge of God and immeasurably valued by him as well. Yes we live in a world filled with terrible hardships, but at the end of this narrow road is found the reality of what is meant by the word, *"Salvation."* ***Matthew 5:13-14 "Happy are you when people insult you and persecute you and tell all kinds of lies against you because you are my followers. Be happy and glad, for a great reward is kept for you in heaven. This is how the prophets who lived before you were persecuted."*** *GNB* It is one thing to be kept in darkness, prevented from knowing the truth of God's gift to mankind, and it is another altogether to know such truth has been offered and to reject it within a spirit of pretense and pride. This is the non-belief identified as atheism. Within the church of atheism we will find some who exhibit anger, loathing, ridicule, and the need to persecute believers; it is these people who know deep within them the truth of God. No matter how they try they cannot defeat conscience that always points to the truth of what is correct and what is not. Yes I understand the argument against conscience being viable only within the norms of a given society. Cannibals may not feel guilt because their society has condoned such behavior, but it does not make it right. I'm certain the conscience although bound and gagged is crying out to be heard. This passive atheist unlike many avowed atheists has not taken a hostile position against believers, rather he has embraced the conflict of war against God, his children and his truth. It makes no sense to go against God if you do not believe he exists! These same atheists have erected statues of the devil under the pretence of mockery; but in truth they have embraced not only the concept of evil but its existence as well. This is exactly the philosophy of those who have identified with the secular humanist preaching, that through its teaching attempts to erase the conscience, simply because they have embraced the idea that there is no morally wrong act that can be committed, providing no harm is inflicted upon another godly realm. One has to wonder how it is someone can knowingly go to war against God and expect to win? How it is someone can be so devious as to think they can keep truth within the confines of darkness when it is shining throughout the universe? Truly these are the children of their father, the devil. The same is true for those who pretend to follow the conduct and overall way of life God desires us to live, while all the while underneath their exterior presentation lives the darkness of worldly precepts. We do not judge (judgment implies the need for punishment and in this God alone is qualified), but surely we can see the truth of deception whenever it raises its ugly head; in this we are certainly not blind and therein our judgment will be correct. Given all of these mislabeled road signs that hang profusely about the heads of mankind it is a wonder we can keep our focus upon the straight and narrow. No matter how we may be detoured into uncharted territory (the man with a compass is free to travel uninhibited) the truth within us will always act as a positioning system bringing us back to our first love, the desire to finish the race and claim the prize of life.

The life of a person should be as the accolade awarded to Nathaniel by Jesus, basically Jesus said of Nathaniel, *"What you see is what you get."* Jesus said there was nothing about him (Nathaniel) that was false. Now that is a truly coveted prize! In the one named Nathaniel we can find neither faker and/or fraud. Unfortunately the world is filled with pretenders and frauds both of which come under the heading of deceivers. Even more unfortunate is the fact that many are holding positions of authority within the churches. These are on a fast track to hell simply because Jesus said that those who cause others to fall would be better off if they were drowned in the depths of the sea. I recently attended a church service, where, within the half-hour sermon the pastor referred to tithing fourteen times. I find that within the electronic church and in many local churches, tithing is a most popular topic that predictably will be included within a certain timeframe. For me the Old Testament practice of tithing, as given to the people from God to Moses, had its purpose, but has since found little use in today's New Testament, which places no percentage on the amount of generosity that should be in the heart of one who follows Christ. As such, a person seeking to follow has found parameters of generosity erected, by emphasizing a tithing requirement many will assume having complied with the edict there is no more required of an official nature. I'm reminded of the account of the widow's offering: ***Luke 21:1-4 Jesus looked around and saw rich people dropping their gifts in the Temple treasury, and he also saw a very poor widow dropping in two little copper coins. He said, "I tell you that this poor widow put in more than all the others. For the others offered their gifts from what they had to spare of their riches; but she, poor as she is, gave all she has to live on."*** When did we forget that it is God who provides for not only the individual but for his church as well? When was it determined by the churches that this form of intimidating persuasion (yes there are some who require tithing in order to be a member of their church) is appropriate? Has someone used, *"the end justifies the means"* mindset in order to place a non-compliance guilt-trip upon church membership? Let me say that another way. If we are wrong in our approach to make a right, it is still wrong. The congress of the United States (it appears) is continually geared to share pork among their selves in order to acquire the vote-count to pass such law that will benefit someone or something. The law may be good but the way it was passed is pure corruption. Thus if tithing (for instance) is introduced to a congregation under the wrong presentation in order to fix a church roof, the outcome may be a new roof, but at a cost totally frowned upon by God. I suppose it became popular when the pretenders found deception to be an appropriate tool affording enrichment of church leaders? There are those who say, "Tithing is God's word and should be followed." Yes it is God's word, but we no longer stone people to death either, and should we do that? Tithing also makes pathways (perhaps unintentionally) that cause and/or produce a puffed-up and prideful attitude in some who do tithe. Sort of like the Pharisee who saw the sinner in the temple while they were both praying, the Pharisee thanked God for not making him like the sinner. It is perhaps these forms of pride that cause consequences separating people from the general assembly presented before God. Tithing can cause the one who tithes to feel more important in the eyes of the pastor, and in doing so the separation is as pronounced in the eyes of God as the Pharisee who believed he was so much better than that ordinary sinner. And here is the most troubling aspect of wedges placed within and throughout the gathering before the Lord in the houses of God: ***Matthew 22: 22-24 Then some people brought to Jesus a man who was blind and could not talk because he had a demon. Jesus healed the man so that he was able to talk and see. The crowds were all amazed at what Jesus had done. "Could he be the Son of David?" the asked. When the Pharisees heard this, they replied, "He drives out demons because their ruler Beelzebul gives him power to do it."*** *GNB* Jesus goes on to school these self-righteous and fearful Pharisees; they feared losing any portion of the accolades usually bestowed upon them by the people, to one who was not one of their group. Jesus tells them, ***Matthew 22:25 But he knew what they were thinking and said to them, "Every kingdom divided against itself will be laid to waste, and no town or house divided against itself can stand."*** *NAB* Having said this let us recognize that the congregation divided by such aforementioned wrongs-committed, in order to achieve a right, is destined to lose the collective power in prayer and worship when presenting itself before the Lord. A voice crying-out in the wilderness is heard, how much more will a multitude? If we could see the road that leads to hell we might cry out for mercy. Many are those who will be told, *"I never knew you."* Yes, many have lost sight of the true message of Christ and they actually think they are accepted in the eyes of God. It is no secret that many have heard the call of God saying, *"Come out from her!"* The falling away of the churches is a fact made clear by the warning in the book of Revelation: *Revelation 2:4-5 "But this is what I have against you: you do not love me now as you did at first. Think how far you have fallen! Turn from your sins and do what you did at first. If you don't turn from your sins, I will come to you and take your lamp stand from its place."* GNB The critical warning above speaks specifically of losing love for God and his truth. Honesty is the only way we can represent the word of God. In general terms it speaks of the need to turn from our sins. Truly the shepherd who misleads his flock is guilty of a most grievous sin. *"We cannot serve both God and money."* Some have managed to find what appears to them as a loophole, in which they can seemingly jump through unscathed, by the omission of the true intent of generosity, honesty, and support of the great commission. Our example is and should always be God our Father, who does not place limitation upon his generosity toward us who love him. From leaders of governments and local representatives we have come to realize there are brightly colored lures that ensnare through corrupt deceptive behavior, but for the one entrusted with the lamp stand of Christ, how great is his fall when such tactics of the world invade his heart?

Here is the meaning of the lamp stand: *Revelation 1:20 Here is the meaning of the seven stars that you see in my right hand, and the seven gold lamp stands; the seven stars are the angels of the seven churches, and the seven lamp stands are the seven churches.* Symbolically the lamp stand is the authority of the church (it is we who are the temple of God, the church), and to have the light within us extinguished is to not be recognized by Christ. *Matthew 7:22-23 When the Judgment Day comes, many will say to me, 'Lord, Lord! In your name we spoke God's message, by your name we drove out many demons and performed many miracles!' Then I will say to them, 'I never knew you. Get away from me, you wicked people!'* Yes, it may be true that many did indeed speak the message of God and did perform miracles in the name of Jesus but when the lamp stand is taken away they will no longer be recognized. *Matthew 5:13-15 "You are like salt for the whole human race. But if salt loses its saltiness there is no way to make it salty again. It has become worthless, so it is thrown out and people trample on it. You are like light for the whole world. A city on a hill cannot be hid. No one lights a lamp and puts it under a bowl; instead it is put on the lamp stand where it gives light for everyone in the house."* GNB Of course we understand that Jesus is using his wonderful way of expression in order for us to realize we have been given truth, and if this truth is lost (we do not accurately present ourselves in the truth given) it is lost. It loses the power to set free those kept in darkness and is trampled by those who desire to keep truth hidden under a bowl.

I SEE

O the blessing that is sight
Behold, the wonders of this life!
Even when our vision fails or is absent from the start
We can see the truth concerning God.
There are many who claim, "I can see!"
But really, they have not sight
They have denied the truth
Contained in God's sunlight.

2 Corinthians 4:3-4 "They do not believe, because their minds have been kept in the dark by the evil god of this world. He keeps them from seeing the light shining on them, the light that comes from the Good News about the glory of Christ, who is the exact likeness of God." GNB

Tithes

Matthew 23:23-24 "How terrible for you, teachers of the Law and Pharisees! You hypocrites! You give to God one tenth even of the seasoning herbs, such as mint, dill, and cumin, but you

neglect to obey the really important teachings of the Law, such as justice and mercy and honesty. These you should practice, without neglecting the others. Blind guides! You strain a fly out of your drink, but swallow a camel!" GNB

Everyone who attends a church knows there is a collection made that is used for the purpose of supporting not only the existing structure, but it is believed to support missionaries and charities as well. And to these we should be giving generously however, when pastors make tithing a requirement for membership, therein we can surely find the voice of Jesus, just as he denounced the Pharisees and the teachers of the Law. There are very many prosperous churches and the pastors live a life of luxury. We see these same churches on the television and there always seems to be a telethon or a pitch for donations, through book sales or partnerships that in many instances take precedence over the very principles that Jesus strongly denounced the religious leaders of his day. It gets worse than that. There are some who are outright frauds. They guide people to place their faith in healing water or prayer cloths or something other than the one who alone is worthy of our trust.

Let's look for a moment at the very first mention of tithing in the bible. ***Genesis 14:20 And Abram gave Melchizedek a tenth of all the loot he had recovered.*** Now, it is written of Melchizedek, ***"He was the king of Salem and also a priest of the Most High God."*** We don't know very much about this king of Salem, and many have looked upon him as a figure that points to the person of Christ. This is done predominantly because the translation of "king of Salem" is, "King of Peace." In addition the king of Salem went out to meet Abram and brought to him bread and wine. Yes it sounds like communion to me, and this is definitely the office of the priesthood and/or church pastor. Again, this look back into the past shows to us the reality of the present. Now having said all of this let us not lose sight of the fact that like the ***poor widow*** who gave everything that she had as an offering to God, Abram, while he tithed ten-percent of the loot taken from those who had captured his nephew Lot, and took with them not only all of the possessions of Sodom and Gomorrah, but all of the people as well; (Lot was a resident of Sodom at that time). Abram kept nothing of the recovered loot for himself! He did this so that the king of Sodom could not say he had made Abram wealthy. The idea that we should give to God the tithe because God will return it many-fold is not really an honest precept. Honesty of course is one of the main precepts that Jesus harshly admonished the teachers of the Law for their lack thereof.

Malachi 3:10-11 "Bring the full amount of your tithes to the Temple, so that there will be plenty of food there. Put me to the test and you will see that I will open the windows of heaven and pour out on you in abundance all kinds of good things." Truly when we hear that God will open the windows of heaven and pour out abundance for those who comply with his laws, what we as Christians must hear are the words of Jesus who speaks to us of the greatest abundance of all; life! Many times in scripture when we hear of gates or windows being opened it can mean the opening of one's mind to the abundance we have in the knowledge of God. People seeking a return on their investment, yes many people look upon the giving of tithes, as an investment guaranteed by God within a given church, these have been misled, by the church. Again, there are many things in the Law of Moses that we do not adhere to today and do not have a place within the preaching of the things that God wants us to focus upon. Namely, the words of Jesus to the teachers of the Law and the Pharisees, *"But you neglect the really important teaching of the Law such as, justice and mercy and honesty."* If we are led to believe that tithing is an investment and requirement (most churches do not make it a requirement but they are persistent in their presentation that it is a biblical principle and should be considered) we are then not being honest with ourselves and/or with God. For the one who places his trust in God there is freedom in abundance. This trust is what we call faith. Such faith must be directed to God alone, for to do otherwise is to find deception. As such, for the one who honestly believes that he is tithing for the correct reasons (not to see a return on an investment as it is portrayed in some churches or because fear is the guiding force, because he has been told it is required by the bible), this person's faith permits him to do so honestly. In this honesty we can present ourselves with confidence and Jesus will not tell us he does not know us. It is our faith that gives to us individual freedoms, (not a license to sin) but a license to become aware of just how much God understands the power of faith entrusted to those who love him. In fact, faith is so powerful that we are warned against placing such trust in the wrong places. There are some areas that God finds disgusting and commands us not to place our faith, such as, ***"divination or look for omens, consult spirits or the dead." Deuteronomy 18*** GNB

The reasoning for this is that for many people, if they should place faith in these areas, and in-turn find a response, therein is the hook of deception and with such a hook they are led into many other areas that God finds to be totally unacceptable. Faith in God has the underlying meaning of recognizing our own dependence upon him. When we recognize our dependence we are then given the means to accomplish the purpose of our lives. Thinking that we are independent is a worldly deception and leads in the opposite direction of finding stability and peace in this life.

Divided

❧

A share a section a division of parts
Severed by feelings opinions and thoughts
Apart and in half the house cannot stand
The kingdom will fall
Whoever hears his-own-drummer answers its call.

East will be west and north will be south
Positions will change as expression and doubt
As birds fly away at the first bite of fall
Its entrance announces to feather and wing
"To another bring color
To another sing songs
Fly away with the wind the last leaf is gone."

The shepherd asleep is focused elsewhere
He cares not for the flock the cry or the bleat
Cares only for self the pillow and bed
Of honey that's flowing and belly that's fed.
With clothing that's warm and roof overhead
The wolf can run wild in the field of his dreams
Until morning arrives with wakening screams
And he is the focus of dividing things.

❧

Mark 3:24-25 "If a kingdom is divided against itself, that kingdom cannot stand. And if a house is divided against itself, that house will not be able to stand." *NIV*

Trust

Who to trust and how much?
Family fails us at times
And friends can be hard to find
A multitude may produce one
But only if the one is not two
We see the outer man and
Hope the inner man is the same.
It can get confusing
Knowing where to place our trust
Contemporary faith is often a bust.
Lord, may it come to pass
Knowledge of your goodness
Enter the hearts of men.
Within the existence of man
Wrought from earth and dust
Within the flesh and sinew
The spirit bone and blood
Within the light of inner halls
Make clear to us as day
The way that we should call
Let all who draw near to you
Find shelter in your thoughts
And find the dwelling place
Bringing peace into the heart.
May Sacrifice as Sabbath Bread
Be offered up in praise
And bring to hearts the nourishment
That comes with trust in grace.

Romans 9:33 As it is written: "See, I lay a stone in Zion that causes men to stumble and a rock that makes them fall, and the one who trusts in him will never be put to shame."

THE GREAT FISHING EXPEDITION

Brooklyn, New York, 1980.
Some neighborhoods have sparse plantings of trees along the sidewalks
while others are unaware of the shade trees produce. Some trees were
planted in backyards by our grandparents who brought with them
the seeds of immigration. My wife's grandparents had a fig tree in the
backyard and when fruit ripened it fell to the concrete patio like heavy
purple raindrops. The Italian immigrant could not take with him the
little fishing boats that dotted the shoreline of the fishing villages. The
language of my parents and grandparents has been lost through the process
of assimilation but some things will always remain. The memories of our
lives and the impact others have contributed remain as anchors deeply
imbedded.

One summer day I heard my wife say, "Take him fishing." Peter
stood by anticipating a positive response from dear old dad. My
reaction was one of incredulity and defensive verbosity. This was a
Saturday in Brooklyn, not a fishing village in southern Italy. "Where
in the world do you think I can take him fishing? Even if we found
some fish they must have already had breakfast! I don't have fishing
gear. What are we supposed to do, jump in and grab the fish?" By
this time Peter (a very bright child), began to reflect within his
countenance the possibility of other activities being suggested. That is,
abandon all hope of fishing and hang out with the other neighborhood
kids. Suddenly, like Moses announcing the Commandments, came the
words: "Take him fishing!" There are times in life when we know the
true meaning of "duteous husband." Obedience is often accompanied

by a measure of fear and it was evident to Peter that the fishing expedition had just begun.

We left the air-conditioned city bus in, "Sheepshead Bay" (famous for seafood and fishing boats) and headed directly for the bait and tackle shop. "Give us a box of worms and the drop line with the plastic float, please." As we walked along the piers the sidewalks were filled with vendors selling their wares. The boats had left earlier in the morning and the tide was low. I asked a woman where it was the fish might be biting. She responded by saying, "Everyone seems to think that the pier furthest down is the place to fish." In fact, there was a large crowd numbering about fifty people on the pier she had recommended. Off we went and found a spot away from the congregated consensus of expensive fishing rods and experience.

"This can't be too difficult son; we'll put the worm on the hook and toss it into the water." With low tide the plastic float and the hook barely reached the waterline. We could see the hook floundering just a foot below the water's surface. After staring with anticipation (for about an hour) at the bathing worm showing no signs of fear, Peter expressed his desire to have lunch. "Dad we aren't very good at fishing can we go and get lunch?" I answered by saying, "You are right my son we are no good at this fishing stuff, but we know someone who is. Let's pray for a fish and maybe Jesus will give us one."

Just after raising our heads from prayer a man walked up to us and said, "When you catch some fish you will need something to put them in." The man pointed to the base of the accommodation ladder that led to a platform below, used to get on or off of the boat at low tide. On the platform was a five-gallon plastic pail complete with carrying handle. I descended the steps, washed and filled the pail with water, carried it back up the ladder, and set it down next to our spot on this, thus far, unproductive fishing expedition. The man was gone. As I looked at my son the line got taut and we knew it was a big one!

We could see the snapper as it struggled against our formidable fishing apparatus. We hauled him in. A perfect sandwich size baby bluefish was added to the pail. We immediately baited the hook again and sent the blessed float sailing. Another strike! Incredibly it looked to us that the fish (just below the waterline) were lining-up waiting their turn to become sandwiches. With great enthusiasm we continued to haul in the little fighters one after the other. Recognizing that no one else was catching fish we realized we no longer needed to attract the fish with the simplicity of a worm. Into the water the line went with naked hook, but still the fish struck with determination. Two teenagers fishing several yards away from us asked, "Hey, mister what are you using for bait?' I answered by saying, "Faith." One young man replied, "I don't believe that!" My response was, "Okay, no fish for you." The other said, "I believe it!" I asked, "Do you want a fish?" He responded positively and so I instructed him to cast his line upon the water! I felt as confident as Jesus telling the apostles to cast out their nets. The confidence came from the fact that Jesus was there with us.

There are times in our lives when we know we are in the presence of God, and this was one of those wonderful moments. The young man was catching fish as quickly as us. By this time the three of us were attracting a crowd, as we praised God for turning a summer day into excitement and joy. No one else caught a fish, and I wondered when the exuberance would end. After all, we only asked for one fish and now we were receiving the bounty of God's generosity. Shortly thereafter I realized the answer, as the party boat that had set out to fish earlier in the day approached the pier for the end of its expedition as well. Peter and I returned home as conquering heroes. As hunters of old fulfilling the hopes of awaiting dependents, we were marvelous to behold, as we carried our catch into the Brooklyn village called, "Bensonhurst."

Of course, my wife responded to our great catch by telling us to, "Get those fish out of here!" Obediently, Peter and I distributed the fish to our neighbors. We regaled them with our story and they received the fish, as if they were among the multitude fed by Jesus, so long ago. Twenty-eight years ago, and I still have the drop line, complete with plastic float and miracle hook. Yes, the memories of our lives and the impact others have contributed remain as anchors deeply embedded.

Rare Find

Diamonds pearls emeralds and jade
Can produce joyous sighs rippling with praise.
There's beauty and brilliance in nature's parade.
The rare find plays music sublime inside the seekers domain.
The music is passing through hands that are grasping.
In vanity's clutches truth is obstructed.

He who listens to a child
Hears the voice of the heart.

Rainfalls passing lightning flashing
Clouds hang knowing their reign.
Unknowing a man when his day began
He and his son would be seeking a fish.
Not only a fish was given
But a faith anchor was delivered.
It permits remembrance of the day
Jesus, and me and little Pete went to the bay to fish.

Unknowing is man a rare find at his feet.
Relenting to please the request of a child.
His wonderment has never ceased.
Prayer was added into the mix
Of baited hook plastic float and a bucket hope.
At once lined-up as if volunteers
Coming toward us in wave after wave
In awe at the thought of Our Lord
Taking the time to fish with the hearts of those
Asking in prayer, saying,
"Lord, we're no good at this."

John 21:5-6 He called out to them, "Friends haven't you any fish?" "No," they answered. He said, "Throw out your net on the right side of the boat and you will find some."

Matthew 13:56 "Are not his sisters with us? Where did this man get all of this? And they took offense at him. But Jesus said to them, "A prophet is not without honor except in his native place and in his own house." NAB

STUFF

Where does this stuff come from? I know about some of the stuff that inhabits my life, but most of it has the appearance of materializing on its own. Every once in a while it dawns on us that we have more stuff than we either need or want. We go to great lengths at times to get rid of it by giving it away, but even that is difficult. At other times of desperation we must resort to becoming creative; people aren't always eager to receive stuff. They ask, "Is the stuff any good?" and, "Why do you want to get rid of it?" Because we want to rid our lives of the clutter, people usually assume there must be a catch, something wrong, an underlying motive for generosity, but in all truth it is what we say, "We don't want it!" I always tell potential recipients of stuff the truth concerning quality and the need for freeing up some room for more stuff on the horizon. Now the stuff that we purchase usually has some staying power, after all, we bought the stuff for a reason. Didn't we? The other stuff that somehow came into our possession most often presents a challenge for disposal. I often think there is a conspiracy behind every smile. I sometimes think there's a darker reality that people are really trying to give me some stuff. I've learned a valuable lesson recently. If you want to give stuff away you have to work harder than it took to acquire it. Anyway, the stuff that we want to give away is almost impossible to give to those who know us. Even more difficult is to try and give the stuff to family. Strangers are more receptive to the stuff we want to give away than those who we love and care for most of all. This of course was the case with Jesus. He went throughout the towns and surrounding areas of his youth giving to people the truth of God, but when he was among his own townsfolk they rejected him and the gifts he brought. Yes, **"The prophet is not without honor except in his native place and in his own home."**

Honor

⌒⌒~⌒

"Step up and sit down this place is for you.
We heard about all you've done and believe it to be true.
There's a child with a spirit that corrupts his speech
And another with a skin disease that causes him such pain.
Please do us the honor of your presence in this place.
It's not much as you can see but all we have is yours.
The goodness that precedes your name has opened up our hearts.
We seek the love of God in this time of troubling stuff."

⌒~⌒⌒

Proverbs 11:8 "The just man escapes trouble, and the wicked man falls into it in his stead." *NAB*

Matthew 2:10-11 They were overjoyed at seeing the star, and on entering the house they saw the child with Mary his mother. They prostrated themselves and did him homage. Then they opened their treasures and offered him gifts of gold, frankincense and myrrh. NAB

STAR SEARCHERS

Dedicating one's life to searching the heavens or just searching for the unknown out of natural curiosity is a good thing. Today we have technical equipment that brings the heavens even closer to our vision and understanding as never before in the history of mankind. Certainly our view of the heavens is wonderful attractive and mysterious. It is the nature of mankind to attempt to understand through discovery the conditions surrounding our lives. Some answers to ancient questions have already been given to man. The origin of mankind as being created by God and our purpose for being has been clearly annunciated to us by Christ. There are many who cannot or will not accept such truth, while others are still waiting for a personal star to follow in order to believe. These live there lives searching for answers among the heavens, in pursuit of what may be too sublime for them. While all the time truth is knocking upon the very atmosphere they breathe. They are seeking a great and mysteriously logical explanation to all that exists except the understanding of God. As such, they search the void of space, and in reward for their efforts they become a part of the void they so desperately wish to penetrate.

Seekers

❧

When our hearts are right what we seek will find us.
If we continually discount and denigrate truth
We'll erect a wall of disbelief made of illusion and grief.
We'll construct a battle plan that places man on top
And never will we understand that God made us all.
The heavens above us like lights that guide our way
Speak to each and everyone,
"This is the day the Lord has made."

❧

Psalm 96:5 "The gods of all other nations are only idols, but the Lord created the heavens." *GNB*

Ezekiel 34:26 "I will bless them and let them live on my sacred hill. There I will bless them with showers of rain when they need it."

BURDENS BATTLES AND BLESSINGS

Some people refuse to see the forest even when a tree falls on them. I sometimes meet people who, it seems their only purpose in life is to complain. No matter what their condition they are constantly seeking a blessing. It doesn't matter to them, they have no idea what form such blessing may take. They just want a blessing. Hearing them might lead one to think they are the most deprived of God's children. Forgotten and left to their own devices. As a child there was an expression for this type of person. It was said of them, "They act like they are starving while it is clearly seen they have a loaf of bread under each arm." They must have attended the same school as the, "Little boy who cried wolf." Sooner or later there must come an awakening and in this conscious state of being find the truth of their lives. One would think by listening to them there is the constant sounding of war drums and the sounds of battle never find an end of day. Unfortunately, this life they live is so occupied by the perceptions of present burdens and battles they rarely find time to recognize the blessings of life. It goes without saying, many of us would not be here today were not for the injection of truth in our lives. Truth is found to be the one and only blessing that guarantees to us victory over all of those antagonisms we call battles and burdens. As Ezekiel says, ***"There I will bless them with showers of rain when they need it."*** The operative word is, "need." Many people fail to see their blessings because they fail to unwrap the presents God has given. Often the burdens of past life experiences clutter up the present and we lose track of the blessings that have been mounting up all over the house. Some of the battles fought today are the very same ones replayed in the mind and hearts of those set free to bear witness to the abundance of God's generosity. By doing so, what happens in many cases, is failure to see the actual misery of others as they are engaged in the life and death struggles present in the world of today. Someone once said, "Count your blessings! You just might be pleasantly surprised."

The King

All voices praise the Lord
Earth to groan and spirit moan
In worshipping the King
Dawn to dark upon the wings of thought
All voices to him sing.
Heaven's gate passing flight angels kneel adore
To Majesty enthroned above, "Holy is the Lord."
Multitudes beyond number shout, "Praise and honor to the King!"
Like thunder from one mouth.
Billowing smoke from censors stoked, the altar of our God.
The Lamb will stand and bring an end to evil's reign.
Silence then, sweet silence, as all can see the King.
Adorned in purple vestments and blessings that he brings.

Genesis 12:3 I will bless those who bless you, but I will curse those who curse you.

Matthew 10:28 "Do not be afraid of those who can kill the body but cannot kill the soul. Rather, be afraid of the one who can destroy both body and soul in hell."

FEAR

I used to love those old science fiction movies from the nineteen-fifties. There was as mixture of suspense, fear and the overall ability to know none of it was true. "Godzilla" never ate Japan and the, "Invasion of the body snatchers" while scary to a kid was never a reality that sparked a truism of fear. Yes, fear can be entertaining when it is we who control it. When it is we who are in control. In fact fear is one of those benefits that within the context of self-preservation affords to us the ability to avoid trouble.

Scripture tells us when we fear God it is the beginning of wisdom. This recognition of God as one to not be set aside and discounted does for us what ordinary fear cannot. Ordinary fear while it is a sort of alert system does not within itself have the means to necessarily negate, that which is threatening us. We find only two options available to us "flight or fight." With fear for God a man finds the means to overcome the fears of this life. ***"If God is for us who can be against us?"*** This statement concerning God being on our side relieves us of the common concerns and permits us to live as sheep protected by the Good Shepherd. I'm not trying to minimize the reality of things that can and do harm us, only that once we realize there is more to life than just the here and now of this existence we are then able to live within the abundance (this to include the totality of life and not just the substances needed for the continuation of the body) that was in-part the purpose of Christ. False security (which is really an illusion) exists for many today in the form of financial wealth or extra heavy doors. None of which is lasting and cannot prevent the inevitable movement toward the next phase of existence. False security is false religion and it exists only because we give to it credibility beyond what it deserves. False beliefs serve only to pacify or to lessen our fears, never are they looked upon as a means through which fear is placed on the sidelines of our former way of life, that was absent the knowledge of God and his concern for our protection against all valid fears.

Shining ray

Hard knock
Hard place
Hard luck
Hard case
Makes us want to flee this place.
Shining ray descends with grace.
Hope is special it's a gift of God in man
A river never ending until we see his plan.
Wide as the universe or tiny as a spark
It confirms the truth of him by bringing home what's lost.
It pierces darkest night and calls to God Almighty to make all things right.
It's the cradle where faith in him is borne, strength within clay vessels
Where emptiness was thought.
It's a constant where defeat in man abounds
Until what was thought forever lost is forever found.

Colossians 1:27 To them God chose to make known to the gentiles the glorious riches of this mystery, which is Christ in you, the hope of glory.

Luke 22:31 "Simon, Simon, Listen! Satan has received permission to test all of you, to separate the good from the bad, as a farmer separates wheat from chaff. But I have prayed for you Simon that your faith will not fail. GNB

ANOTHER LEVEL OF REALITY

He had dreams before some even had colors. Most were the ordinary patch-quilt variety that vanished from memory with the first light of a new day. A few were deeply spiritual wherein the closeness of God left indelible faith upon his soul. Nightmares also had their time to visit and fade from consciousness. He even shared the common dreams of others that made aware the unrealized potential of his life. But it was the nightmares mostly that gave birth to the practice of, *"Now I lay me down to sleep."* It was the part about the Lord keeping his soul that gave him the most comfort, and in this comfort he had rested free from bad dreams for many years. This man had felt secure in the protection of God, his purpose in life, and the attitude he carried in his Christian walk, until he was shocked from the complacency that attempts to deny the reality of war.

He had long ago realized the constant change within himself as each part of the whole struggled to dominate the others. Constantly shifting in thought from the carnal, natural and spiritual man. It is the biblical truth embedded in him that for the most part kept an even-keel to his ship of life; denying by God's grace the negative aspects of human desire set upon capsizing and bringing down to the depths the victory won by Christ. He knew that faith in the mercy of God provided fuel to keep movement of his ship toward the goal of eternal life in Christ. This night, his ritual complete, *"I pray the Lord my soul to keep,"* he assumed the position upon his bed that never failed to close the curtains of reality and give free reign to the subconscious state of sleep.

Through the darkness, came the gentle call of his name, saying, *"Wake up."* The words spoken brought awareness and he entered a dream within a dream, revealing a deeper reality of the condition of life. Physical as well as thought were immobilized upon his bed. All of his senses were focused as fear alerted him to the presence of evil. Looking out from the confines of his bed, into darkness that no longer was the security of his home his fears mounted. He felt the weight of evil as it laid its head upon the foot of his bed. Panic arrived as a hissing mass touched his body. The stench of its breath eroded the knowledge of dream into the harsh world of another reality. It is this detachment of anchor that caused the panic to swell into scream proportions. He had no time for fancy prayers, nor could he remember any! Only one word was formed in his state of fear, "Jesus! Jesus! Jesus!" Over and over in his immobile state he assaulted the evil with thought. Into the vacuum of another reality the holy name resonated from his heart! Movement came back to his thoughts, as his body lay frozen from the natural effects of sleep. He gazed upon his sleeping body as he left the bed and entered a room that was not his own and followed the evil toward the exit from this place. As he looked into the darkness he saw nothing but heard the voice of multitudes without number. It is into this body of complexity that the evil had entered, like a malignancy undetected and protected by the sound of man's own voice. Upon awakening into conscious awareness it was impossible for him to differentiate between wakeful reality and the deeper level, both had assumed the level of truth.

Most dreams are discounted and placed into indecipherable fragments that fade into the fog of memory. However, the entrance into such a level of deep awareness brought understanding to the length evil will go in order to torment and corrupt was made fixed within his mind. He knew now the meaning of an evil force loose upon the earth seeking to destroy, and in this knowledge his vigilance was increased. He has always been able to see evil in the world through the actions of mankind but this was apart from man. The reality of God had for a long time been not only accepted as truth but was imbedded within him. He had not given much recognition to the Evil One. His thoughts in this area were acceptance but then quickly moved on from there. Just as life becomes repetitive and we seem to operate on automatic so it is with faith. We find faith in us and we believe it to be secure and able to keep us safe from such intrusions of in your face evil. All of this is true but there may come a time for us to confront the reality of not only our purpose in life but the unceasing war taking place all around us. When the enemy walks into our home and boldly awakens all of our senses with the reality of his power, it is then we fully understand our need for reliance upon God. The complacency of our lives quickly dissipates and we are placed once again upon a wartime footing. When we least expect it we may be tested, sifted like wheat as a farmer seeks to eliminate the chaff. So it is with the Evil One who desires to find the bad in us and with it the hammer of condemnation. To be placed into the sieve of evil's judgment, what will be found is perhaps not so much good. In this small amount of good, if any at all, the accusing finger of condemnation will seek to pronounce to us our failures. Such condemnation can leave us as a deer in the headlight of an oncoming vehicle, paralyzed and unable to run to the safety of the trees. If we keep our faith close to our heart and mind we will always be mindful of the tree of life that clothes us with the righteousness of Christ. It is the vision of this tree embraced by Christ that gives to us the ability to cry out in the night, Jesus! Jesus! Jesus! At the sound of his holy name all evil must depart from us and no longer can it find entrance into the restfulness of sleep. You see it becomes evident to us that we are no different from the biblical figure called, *"Job,"* he was tested and suffered greatly for his close relationship with God. So it is we also may be tested in a most direct manner. We may want to ask why God would give his permission for us to be tested and examined through the eyes of evil? Well, apart from the enhanced awareness that it will bring to us we must understand that God has the knowledge we need to be awakened from the complacency of a peaceful mindset. The closer we come to God the greater we are placed into the forefront of the battle. Jesus is unlike other generals he leads from the front. *HE LEADS IN THE HEART OF BATTLE WHERE THE FIGHTING IS MOST INTENSE. IT IS THEN WE ARE MADE CRITICALLY AWARE OF OUR SURROUNDINGS—THE ENEMY IS CLOSE ENOUGH FOR US TO SEE CLEARLY.* Corruption not only has a look of death but it smells uniquely identifiable to all it comes into contact with. Attempting to mask the odor is impossible. Adding an air freshener will not erase its foul presence; it will only heighten the degree of nausea invoked. We then are moved to bury the source with the fresh air of truth

279

Wake up

We can get so distracted by the land of the living
The going about of everyday life
We sometimes forget our purpose
In the repetition that seems to never die.
Rise up with the sun eat breakfast and run
Perform some meaningful task for those who employ
Go home and rest until the new day arrives.
Something is happening beyond my vision to see
Within the time allotted we often call, "free."
A sifting or testing is ongoing for us
Because we've placed all trust in God.
The reality of life is not put on hold
When the blankets are pulled up over the cold.
When the day has come to an end
And sleep is wrapped around the edges of the bed.
It's then we are made deeper aware
Concerning the darkness seeking to snare
Seeking to capture and poison the soul
Immobile it makes within the abode.
We can smell the stench a slithering makes
The vile intent of the hunting of snakes
Into the place we thought was most safe
In mind and the heart in the home our God made.

A fighting of will to call out for help
Forcing the thing out into the night
Where others are not given a clue
This monster of hate wants them too.
Wake up!
Don't be found dreaming in daylight or night
Keep your sword at the ready the truth that is Christ.
Tucked under the pillow and deep in your head
Just in case another reality enters your bed.
You too, can shout out for help.

"I'll never leave you," are the words he spoke.
Strength for the body the mind and the soul!

Luke 21:24 Be careful not to let yourselves become occupied with too much feasting and drinking and with the worries of this life, or that day may suddenly catch you like a trap.

Hebrews 13:1-2 Keep on loving one another as Christian brothers. Remember to welcome strangers in your homes. There were some who did and welcomed angels without knowing it.

THE VISITOR

The seventies saw a blizzard in Brooklyn New York. Of course the rest of the east coast had also experienced it as well. I was working the midnight watch at Long Island College Hospital as a stationary fireman. During the course of my duties that included checking the outside buildings for proper environmental norms (especially heating) on this snow filled night, I had occasion to pass by the emergency room waiting area. There was only one person in the waiting area (the snow outside precluded mostly everyone from attempting to get medical care) and he definitely looked as if he was in great need. His appearance was one that brought to mind many questions. How did he get here and when? How could he have survived outside in this cold? He obviously did not drive or was driven here, in fact nothing was moving out in the street, the snow was that deep.

He wore an old short sleeve shirt that must have been a prize possession of someone from Hawaii and his pants were held in place by cord instead of a belt. His shoes were loafers that surrounded feet having no socks. His head was bald and his facial features cried out with pain without making a sound. At that moment of my assessment the security guard was about to remove him from the premises. It was his duty to do so, since the man had not indicated a need for medical attention and the hospital policy did not allow for vagrants. As he was leading the man to the door and out into the freshly fallen waist deep snow I said to my friend, "There is a place on this earth for all of God's children." Having said this, I asked him to not send this man into the cold. It was at this time that the man fell to his knees

282

and grabbed my leg in thanks. He said to me, "God bless you." I was shocked more than anything and asked the man to get up. I told him I was the least of God's children and helped him to his feet.

After sitting him back down in the waiting area I told him that at five o'clock the restaurant across the street from the hospital would be open and we could then get a breakfast special. The special consisted of egg on a roll and a container of coffee, all for a dollar. He wanted my new hat. He expressed to me that he was a Jew and did not have a hat for his head. I thought to myself that is not all you are lacking. Unfortunately for the man it was a new hat and he had no chance of getting it. However, I told him that I had a hat and other clothing for him in my locker in the boiler room, and I would give them to him after my duties were complete at breakfast time. I inquired as to why he was so poorly dressed in such weather? His reply was that he had gone to a synagogue but was not given anything. Thinking this to be strange, I continued with my rounds.

At five o'clock I went back to the man and we went into the restaurant where Nick, the owner, was just getting the grill hot. The man and I were the only customers in the restaurant at that time. I ordered two specials and told the man to wait for a few minutes because I had to go back to the boiler room to get his hat and clothing.

Upon my return the man was gone. I asked Nick, "Nick, where is the old man I came in with?" His reply to me was, "Pete, you didn't come in with anyone." I said, "Yes I did I ordered two specials and said I would be right back." Again Nick said, "Pete you ordered one special and here it is." As I left the restaurant I looked up and down the street filled with waste high snow, and all that I could see was my footprints alone.

Talk about being baffled, I went back to the hospital waiting area looking for my friend the security guard. I told him I lost the old man that was allowed to stay inside from the cold. His reply to me was mystifying. He said to me, "Pete, I thought you were going to breakfast with him, how could you lose him?" "You don't understand," I replied, "The man just disappeared and Nick said I went into his place alone." "He probably didn't see him" was his logical explanation. I then realized something was missing besides the old man, the explanation of it all. I felt sadness over the fact I had not given my hat to him when he asked for it. I don't understand what happened that night, but what remains with me is this: Sometimes we only get one chance to do the right thing. I should have given that man the hat for the obvious reason, but also because my wife disliked it. Yes, sometimes we only get one chance.

Soul Man

⌒⌒⌒

Talk about a mysterious stranger
This man was a complete puzzle.
No one saw him come or go and it seems
Not everyone saw him at all.
The weather didn't keep him down
But he did look so badly frowned.
I suppose being dressed for summer in a blizzard
Can cause anyone to lose heart
But where did he come from and to where did he depart?
What was his purpose seeking shelter in the waiting room?
Why did he leave himself open to the storm?
Why didn't he go back to the room or wait for my return
With clothing to keep him warm?

He may have been seeking to learn truth in the hearts of men
On such a windswept night
Where even the homeless find a bed.
I guess I'll never know but always can surmise
From the evidence presented by that old man, God bless his soul
Opened up my eyes to a mystery,
God may have authorized.

⌒⌒⌒

1 Corinthians 4:1-2 Thus should one regard us: as servants of Christ and stewards of the mysteries of God. Now it is of course required of stewards that they be found trustworthy. *NAB*

Hebrews 13:1-2 Keep on loving one another as Christian brothers. Remember to welcome strangers in your homes. There were some who did that and welcomed angels without knowing it.

Book 2

SPIRITUAL PEARLS

For

NATURAL OYSTERS

Crossroads

The straight road is easy to follow
Sun by day and lamp by night
There's nothing to balance upon the scales of life.

A troubled man seeks a way out
Up and down east and west
The crossroads beckon saying, "This way is best."

All is but testing for footfalls solid
Listening to off roads inviting a rest
Wandering the back roads away from the path
Snowfalls that follow erase all our steps.

A wayward point alone isolation
Captures visions presented in time
Entraps the journey as dead end signs
Slows the rhythm underbrush grabbing
Crossroads deny that life can mean sadness.

Life is hard.
A painted sun gives not warmth.
We know there is sweet and sour courage and fear
Right and wrong laughter and tears
Weak and strong hatred and love
On the crossroads of life the lessons are tough.

For those who have left the surety of narrow
The crossroad speaks, "It's better tomorrow."
The straight path is the shortest of lines
No intersections or impossible climbs
Decisions come with sunshine or rain
But many a storm is for man's gain.

Proverbs 12:28 In the way of the righteous there is life; along that path is immortality.

Tomorrow

Tomorrow is a myth
It neither lives or dies
A circle spinning
A carrot on a line
A cart without a horse
A race without a prize
Game without beginning
A line without end
We live this life God gives
As if tomorrow is a friend.

A distant voice calling across the ocean time
Her tone is pleasant timbre but deep within lives lies
A play without actors
A view that captures
Night turns into day and daytime has its curtain
We live this life God gives as if tomorrow is for certain.

Tomorrow is forever as infinite as thought
It can't be encapsulated traded sold or bought
Cannot be touched or faded but in a breath is gone
We stand upon the present looking forward and/or back
Tomorrow is the moment without evidence of tracks.

Luke 12:16-21 And he told them this parable: "The ground of a certain rich man produced a good crop. He thought to himself, "What shall I do? I have no place to store my crops." Then he said, "This is what I'll do. I will tear down my barns and build bigger ones, and there I will store all my grain and my goods. And I'll say to myself, "You have plenty of good things laid up for years. Take life easy; eat, drink and be merry." But God said to him, "You fool! This very night your life will be demanded from you. Then who will get what you have prepared for yourself? This is how it will be with anyone who stores up things for himself but is not rich toward God."

Mirror

It's necessary to be jostled and bumped
Scraped and confused
Beaten battered broken and bruised.
Weakness and pain strengthens a man.
It brings understanding where imperfect can't live.
What would we know of trouble and pains?
Secured in the Garden no cares or complaints.
A world of disappointment often means hurt.
It's a good thing to be found wanting
Imperfections are identified it keeps the rebuild ongoing.
Who can understand perfection or life?
We learn with one foot in front of the other
Viewpoints change.
"Mom, you are walking too fast"
And then,
"Son, wait for your mother."
Perfection is a word we can only begin to emulate.
A child wearing daddy's clothes finds delight in a mirror.
He and daddy appear the same
Acting like him makes appearance improve.

1 Corinthians 13:11-12 "When I was a child, I talked like a child, I reasoned like a child. When I became a man I put childish ways behind me. Now we see but a poor reflection; then we shall see face to face. Now I know in part, then shall I know fully, even as I am fully known."

Matthew 5:48 "So be perfect just as your heavenly Father is perfect."

Reputation

⌒⌒⌒

It seems everyone wants recognition upon the world stage.
Normal behavior or weird
The aim is the same, notoriety and fame.
No one thinks of reputation until is has been shredded
And once it has been ruined how can we go back and get it?
Celebrity and stardom often asks a hefty price,
"Do what I ask and I'll put your name up in lights."
Symbolic power in blackened limousines
Stakes a claim, "role model" to emulate achieve.
In the glitter of existence the heart finds no reprieve from the
Prideful stings and blisters the put-on passion of the weeds.
The glory of God is his excellent reputation.
Why then is he not the role model for all generations?

⌒⌒⌒

**Ephesians 4:17-18 So I tell you this, and insist on it in the Lord,
that you must no longer live as the Gentiles do, in the futility of
their thinking, They are darkened in their understanding and
separated from God because of the ignorance that is in them due
to the hardening of their hearts.**

Not By Sight

It can move mountains uproot trees
Call upon strength and bend a knee.
It affirms life uplifts what's down
Whispers gently to hope as an only child.
It sets the foundation solid the ground
Withstanding the wind of future and now.

The sun announces a way to be found
Through mountains and valleys deserts and maze
We step ahead one foot in front of the other
On the pathway of light blessed by truth
With eyes on the prize eternal as space
Forward we walk in protection of grace.

2 Corinthians 5:7 "We live by faith not by sight."

Brownstones

High stoops resembling box seats in theaters
Call out as pyramids to majesty that was.
Kerosene heaters threw heat like the major leagues.
Deliverymen carried heat upstairs.
Lath walls had the strength of a fortified city.
Fire escapes had dual purpose—both gave relief from the heat.
The top of the high stoop steps was the platform to view activity below.
Kids waiting the year they would be allowed to play stickball in the street.
Some hits soared high over majestic manhole covers that rivaled the
artistry
And craftsmanship of ancient sword makers
Dependable and unnoticed by tail finned motorists.
Skylights led to the roof, vertical ladders, auxiliary clotheslines, stargazing
and hope.
Clotheslines connected neighbors and all of the telephones were in booths.
If it got too cold dungarees froze.
Mom attempted to iron the damp out of the pants.
As we looked on asking in our underwear, "Is it dry yet?"
Everyone cuffed jeans in neat folds above high top sneakers.
Dungaree jackets became billboards for neighborhood artists
After many wash cycles the dungaree blue began to fade.
Socks and shorts were washed with brown soap and washboard.
Eyebolts were the anchors connecting brownstone and backyard poles.
Clothespins and rope replaced by machines
No matter the direction of tumble it could not rival hang drying
That smelled clean and untroubled.
Brown soap, brownstones, hardwood floors and hard hope, meant work
harder.
"The fruit wagon! Go downstairs get two tomatoes, and a head of lettuce
Here's a quarter, bring back the change."
Some brownstones were heated with a coal-fired furnace
Someone had to rake and dump the ashes.
Coal was delivered through guillotine doors on slides into basements
yawning.

Gray cinders reincarnated to battle snow as it mocked rear wheel drive vehicles.
Brownstones had a banister like Steeplechase Park, a fireman's pole with a different arc.
It produced a laugh that ran through the house, a covenant between tradesman and child.
I'm sure they were also built in Manhattan Bronx and Queens
But Brooklyn was the borough of, "Kings" thus brownstones ruled.
Only the ferry went to Staten Island, it cost a nickel to get lost in paradise.
It has been said, "Every gain has its price."
Brownstones were not built on Staten Island.

John 14:1-2 "Do not be worried or upset," Jesus told them. "Believe in God and believe also in me. There are many rooms in my Father's house, and I am going to prepare a place for you."

Nightmare

I dreamt I was rich.
They toppled the system.
I slept in a room full of cash.
It was locked from the outside.

I won a huge lottery and had a mansion built.
A great wall was built to surround it.
Outside of the wall a moat was dug.
The finest of electronic surveillance
Was installed within the wall.
The firemen waved.

The trunk of my car was filled with gold bars.
It was repossessed.
I found a brown paper bag filled with bearer bonds.
In a cold articulate voice I heard, "This is a stickup."

While diving I spied a treasure chest.
Hundreds of sharks suddenly appeared.
Lastly I found myself poor.
The telephone rang only to remind me.
I had so many bills I kidnapped my mailbox.
This I knew all too well.
Sleep at last, thank God.

Matthew 6:19-21 Do no store up for yourselves treasures on earth, where moth and rust destroy, and where thieves break in and steal. But store up for yourselves treasures in heaven, where moth and rust do not destroy, and where thieves do not break in and steal. For where your treasure is, there your heart will be also.

Peace and Pain

From the beginning the start of man's days
Innocent thoughts and innocent ways
Capture a leaf as it sails on the breeze
Sleep in the shade or bathe on the beach
Speak with a lion or swim in the deep
All this and more was given to man
From the beginning as strength in a friend
Grace and peace was always the plan.

Descent into bondage distrusting grew
We looked upon others with cynical stares
We carried the burden of failure to listen
We stumbled in darkness without healing rays
From the slip and the fall came the wrong and the pain.

Genesis 2:15-17 Then the Lord God placed the man in the Garden of Eden to cultivate it and to guard it. "You may eat the fruit of any tree in the Garden, except the tree that gives knowledge of what is good and what is bad. You must not eat the fruit of that tree; if you do, you will die the same day.

Calling

⌒⌒⌒

To be called to serve requires God's strength.
Such strength is derived from the knowledge of truth love and majesty.
It's knowledge given to see hurt hunger and poverty.
It's the vision that comes with forgiveness.
It's really a call to live in the kingdom.
It's an offspring maker
And a birthright stamp
It's a kiss for common man.
It's a blessing and kind of frightening.
You see such a call comes from God alone
Transforming flesh and bone into kingdom priest and home.

⌒⌒⌒

Acts 9:4-6 He fell to the ground and heard a voice say to him.
"Saul, Saul, why do you persecute me?" "Who are you, Lord?" "I
am Jesus whom you are persecuting," he replied. "Now get up and
go into the city, and you will be told what you must do."

The Johnny Pump

Turn the diamond shaped wrench
With the water's rush cheers of joy and relief from the heat.
A stream of cool, delivered through an old Coke can.
We didn't need sprinkler caps back then.

Rivers were formed in the gutter
Popsicle sticks rode the waves
Some kids built diverting dams
And all breathed relief as the river cooled feet.
Water projected two stories high
A hypnotic dance under bright sunny skies
Carrying the promise to all that was dry.

"Wait, don't wet me!"
Came a sometimes plea
From a passerby attempting to flee.
Laden with brown shopping bags
Pleading mercy to the one controlling the can.

Old milk cartons spread the word
Delivered with purpose to those who observed.
Nothing was truly safe from the game
Not jeans, shoes or bebop hats
Not hairdo dogs or lips that flapped
All were bathed in the cool misty spray
When the pump we called "Johnny" came out to play.

We called the fire hydrant, "Johnny"
It wasn't a pump at all.
We were just kids in the heat underneath a waterfall.
Bare feet sometimes slipped and sneakers sloshed
Dogs barked and peopled warned, "You better not!"
Yes, that was a common song.
Opened windows were quickly closed

Cars slowed seeking a free wash
Kids wore bathing suits in the street
Shouting with dancing feet.
To the sound of the water's beat they screamed!
In the heat of the day on blacktop beach
On the south side of Brooklyn with friendships so sweet!

Proverbs 18:24 "Some friendships do not last, but some friends are more loyal than brothers."

Mind Dancing

While you were gone I played in my head
I danced all around until the right words were said.
Truth interjected a backhand return
Denouncing deception concealment and wrong.
I dithered and bickered back stepped and crawled
Within the darkness with back to the wall
A side-swing solid and strong
Caused me to stare at all that was wrong.
Frozen and captured unable to move
Truth hit the heart with positive proof.
I knew it was useless to continue this way
With sun shining brightly on all of my ways.

**Acts 17:30 In the past God overlooked such ignorance, but now he
commands all people everywhere to repent.**

Resolve

In my eyes you may see he who blessed this life
With children's smiles that grace the heart
Sparkling with love and trust.
With older folks that watch and pray
With knowing brows and caring ways.
Colorful rainbows shooting stars
Chirping birds in praise of God
Let all in nature see his ways
As a book on every page
Speaking truth of God and grace.

Matthew 5:13-15 You are the salt of the earth. But if the salt loses its saltiness, how can it be made salty again? It is no longer good for anything, except to be thrown out and trampled by men. You are the light of the world. A city on a hill cannot be hidden. Neither do people light a lamp and put it under a bowl. Instead they put it on its stand, and it gives light to everyone in the house. In the same way, let your light shine for men, that they may see your good deeds and praise your Father in heaven.

Green

⌒⌒⌒

It's the color of hope.
It's the sight of renewal throughout creation
Confirming truth and love embracing.
It's rain that falls intently
A soothing breeze in early morn
It's shelter from uncaring storms.
A kiss assuring hearts to dream forests of abundant green.

From heaven's throne he came to earth secured in wisdom's tome.
Concerned for the lost thirsting for water at the root.
In hardened clay and detoured dreams
On dusty roads that take us to nowhere
We cry to God
When here below all else fails our means
It's then we know
It's love that keeps life green.

Evergreens in splendor display mercy throughout winter.
Others decrease in green with sighs.
Captured by the cares of life
Without love it withers and dies.

⌒⌒⌒

Luke 23:31 "For if they do these things when the tree is green,
what will happen when it is dry?"

Progress

We learn to walk before we run
We emulate sounds before we speak
We gain understanding before we teach
We find peace with God before we preach
We know defeat before victory's song
We walk in the dark before light is shone.

A foundation is laid at the outset of building
Materials are chosen designed to conform
A blueprint presented weather's a storm
Honest designs will always prove true
Will always produce a much better you!

Proverbs 16:22 Understanding is a fountain of life to those who have it.

Priority

Pay for the car or wear out the feet, buy medicine or eat.
Send a man to the moon plumb the depths of the sea.
Build stadiums for sport or pulpits to preach.
Both have microphones and an audience to reach.
Capture the sparrow and study its walk.
Clothe the naked with burial cloth.
Feed the hungry a musical dirge.
Send a limo for the final lap
Then cover the loss with dirt.
Celebrity shakedown champion's a cause
All is as smoke that billows and chokes
Caught in the wind of bluster and chatter
Churning a fly in with the batter.
Struggles in life are denied attention
As ears plugged with cotton and glasses tinted.
Efforts to solve the ills of the day
Are but footnotes in priority's way.
Give to the poor and still they're forgotten.
Angels of mercy dispense crumbs.
Research grants for ridiculous things
Are not aware of chemotherapy's stings.
Who can deny the hunger of a child?
It's easier when the crying is at night
When the world is asleep.
The sun is shining and the snoring is deep.
Research sounds like pickpocket it matters not the subject or topic.
Push the cash and examine a dream filled with a heartbreak and cavern
of screams.
Hooray for the children abortion is free.
Hooray for the children.
They gave their lives for a really grand plan.
Examine their cells for the good of man.
Hooray for the children.
They never had a chance against hypocrisy's dance.

Does priority end at the property line?
Build a fence and stand on top.
Where it leans jump!
Watch out for that stump
Another reminder of what was.

❧

Matthew 6:24 No one can serve two masters. Either he will hate the one and love the other, or he will be devoted to one and despise the other. You cannot serve both God and money.

Hard times

⌒⌒

Hard times are mostly made of an irritant called, "Trouble."
It comes to us unexpected and sometimes with notice.
We should ask ourselves, "Where does it come from?"
One place is from the heart.
A hardened heart invites it and all its friends.
All of nature suffers when a hard time shows up.
It's like the rippling of a lake when it feels a rock.

It's a fact of life
When self is center stage love grows cold.
The fireplace absent fire
Permits anything approach.
If only man would understand
Pushing to the edge invites a need to fly.
If only he would think before he leaps.
The hard times would lessen or say, "Goodbye."
There is confusion and deception planned sublime
Causing man to grasp for air and sky.

Hard times are like running in a race that never seems to end.
We know deep within our heart we have to find some rest.
Hard times are like a slow motion dream awaiting the end of the fall
Or like running away from a chasing call.
What does it all mean?
Wake up!
Without the truth of God your direction is pointing down.
And as we all know
It is a hard time when man hits ground.

⌒⌒⌒

1Timothy 4:1 The Spirit clearly says that in latter times some will abandon the faith and follow deceiving spirits and things taught by demons.

Eternity

Who can envision its end?
Who knows its height depth or enormous breath?
Who can get in front of it or run completely around?
Who can think fast enough outpacing it with leaps and bounds?
Who can make a dent in it to say a step was gained?
Who can find a place boasting captured ground?

When does
Eternity find its end
Forever find a limit
Bottomless a foot
A note finally fall
Forever show its face?

Within the plan of God
Movement heeds, "halt"
All things shall bend a knee
In the presence of the Lord!

**Acts 13:47-48 For this is what the Lord has commanded us:
"I have made you a light for the Gentiles, that you may bring
salvation to the ends of the earth. When the Gentiles heard this,
they were glad and honored the word of the Lord; and all who
were appointed to eternal life believed.**

Simon's thoughts

It's injustice!
He's barely recognizable.
I know this man he's not a criminal.
Where are my sons?
I pray they are not near the city.
Never have I seen such a crowd gather for death.
I'm stunned.

Crowds in the streets
Soldiers uncaring
Droplets of blood at my feet
Words thrown like daggers
Piercing and wounding
They cause him to stagger
Off to the left and off to the right
Leaning forward and back, ever forward
Headlong in flight
Cobblestones greet him
As a betrayer's kiss
Cold and deadpanned
As if saying,
"Greetings brother."

Matthew 27:32 As they were going out they met a man from Cyrene named Simon, and the soldiers forced him to carry Jesus' cross.

Penetrating Vision

⌒‿⌒

"Roses for lovers and lovers for roses," is what I heard the man say.
While advancing his words were enhancing the beauty in their display.
I never knew roses possessed of such color and fragrant bouquet.
The aroma inviting but warning:
"Be careful of what's hidden within."
I was unheeding so found myself bleeding
From a thorn penetrating my skin.
The pain that it brought went straight to my heart
With thoughts woven of thorns on his head
By love he was driven with no roses given to receive pain in my stead.
Yes,
"Roses for lovers and lovers for roses," is what the man said.

⌒‿‿⌒

Matthew 27:27-29 Then the governor's soldiers took Jesus into the Praetorium and gathered the whole company of soldiers around him. They stripped him and put a scarlet robe on him, and then wove a crown of thorns and put it on his head. They put a staff in his right hand and knelt in front of him and mocked him. "Hail, King of the Jews!" they said.

Absolute Vision

It's curious to hear a man say, "I can see."
The older I get the more my vision decreases.
What about insight?
Can a man see if he will not recognize a need for forgiveness?
Many times in life we make a mistake and ask of others, "Please forgive me."
There's a blindness of the mind that precludes understanding our need to admit to wrong.
We will not see God's justice, steady certain and sure.
Tempered and honed is man's position well within our comfort zone.
There is nothing to bother or upset as long as there's no wrong.
Drifting is man's position nothing is fixed except for death.
It is curious, there's an absolute he'll accept.
God, as absolute he will quickly reject.
Denying is man's vision until God's patience is spent.
Shouldn't we be able to see, it's to God we must repent?

2 Samuel 22:8 "The earth trembled and quaked, the foundations of the heavens shook; they trembled because he was angry."

Understanding

What do we really understand?
What can the intellect comprehend?
Within the physical much is put to bed.
Abstract finds its place in words that say, "I guess?"
All we think we know and all we hold as proof
Are but lines sent into space without understanding truth.

Laws caressing nature's breast
Bring limitation beyond our strength.
High wind overhead brings to trees a glance
Heights beyond their reach beyond their longest branch
Beyond the grasp of man learning proves his need
Proves his understanding is no different than a tree.
The wealth of understanding finds truth in humbleness.
Established roots find water where none was thought could flow
A man finds understanding allowing him to know
The root of wisdom's planning permitting trees to grow.
We know for certain
Deep within the soul
Deep as thought perceived
Deep and solid driven
The new life we received.
We know there is power in conviction
Joy in holiness
Truth in words of wisdom
Peace in freedom gained
Life in union given
Through the word of God proclaimed.

Reliance upon our own understanding
Denies there is darkness and denies the morning's light.
Understanding finds a fragrance that leads to life's intent
That brings to us the answers we could never get.
When all we thought as surety finds removal of the veil

Our thoughts are then exposed as illusion's darkened pall
It's then we comprehend the meaning of what's real
Understanding forged with wisdom gives truth its constant zeal.

❧

Proverbs 3:5 "Trust in the Lord with all your heart. Never rely on what you think you know. Remember the Lord in everything you do, and he will show you the right way. Never let yourself think that you are wiser than you are simply obey the Lord and refuse to do wrong."

Bells

❧

Bells announce trouble joy and life
A special octave in the ear
Movement back and forth its beat
"Attention!" They make clear.

O God,
Let them ring salvation's song to those who slumber deep.
Into the heart that hurts let them gently speak.
For those whose hope has faded let them make a trusting sound.
Let them pierce the deafened soul as arrow pierces dark.
And when they make a mournful moan their echoes ring with hope.
As an earthquake tremor leaves no avenue of doubt
Triumphantly into the dark bring light where none was found.
Let their ring of truth remain present throughout time.
Let them pierce the silence that brings emptiness of days.
And let them ring out loud the joy of thanks and praise.
Louder still their ring as heralding profound
Their truth extending outward as ripples on a pond.

O man,
With just a tiny cry God heals a broken heart.
No need for ringing bells to race among the stars.
With just an outreach thought renewal of the lost.
With just a thought his way a pathway then is found.
With ringing of a bell the head is lifted high
Up into the heavens with recognition's rhyme.
It's then their voices find echoes of renown
It's then their chime declares the lost has now been found.

O bells,
Of trouble joy and life sound with battle's might
Speak, "be gone" to valleys steeped in shadowed forms.
Speak with pleasant timbre erasing downward frowns.

With unerring splendor to the world announce,
"The Son of God has come and with him is your crown."

1 Peter 5:4 And when the Chief Shepherd appears, you will
receive the crown of glory that will never fade away.

Arrogance

Unwillingness to yield to truth suggests
A fool dressed in ignorance defiance at large.
Passing through testing temperament
With violence as a guide
Will find the well of arrogance is really dry.
Wisdom's scalpel cuts to view inside.
God pruning his garden and discarding what he will.
He keeps the wheat and weeds are fed to flames
Eternal is the fire that never kneels or wanes
The grave is found unyielding where many lost their name.

Matthew 23:31-33 So you testify that you are the descendants of those who murdered the prophets. Fill up, then, the measure of the sin of your forefathers! You snakes! You brood of vipers! How will you escape being condemned to hell?

Full circle

O green fields
Great ears rising
Ever pleasing and seeking
In silenced crowned.

Gathered processed stored and shipped
Consumed by hunger found.

Returned again from whence it came
Earth
Dust
Ground.

Ecclesiastes 12:7 "And the dust returns to the ground it came from and the spirit returns to God who gave it.

Blacker

Black the widow's cloth like sack of old
Declaring undying love to a starving world.
Black the hole in space theory's thought accepted
Black again the place where love is found rejected.

Black the ancient plague, sin from its first day
Drumbeats of clarity a mounting mournful dirge
Souls in darkness held as roll call rings her bell
Sounding for the multitudes of residential hell.

Black the unheard cry that fails to reach a friend.
Black the beggar's bowl left wanting in its day.
Black the heart and soul leading man astray.

Black the high-hat novelty
A show for commonality below the stratosphere
Begins to know what's needed when air becomes so rare.

A web of woven strands, knit one, purl two, camouflaged as truth
Denies the find of guilty as shadows sometimes hide
Beneath a sword hung overhead, saying,
"Sever yourself from pride."

A hole piercing hull points direction to abyss
Into black unending where none are ever missed.
Black the sailor's sea and black the eye of war
Black the robes authority in rooms of hearing worn
Deaf to truth pronounced in God's clarifying voice
A failure of the heart is revealed as cause.

Black the core of man construct of willful wrong
Black as pitch the night when starlight's beam should fail
Fleeing as if thieves revealed behind a veil
Far off suns and meteors, stars of shooting fame

Comet tails of ancient lore, with or without names
Shall find as did the "rich man" reduced to deal with flames
Finds within the darkness the props in movie scenes
All are just illusions of counterfeiting dreams.

Hurtful moving steps diminished until ceased
Hide inside the darkness as a lamp whose fuel is spent
Find a blackened spiral, no beginning and/or end.
Black the day shall come with herald's trumpet strong
Black the day unveiling righteousness to song
Black the pall so cast in the field of poison's call
All who seek a warm embrace are moved by siren's call
Along the outer edges the slippery slope of wrong.

Black will come the day when caustic tears proceed
From the eyes of man whose vision seeks applause
From actions deemed creative overcoming truth with flaws
Held in headlights of attraction with a promise, "Satisfaction."
That's never heard, "Enough!"

Black the day shall come when mankind finds despair
Within his mournful cry that finally understands
The black that held us captive is gone when Christ appears!
Black has scoffed at sacrifice in ridicule of mercy's grace
Has looked the gift eternal life and laughed into its face.

Black is Judgment Day
For those whose hearts have looked away
Whose voices call to rocks and say, "Hide our souls away!"
A great divide is formed appeals cannot be made
There is no higher court or place to buy delay.

In the black of darkness held in webs of self-made weave
The tortured souls cry out as a victim in a trap
Finds no escape by any means, cannot attempt advance
Forlorn, alas forlorn the hope for them has passed
Beyond the time forgiveness

Beyond the time of reach
Into the time of nothingness
As black as God perceives!

⁓⌣⌣⁓

Revelation 6:12-15 And I saw the Lamb break open the sixth seal. There was a violent earthquake, and the sun became black, like coarse black cloth, and the moon turned completely red like blood. The stars fell down to the earth, like unripe figs falling from the tree when a strong wind shakes it. The sky disappeared like a scroll being rolled up, and every mountain and island was moved from its place.

Lukewarm

A focused flame is radiant specific
Like a laser of truthful intent
Burning away at darkness formed by ignorance.
When fire in a man grows cold
It signals an empty pit where once a fire roared.
It's filled with ash and worldly ways that will not heed a torch.
Denying waves of kindling sparks—even clustering of stars go dark
When denied as the handiwork of God.
Calmness in the place where the heat of truth belongs
Says, "How far is it before you notice the fall?
How much distance must be placed between a man and God
Before his need is fathomed, before his life is lost?"
Uncaring in the mind shouts, "There's no one home!"
Uncaring in the heart says, "Just leave me alone!"

Man enjoys comfort until his poverty's made known
Failing to buy a moment at the end of life's road.
Fails productive action acknowledgement of sin
He fails to see the line of truth in the breath he holds within.
He will deny the sun and moon and universe of stars
Until the ashes of his ways declares a total loss.
Hot or cold can find acceptance.
A life that's heated up from one that never was
Enters beginning without ending by the firewood of love.
Hot says, "Yes, I'm saved," hallelujah filled with praise!
Cold is a life that's chilled by the winter of his ways
"All for naught" is spoken in the view of what remains.

A tower built upon illusion's wealth fails to be concerned
Has self-satisfaction to blind the heart and soul and mind.
Has failed to understand a tower's just so high
It can't protect against the power of envy greed and lies!
Slowly the ember dies a crackle as a shout,
"Quickly the heat has left you, lukewarm within without.
Above the flames you flew and now are nowhere found."

Revelation 3: 14-19 To the angel of the church in Laodicea write: These are the words of the Amen, the faithful and true witness, the ruler of God's creation. I know your deeds that you are neither cold nor hot. I wish you were either one or the other! So, because you are lukewarm—neither hot nor cold—I am about to spit you out of my mouth. You say, "I am rich; I have acquired wealth and do not need a thing." But you do not realize that you are wretched, pitiful, blind and naked. I counsel you to buy from me gold refined in the fire, so you can become rich; and white robes to wear so you can cover your shameful nakedness; and salve to put on your eyes, so you can see. Those whom I love I rebuke and discipline.

Renew

❦

Renew the moment of your grace that brought me to my knees.
Renew the childlike faith of when I first believed.
Joy was in my heart like finding a lost friend.
See how far I've fallen, how I've failed to grow
See how weak and feeble I stand before you, Lord.
Draw close to me.
Although I seek my faith is weak
Like fire that's grown cold.
As coal turns gray around its edge
And is forgotten at its core
Somewhere I lost my way
Somewhere I lost my cross.
In the knowledge of my loss
My voice cries out in pain
"I cannot live with halfway home
Or halfway in the grave!"
Send the fire lost into this waiting heart
Renew my faith with binding cord
Renew this man, O Lord.

❦

Ephesians 6:18 And pray in the Spirit on all occasions with all kinds of prayers and requests. With this in mind, be alert and always keep on praying for all the saints.

Missing Link

⌒⌒⌒

Sifting sorting and searching
To make the theory complete
Digging for gains in the remains
Of societies long gone and past
From the grave they do seek volumes to speak
Deserving of worldly applause and acclaim
Never stopping to think their missing link
Cannot be found in the grave.

⌒⌒⌒

Romans 1:20 For since the creation of the world God's invisible qualities—his eternal power and divine nature—have been clearly seen, being understood from what has been made, so that men have no excuse.

Memories

❦

Some memories speak gentle in the ear.
Others mock with laughter remembrances of fear
That kept us moving deeper into the night of gloom
Until God gave to us his mercy
And rolled away the stone
That held us weak and captive
With bindings self adorned.

❦

Isaiah 9:1 "The people who walked in darkness have seen a great light; upon those who dwelt in the land gloom a light has shone." NAB

Dependence

We can't walk on water because we can't walk alone.
What we permit defines us and what we ignore blinds us.
Truth gives us wings and wrong denies the King.

The illusion of independence
Puts all in arm's reach
Printed in self-help books
Dangled in our face
Like fishing lures and baited hooks
Presented by the learned as all we need to pass
Alas, empty words find vacancy as sunshine goes through glass.
All there is and nothing more finds need to understand
The giver of all truth did not begin with man.

Plant a seed and watch it grow, harvest it in time
As long as rainfall finds the land a grain of wheat will grow.
As long as sunshine's presence denies to us the cold
A tree invites with branches to all in nature's plan
"Come, enjoy the offerings" the gifts from God to man.

Be mindful of the river's flow and seasons understand
For what we think is ours alone will pass from hand to hand.
Wisdom of God's design makes us aware of our dependence.
Absent understanding the life we live finds end
As thought concludes a sentence
As ink is drained from pen
The breath of man releases flesh to dust again.
Reliance upon God is what we need to stand
Walking upon water needs his outstretched hand.

**Luke 11:2-3 He said to them, "When you pray say:" 'Father,
hallowed be your name, your kingdom come, give us each day our
daily bread.'**

Blindness

It's one thing to not understand her call.
In this we can certainly ask, "Who are you?"
It's another to pretend to be her friend and then ignore her hand.
Wisdom's soul resides in truth a covering for the earth
In this the heart will soar to unimagined heights
Will capture thoughts as pearls shining in the light
Will bring to man happiness undaunted by life's night.

Wisdom's arrival may cause a covering of the eyes denial or surprise
Like exiting a darkened room confronted by daylight.
Some may seek to go back inside where ignorance hides.
She may cause a hardening inviting pride to reign
A failure to learn as rocks repel the rain
As flame gives rise to burn, man's hand is pulled away
Allowing truth to calm the agony of pain.

"Better to hide in the dark with imagination," they say.
Defense of illusion is a cardboard smile picture perfect.
A cry without sound is found wanting
As a caged lion views his feast jaunting
As a painted landscape with neither height nor width or depth
Illusion finds a viewer where desire should not tread.
Traps set and longing to bite and rip and shred
All who fail to understand the overtures so blessed
Within the call of God's own voice to all seeking rest.

Ignorance of God is true blindness.
It's just a few steps away from mindless.
"Take heart," we say
God answers all in wisdom's dawning
None are turned away as sure as daytime sees the morning.

Job 28:28 And he said to man—"The fear of the Lord—that is wisdom, and to shun evil is understanding."

Corruption

We don't need to mine for it
To search the earth for signs of it
It makes a sound of brokenness
Has held its grip with mocking song
Since man first heard a serpent's tongue
Revealing what is right and wrong.

A process born of prideful man
Continues on 'til breath has failed
Awaiting then a call to rise
To face pursuits of useless gain
Find corruption of its fame
Within the flame of utter shame
Reduced in truth to withered rags
As if placed inside a vat
Of caustic and corrupting acts
Speaking laughter's hurtful smack,
"Gotcha!"

Lies as hooks that lure
With fancy suits and overtures
In this the laughter sounds as screams
Absent of the worldly dreams
Judgment sounds it mournful bell
Pronouncing clear, "Eternal hell."
As honest as a mirror's face
The life we led cannot be hid
Not in the heart or in the grave
Truth will speak each thought in waves.
On the last and final day
The straight and narrow path appears
Reminding of the broken ways
In defiance truth and grace
Bearing witness loud and clear,

"The Word did come you would not hear
Your clothing now as rotted rags,
Instead of robes of righteous acts."

⁓⌣⌣⁓

Jeremiah 13:6-7 *"After a long interval, he said to me: Go now to the Parath and fetch the loincloth from the place where I had hid it. But it was rotted, good for nothing!"*

Matthew 6: 19-21 *"Do not store up for yourselves treasures on earth, where moth and decay destroys, and thieves break in and steal. But store up treasures in heaven, where neither moth nor decay destroy, nor thieves break in and steal. For where your treasure is, there also will your heart be."*

Denial

"My friend,
God is the creator of all things good."

"So you say,
I deny the statement refuse to admit to it.
I'm unable to understand why you just won't quit.
You're trying to make me see what is just not there!
I need tangible solid visible proof
Examined by a microscope and x-rayed to its core
But what is just invisible leaves me no recourse."

"My friend,
Recognition of God's truth consists
Of having been convicted and convinced
Without the witness sight demanded by a man
It is within the strength of faith
Laid bare for all to see
Upon a cross of wood
And nails of crimson pain
Dripping to the earth one drop and then again
Causing dead to rise with praises to his name."
As thought proclaims, 'I think therefore I am'
There's no need supporting beams or a pulpit grand
A solitary strength denial cannot mask
Truth and holiness, is the great, 'I AM.'

My friend,
Denial has a sister that makes us run from God
It is the mark of sin we've carried from that day
We heeded not his voice then sought to run away.
It takes us to a blackened hole deep within man's soul
It sings a song of coffin pall in beats of melody
It dances with a jester's smile and leads us to defeat.
At last the shadow's veil is lifted from the eyes

Within the declaration, 'I am the resurrection and the life.'
Tangible reality that's visible to sight
Jesus."

~~~

Matthew 10:32-33 "Everyone who acknowledges me before others
I will acknowledge before my heavenly Father. But whoever
denies me before others, I will deny before my heavenly Father."

End time racers

Run the good race for the prize
Run the bad and be disqualified.
The world appears as a ghetto
A dog eat dog existence living for the moment
Chasing one's own tail never satisfied
Always there's desire to take another bite.

Everything in life has two sides
Presents to us a choice of wisdom and/or lies.
The choices that we make
Bring us joy or suffering
Like arrows to the heart
Its sting burns as fire
Consuming with a roar
Attacking unrelenting
Improperly stored
Like a linen cloth placed under rocks
Beside a river's bank
Seeing not the sun
Ragged it becomes
Stored in the dark with moths.

The good that we do
Will be worn as white robes
Proclaiming to God,
"The armor that you gave
Kept me from all harm.
Thank you for permitting light into my eyes.
Thank you for salvation laid bare upon a tree.
Thank you for the mercy that came to set me free.
Thank you for eternity stretching faster than is thought.
And thank you the good things you placed upon life's road."

I Corinthians 9:24-27 Do you not know that the runners in the stadium all run the race, but only one wins the prize? Run so as to win. Every athlete exercises discipline in every way. They do it to win a perishable crown, but we an imperishable one. Thus I do not run aimlessly; I do not fight as if I were shadowboxing. No, I drive my body and train it, for fear that, after having preached to others, I myself should be disqualified.

Competition

〜〜〜

Everything in nature competes
It is a way of life that says, "Don't expect to eat, if you sleep."
A man is entitled to his wage but a sleeper has nothing to claim.
Without competition a man will come to errant ways.
Without purpose there is folly and in folly there is ruin.
A wolf will hunt by day and howl at the moon
Giving praise for his labor or lamenting hunger's song
It is the way of life, in struggle forage on.

〜〜〜

2 Thessalonians 3:7-10 For you know how one must imitate us.
For we did not act in a disorderly way among you, nor did we
eat food received free from anyone. On the contrary, in toil and
drudgery, night and day we worked, so as not to burden any of
you. Not that we do not have the right. Rather, we wanted to
present ourselves as a model for you, so that you might imitate us.
In fact when we were with you, we instructed you that if anyone
was unwilling to work, neither should that person eat.

Lamentation

Where is the innocence that partnered with our youth?
Why have the former days passed away as fools?
The young are fed a tray so bland denied of bygone days
Absent is the fruit of truth replaced by errant ways.
Veils of reconstruction filled with emptiness and lies
Lead the youth today with corruption's song of rhyme.

There was a time man found shock with wrong
But now we find him bound and gagged hiding in the dark.
Callous grown so hard it suffocates the heart
Inwardly he runs and covets what will spoil
Refusing to acknowledge just how far his fall.
Absent is the meaning of the sting of sin
Denial of the conscience pursued with strength in vain
Forgotten are the days of youthful joy's refrain
Emptiness and shadow in the place where sunlight reigned.

There are cracks in the foundation and the paint is oh so dry.
Columns leaning left attempt to justify
Lies on big wide screens in colors that deny
The truth of what remains in the ruin of mankind's lives.

Cardboard smiles and silent schemes belie our present days.
The clapper fails the warning bell one step away the maw of hell.
Why hasn't reality dispelled the painted face?
Why has man allowed God to be replaced?
What on earth has happened to the voice of truth and grace?

Modern hope is illusion that cannot change or save
Offering confusion in this the end of days.
The land that was so blessed finds tears that never dry.
Offerings of peace and love are packaged in lies and pride.
He sets his heart among the stars away from cares that plague
And welcomes dead of night applauding wicked ways.

Briefly he does soar until heaven's voice is heard,
"O man, you sought a pedestal to shine above as stars
Moments in the starlight have caught and bound your heart.
Illusion found a home and slight of hand declared,
'Pay no heed the storm that thunders in your ear'
(Soon, you will be lost as days that were so dear)."

~ ~ ~

Job 29:1-4 Job began speaking again. If only my life could once again
be as it was when God watched over me. God was always with me then
and gave me light as I walked through the darkness. Those were the days
when I was prosperous, and the friendship of God protected my home.

Testimony

Where can I begin?
How to speak the way of forgiveness and grace?
Enemies on every side demons of this life
Alcohol gambling false thoughts debts and strife
Attacking unrelenting no freedom from regrets
Vicious undertakings sealed in every breath.

The things that remained: children wife and life
All were held as hostage through evil's ruling bite.
At the time of very last a voice is heard that said
"You're lost, this is your chance receive
Truth will set you free if only you'll believe."

I knew nothing but his presence then so in my heart I called and said,
"Lord, destroy my enemies and crush them in the ground!"
But then the voice said, "No, that's not how love is found."

To my knees crying soft once again my heart invoked.
"Lord, I know nothing, let your will be done forgive my outburst rude."
In silence peace secured within the inner halls
As my wife sang praises in words the angels knew.

Amazing transformation escaping spirit's tomb
As a newborn wakening the confines of the womb
Stability like a seed transformed sprouting forth its shell
Former ways denied as I was saved from hell.

Three days of mourning for the past where I was blind
For all the things I now see rushed shudders to my mind.
At last upon my feet in scripture found a feast
And from the ashes of that life walked out a brand new me!

Matthew 6:9-13 "Our Father in heaven, hallowed be your name, your kingdom come, your will be done on earth as it is in heaven. Give us today our daily bread. Forgive us our debts, as we also have forgiven our debtors. And lead us not into temptation, but deliver us from the evil one."

Greener and Meaner

"Mankind is the great despoiler of the planet.
All is dying on this earth we share," they say.
Someone must be lying
Since the grass comes back each year.
The trees are still producing shelter leaf and fruit.
The ground that brings forth produce is still provided rain.
The sky above in concert with sun and cloud look down
Still we hear the voices in mournful gait abound.

Anger fills their faces as if God were not around
And from pretentious rulers who know not loss or pain
"The sky, the sky is falling" rings constant in refrain.
"We need a lot less people," is what they say,
Spoken within whispers underneath their made up face.
"We have to save the planet we must save the human race."

Still everything grows up grows old and dies
Except, the little heartbeats that have been denied.
Why is there such panic when a newborn baby cries?
"Exhaled breath will cause our death," they say.
When did man forget to look to God and pray?
Amazing, we can't turn one hair the color gray.
We can't make it rain or bring to earth a storm
But we can save the planet by choosing who is born?

"Reduction of their number is a right we can afford
Teach them to demand for free more and more and more!
Teach them how to vote for table food and pie
As we remain on mountain tops worshipped and adored.
It's not selfish mean or evil but prudent freedom's chance
Advancing to the people hope and change in this great land."

Teardrops never dry when decisions say goodbye
And forgiveness is not given to deception's evil lies.

~~~~~

Isaiah 2:9 "Everything will be humiliated and disgraced. Do not forgive them, Lord!"

Opened Books

Recordings and books look into the matter
Searchers and seekers digging to find
All that transpired throughout eons of time.
It can't be done with hands of man
Not with printing of great books
Not by professors with endless discourse
Not with stone carvings or markings with pen
The mind records all actions deeds and thoughts of men.
Opened books are read with praise or shock.
All things must end when time cannot find a clock.
At the restoration of man seals are unlocked.
Books are opened names are read
Deeds revealed rejoicing or dread
Heads uplifted or hung in regret
All that was done in the soul of a man
Is seen in an instant without picture printer or pen.
The spirit-mind imprints life with vision and breath
First thought to last
Unfading,
Simply weighing life.

The spirit speaks in language well known
It cheers from the heart cries and/or moans.
The book of this life is not written in stone
Not printed with ink or stored in great tomes.
The life of a man is much more than flesh
When books are opened a light is revealed
Shone into the darkness where nothing's concealed.

Deceptive corruption ragged and soiled
Thoughts hidden from others in pockets sewn deep
Shocked and confused amazed to find
Unfolding of records held tightly so long.
A laser for deeds thought privately owned
Searches the past as a miner seeks gold.

Revelation 20:11-15 Next I saw a large white throne and the one who was sitting on it. The earth and the sky fled from his presence and there was no place for them. I saw the dead, the great and the lowly, standing before the throne, and scrolls were opened. Then another scroll was opened, the book of life. The dead were judged according to their deeds, by what was written in the scrolls. The sea gave up its dead; then Death and Hades gave up their dead. All the dead were judged according to their deeds. Then Death and Hades were thrown into the pool of fire. (This is the second death.) Anyone whose name was not found written in the book of life was thrown into the fire.

Justice

Suffering and shock stuns the soul
But justice like a clock ticks ever in the bones
Resolute in purpose recompense assured
By God, who is Judge Strength Sword!
Mourn to break the knot of pain
Barbed awareness in the veins
Free the spirit from the cold
As a dagger rending flesh
As an arrow pierces storm
As light defeats the dark
Mourn to break the knot.

Mourn for the souls who fled to heaven's door.
Mourn for the heroes who are no more.
Mourn for all creatures and birds upon the wing.
Mourn for the earth that had not a voice
Convulsing from the life that ran into fertile ground
In rivulets of crimson making not a mourning sound.

Within the ash of the grave voices call as crashing waves.
Resonant the sound to hands stretched forth to flame.
Swift is justice to hearts of stone and evil ways.

To eyes in darkness light is shone as eagle wings take flight.
Wisdom as her guiding force fed by silent lives.
Voices free of mourning moans cry, "justice!" at God's throne.
It's love that's feared in fortress stone sending tremors to the bone
Breaking boulders at the root with the hammer strength of truth.
Announcing boldly,
"Time to pay.
There's nowhere to run,
No hiding place!"

Peter F. Serra

Isaiah 9:7 He will reign on David's throne and over his kingdom, establishing and upholding it with justice and righteousness from that time on and forever.

In memory of The Twin Towers, September, 11, 2001

Honesty

⌒⌒⌒

Skies of menacing gray
Portraits in clouds drifting away
Tomorrow's dawn is opening gates
Singing is heard from white doves at play.

Rapturous pounding drumbeats of rain
Exploding in thunder along the plain
Descending in triumph into the heart
Honesty's day is a cleansing from God.

Honesty bonds people together
Like adversity and hard times
Mind to mind and heart to heart
Fabric sewn as marrow and bone
Heavy and taut the fisherman's knot
Honesty.

⌒⌒⌒

John 3:3 In reply Jesus said, "I tell you the truth, unless a man is born again, he cannot see the kingdom of God."

Homeless

⌒〜⌒

Homeless bones haven't rested for so long.
Clothes torn and tattered from constant weather worn
Joints are most pronounced like rusted hinges creak
It truly is amazing from these bones I do hear speech.
"I'm sorry to intrude but you see I have this need
That keeps me always asking, well, really it's a plea."

Have mercy on these bones in dire haste
Going this way that but never going any place.
Have mercy when you hear the voice of need
Knocking upon your heart
For the one who is knocking
May be of the flock of God.

⌒〜⌒

Hebrews 13:2 Do not forget to entertain strangers. For by doing so some people have entertained angels without knowing it.

Matthew 8:12 Jesus said, "Foxes have holes and birds have nests, but the Son of Man has no place to lay his head."

Word

Tapestry of clarity
Truth certain
Turn the page
Draw the blinds
Raise the curtains.
Love is calling.

Hunter proclaims
"All in the game
Swift and slow alike
Slick and naïve
Old and brave"
In the hunter's sights
Hunter denied.

Closed doors receive a knock.
Camouflage revealed.
Dead men drop to their knees.
Common clay bathed in light
Crystal is the word of God.
Hunter denied.
Turn the page
Draw the blinds
Raise the curtains.
Love is calling.

Luke 11:27 As Jesus was saying these things; a woman in the crowd called out, "Blessed is the mother who gave you birth and nursed you." He replied, "Blessed rather are those who hear the word of God and obey it."

Bedtime

―――⌒∽⌒――――

"Now I lay me down to sleep"
Aware of places deep.
Reality the pillowed bed
Mindful places dark and dread
Conscious dwelling fixed as flint
Sealed within deep with strength
Nothing fancy straight and plain
"Reside with me, O Holy Name."

Faith in grace
Steadfast shield
Humbling truth
Dispatch in haste
Evil from this place
Spirit Sword knowledge swift
Steadfast love upon my lips
Readiness within my feet
Helmet fastened slumber sweet
"I pray the Lord, my soul to keep."

―――⌒∽⌒――――

Revelation 2:12-13 To the angel of the church in Pergamum write:
These are the words of him who has the sharp, double-edged
sword. I know where you live—where Satan has his throne. Yet
you remain true to my name.

Buttons

❧

Button eyes button nose and buttons for your clothes.
We have buttons for the doorbells that call our friends to play.
There's the buttons for machinery that we use each day.
Buttons causing internal massive blasts
Must be discarded in a way
That ensures a final resting place forever in the grave.

❧

Proverbs 16:32 "Better a patient man than a warrior, a man who controls his temper than one who takes a city."

My God

My God, my God, my God!
Is the witness, concerning Jesus.
In you, O Lord, is fullness of the Father.
You chose to live the plan embodied in the, "Son of Man."
To walk the earth humble most as love to serve without a boast.
Creation's fall restored by you
Death could not compel to stay
Could not keep in bondage of the grave
All worship and unending praise to you
My Lord!
My God!
Always!

John 20:28 Thomas said to him, "My Lord and my God!"

The Dog

⌒⌒⌒⌒

The dog is man's best friend.
Its been that way since the day God created them.
The patience of the dog is something great.
It displays a confidence that only comes with faith.

The dog knows not limits to express his love.
Perhaps it is a special gift that comes from God above?
It's true man gave names to those with hair tails and paws
But when he saw the qualities instilled within the dog
He may have lifted up his hands and said,
"Thank you Lord!"

Perhaps it's not coincidence man named his friend, "Dog."
You see it's just the opposite of the way that we spell, "God."

⌒⌒⌒⌒

Genesis 2:19 Now the Lord God had formed out of the ground all the beasts of the field and all the birds of the air. He brought them to the man to see what he would name them and whatever the man called each living creature that was his name.

Salami Vision

❧

The monk approached his brothers to tell of his intent.
"I shall fast for Lent!
Salami shall be purchased, its purpose to suspend
From the ceiling of my room, my resolve to test!"
After many days his hunger did increase
And so began the practice to the salami he would speak.
He paced in little circles beneath the enemy displayed
In pangs of hunger mounting upon his knees he prayed.
Many days of sleepless nights and fanciful flights
To banquets of the mind, as aroma beckoned, "Take a bite!"
The fast was almost over, his brothers watched as admiration burned
With victory thoughts increasing, "A feast the monk has earned!"
Good Friday morning they heard a primal shout
And found the monk of mention with the salami in his mouth.
Though your intentions may be righteous take care not to start
To hang around with salami that will tempt you and eventually break
your heart.

❧

1 Corinthians 15:33 Do not be misled: "Bad company corrupts
good character."

Eyewitness To A Cooking Lesson

"Isabella, do you want to help me cook?"
"Yes, grandma."
"Good, now stand on the chair and wash your hands.
Use the paper towels.
This is how to cut the mozzarella, use the butter knife.
Dip the cutlet into the eggs.
The breadcrumbs are next-cover them up all the way.
I'll put them in the pan.
Wipe your hands give me a paper towel also,
Thank you.
You are a big help for Grandma.
We can clean up after the frying.
Stay away from the stove it's hot.
You don't want grandma crying."
"Grandma, can we make the little meatballs too?"
"Okay, wash your hands,
I'll get the chopped meat."
Witnessed by Grandpa. Grandma and Isabella, age 4

I Samuel 9:23: He said to the cook. "Bring the portion I gave you and told you to put aside." So he took up the leg and what went with it, and placed it before Saul. Samuel said: This is a reserved portion that has been set aside, for you. Eat, for it was kept for you until your arrival; I explained that I was inviting some guests."

Inward Flight

⟨~⟩

Worn and hurt the heart deserts
Creates a callous room
Despair's call finds forlorn
As life is entombed
Darkness, comfort's shield
Denies the fertile fields love attended.
Life is suspended as drought replaces bloom.
Pity the inward traveler
Confined by poor eyesight
Eyes inside groping
For eddy's in the night
Shadows beckon,
"Move deeper into night."

Pray for the inside dweller
Knowing not this freedom thought,
"Life is expression outward
From creation's time of birth
Understanding brings us comfort
And underwrites our worth."

⟨~⟩

Joel 2:32 "And anyone who calls upon the name of the Lord will be saved."

Roasting Spuds And Other Lost Arts

❦

Flipping baseball cards was different from today's road-rage bird.
Shooting marbles, bottle caps filled with wax, different from drive-bye's ending in bang.
Girls loved Buster Brown's, socks neatly folded, guys walked with a "bop" to flaunt it.
Poodle skirts jumped "double-dutch" a "hop" was a dance.
Crashing parties caused trouble and throwing of hands.
Kids roasted spuds over fire with sticks, little hobos little cares.
We wrapped it in tinfoil if we could get it.
Marshmallow roasting was quick, the hungrier we got the spud only got hot.
We kept the fire going with twigs, "Chunky" wrappers and popsicle-sticks.
There was no hurry we were kids.
The game of "Kings" was played with a high bouncer against a wall and inside of boxes.
A "killer" scored an automatic point other killer's went upstate and wore uniforms.
We always remembered the "boys upstate" sacrificing a sip of what they couldn't taste.
Who were they anyway?
The high bouncer ruled in the streets we watched on the sidewalk for a two-sewer blast.
Who could have guessed we would be looking at the past?
The "Pinky" had measles, with the high bouncer it couldn't compete.
With hands we played "stoopball" with feet "kick the can."
"Buck-Buck" jumped high onto backs unaware.
"Pillow's" watched the finger count, number one in the line guessed loud!
Sidewalks were squares of Pennsylvania Slate that glistened from the rain.
Streets had cobblestone in some places, a bumpy ride for bicycles scooters or skates.
Little kids jumped on cracks and would cry-out, "We broke the devil's back!"
A kid jumps on, "Crack" today and he gets hurt.

Electrified buses had overhead cables steel wheels rode on rails sunk into the blacktop.
Long pole connectors like bug antenna searching on the street they called, "Bergen."
Hitchhiking at the rear of the electrified bus was easier than others.
If the driver failed to stop, pulling the cable meant immediate halt.
Away we ran from the invalid bus as the driver repositioned the cables and cussed.
The grocer totaled the bill on a brown bag in pencil.
Top-shelf items were captured by the a "grabber."
A mechanical hand extension, it was a clever invention.
We waited patiently chewing a slice of American cheese.
The grocer filled the list easily.
The butcher's floor was sawdust over black and white tiles.
Cutlets were flattened to thickness by order, momma knew how to supervise.
"Yoyo" was a kid's toy, not a greeting, and teachers actually taught.
Subway seats had bamboo weave old folks had worth.
Hammer and nails box and board two halves of a skate and off we roared.
Skates had a key and clamp one size fit all like light from a lamp.
Little Red Riding Hood was hit with lies, big nose, big teeth, big eyes,
Now the hoods are in SUV's, big wheels, big deals big rides.
Lost in time are the old ways.
"Cats eyes, jumbos, purees, cracked top and carpet guns"
Were played in "PF Fliers" ripped jeans garrison belts and chewing gum.
Back then life was tough we worked prayed and played hard.
Bruises healed, new days were faced with zeal hoping for snow and, "King of the Hill."

Matthew 18:2-3 He called a child over, placed it in their midst, and said, "Amen, I say to you, unless you turn and become like little children, you will not enter the kingdom of heaven."

Material Thing

"Listen man, in this life you lose!
You scramble for pay and pay with your life's work.
The winter of your days is laden with loss and then you die.
'Eat drink and be merry' sun up and down
There is no right and wrong or conscience to be found.
Take your fill today there's nothing in the ground.
There is not afterlife not judgment of the proud.
There's not a step beyond
There's just the here and now!
A moment in the sunshine's ray
Says, 'all things are allowed.'
Don't let the moment pass lest darkness weave a shroud.
Come take hold my hand 'til mourning sounds ring loud.
Life is just a moment.
What was done is gone.
There's nothing to regret.
When you go underground."

"Listen, Material Thing, when will you understand?
Your vision is omitting the truth of God's great plan.
Illusion and poor vision is what you offer man.
Nothing is for keeps except the soul God gave.
A man must find the Truth in order to be saved.
Yes, the body meets the ground but then the spirit soars
To heights you can't imagine to meet the risen Lord.
How correct were those long gone kings?
Pyramid tombs secret rooms and window to the stars.
Dead man's bones misplaced hope most precious truth not met.
When their eyes did close they failed this earthly test.
The weight of gold and silver did not add a breath.
Pay attention, O voice that shouts, 'collect and get!'
Many have felt your pull and fallen for your lies.
But truth declares to everyone, 'open up your eyes!'
Material things will not ease a fire's breath.

357

They will not bring an end to desire's nagging call.
Hunger seeks not rest until the curtain falls!
Dead man's schemes lavish dreams and calls for more and more
Perish into dust with the lies you told to us!"

Luke 22:31-32 Simon, Simon! Listen! Satan has received permission to test all of you, to separate the good from the bad, as a farmer separates the wheat from the chaff. But I have prayed for you, Simon that your faith will not fail. And when you turn back to me, you must strengthen your brothers.

Wormwood

The courtroom is silenced for judgment to be heard.
The gavel makes its sound attention is called.

Set into motion from beginning of time
And grabbed by the hand of God
Hurled down to the earth with judgment in mind.

The courtroom is filled with anticipation.
The Judge breaks open what's sealed.
All of those found faithful are robed and healed.
Filled with thanksgiving for the moment at hand
A third of the living will perish
According to God's great judgment plan.

"Fill the container with fire and throw it down to the earth.
Throw flashings of lightning thunder and quakes
Down on the earth upon rivers and lakes
Spread upon oceans and deep into caves
Nothing will hide the arrival of fate.
Nothing pretends it's just a mistake.
Not happenstance or pure common fate.
Deception and lies cannot escape
The arrival of 'Wormwood'
From the vacuum of space
The end of evasion
The end of grace
The end of pretending God's been erased."
Truth is now found
Hurled from space
The star called, "Wormwood"
Down to the earth to mark her disgrace.

Revelation 8:10 The third angel sounded his trumpet, and a great star, blazing like a torch, fell from the sky on a third of the rivers, and on the springs of water-the name of the star is Wormwood.

Gateway

❧〜〜❧

With every thought the gateway appears
Entrance into infinity's maze
With every turn new light arrays
Paths well traveled from beginning of days.
Others untouched, remote from man's sight
Sudden appearing as news across waves
Bidding us enter illumined intrigue
A starburst speaks to darkness with flares
A message of light needing no definition
Its presence alone proves its existence.

No matter which way I look, outward or in
The gateway appears, as if saying,
"There is no end."

So infinite is thought
Narrow at times pointedly focused
Or a mirrored diadem
Broadening the spectrum given within.
Reflecting transferring one to another
Saying, "God is waiting to meet you my friend."
The doors that are opened
Have thresholds called, "blessed."
Surely the answers are not mine
And the questions come from a place
Awaiting the seeker to find.
Conclusive and unwavering proof
Within the gateway divine
Containing all truth for body soul and mind.
Jesus.

❧〜〜❧

Matthew 8:13 Enter through the narrow gate. The gate that leads to damnation is wide, the road is clear and many choose to travel it. But how narrow is the gate that leads to life, how rough the road, and how few there are who find it.

Unending

I see no difference above or below the ground
Dead is dead if there's no one home.
An empty shell finds little worth
Nighttime bows to morning and daytime has its song
Echoes fade as drifting clouds portraits for the mind
The life of man is unfulfilled bleak and oft times wrong
Until his course is altered and rescued from life's storms.

A man hears laughter mocking, "Life is brief."
Until he finds himself he cannot be complete.
Until someone he finds understands the way he thinks
Life is just a journey ending in defeat.

It's more than, "Start and Finish."
It's continuous as thought.
More than just a passing breeze in summer's heat and rays
More than shelter from the cold in winter's falling flakes.
Eternal breath is captured outpacing reach and length
Upon the wind is carried beyond laughter's mocking breath.

Everlasting has not broken lines
Is removed from the concept that is space and time.
No need for a rewind to keep the counting strong
Unending ever stretching
Beyond finite leaps and bounds
Expressed within the Prodigal's eyes opened wide
Unending finds beginning in God who gave man life.

Just as air permits man breathing
Connecting inside and without
So too the voice of wisdom saying,
"Unending is God's love."

> *As in the beginning*
> *Where death had not a sting*
> *Truth is everlasting*
> *And life to man it brings.*

John 3:16 For God so loved the world that he gave his one and only Son, that whoever believes in him shall not perish but have eternal life.

Legacy

~⌒~

Who knows when the beat of life shall cease?
What then should we say to those we have to leave?

"My children listen to your father as I pass along to you
The reality of life that was given in my youth
At the age of thirty-three God did come to me
And speaking words convincing my soul was then set free.
Belief became the anchor denying drift in waves
And calm within life's storms has followed all my days.
Truth was all around me cutting through life's fog
As a beacon shining with warning and with love
I focused on its light and danced within my heart
And ever since that day I knew where I belonged.

Pay attention to the truth that others will deny
God is always with us every moment of our life.
Unless a man seek wisdom his days find emptiness
Filled with uncertainty and laced with happenstance.
Absent a foundation that keeps an even keel
Sometimes he can capture the object of his prize
But mostly there's an emptiness caused by stubborn pride.
And when the final beat and darkness fills his eyes
The failure to embrace God's truth comes as great surprise.

Follow the example of knowledge right and wrong
It lives within your heart and sings a gentle song
Absent condemnation the peace of God is found.

When life finds falter unsteady is our walk
The impact that then follows sings a nagging song
Harrowing in content leaving scars and tracks of wrong.

They never are forgotten but lay anchored in the deep
Returning without warning to break our restful sleep
As apparitions moaning lamentation for what's lost
They cry loudly accusation of a life lived in the dark.

363

Alas they are but echoes ringing in the mind
But still they carry impact of a former time
Opportunity came knocking and no one could it find.
Heed the voice of wisdom and sleep will then be sound
Without tossing frightful nightmares that echo days long gone
Denied the peace of God by the pull of wrong.

Limit the anguish bucket let it not be filled
And life will find true meaning even when uphill."

**Proverbs 19:20 Listen to advice and accept instruction, and in
the end you will be wise.**

Mary Listens Martha Works

There's a time to listen and work.
Work is important it visits us each day.
Listening finds its worth in many different ways.
Both are valid and embraced by life's demands.
We listen to compete and work to eat.
It has been said,
"Listen to learn and learn to listen"
In this there's happiness.
Both know how to add and at times subtract.

Overtime pays premium, as does a whisper in the dark
That stops a forward movement that keeps us from a fall.

The proper time to work is at times very near.
At times we're called upon to bring everything to bear.
Emergencies arise as smoke into the air
It's then we hear understanding's sisters,
Crystal and Clear.
A man must find the time to listen
To the urgencies that oft times fail our sight
But in a word of truth opens up his eyes.

Troubled by innocence and wrong is the seeker's mind
Searching for the truth that calms the rising tide
Searching for forgiveness and calm within the soul
Searching outward in the world and deeper still inside
And when we hear the voice so sweet it's time to rest recline
At the banquet table prepared for us by God.

Luke 10:38-42 As Jesus and his disciples were on their way, he came to a village where a woman named Martha opened her home to him. She had a sister named Mary, who sat at the Lord's feet listening to what he said. But Martha was distracted by

all the preparations that had to be made. She came to him and asked, "Lord, don't you care that my sister has left me to do the work by myself? Tell her to help me!" "Martha, Martha," the Lord answered, "you are worried and upset about many things, but only one thing is needed. Mary has chosen what is better, and it will not be taken away from her."

Vanity

⌒⌒⌒

There's a malady under the sun that approaches with images produced by shallow hearts having little knowledge of self worth. In the young it speaks of perceived defects having no remedy for achieving perfection as others envision it. In the old it brings a blindness the makes it impossible to see the beauty of gray. There's a rebellion in man that refuses to acknowledge the inherent mandate of the human condition, and in each passing year it taunts those so afflicted with vanity. Indeed why can't man see the beauty of acceptance and the humility inherent in all things under the sun. Shallow and thin is thought that cannot venture beneath the skin where is found the deep and lasting beauty that has no time for age.

⌒⌒⌒

Beauty

❦

Stepping out and stepping loud
Flashy kicks neon crowd
Talking trash without a sound
What to do when it comes crashing down?
Beauty.
With every step you bowed
To vanity so proud
And it got you what you wanted
Notice from the street
And in the bowing you would flaunt it
To faces passing fleet.
Beauty.
The hip-hop in the step is gone
It had a time to visit
The mind recalls the shallow talk
Amazed through present eyes, "surprise."
What to do when it dies?
Beauty.
Now the days of nothing praise
All is gone and muted
In its place you find the grace
That always seemed elusive.
Beauty.

❦

Ecclesiastes 1:2 "Meaningless! Meaningless!" says the teacher.
"Utterly meaningless! Everything is meaningless."

Fools Gold

Gold stabilizes countries as a currency of worth.
It is fashioned into jewelry for those who wish to state,
"I am wealthy and that makes me great!"
Look at all this stuff that's draped pierced and worn.
That's put on for display with a message that is known.
"Success is acquisition and it takes me where I want!"

Yes, in some designer's fashion there are religious overtones
Declaring allegiance where nowhere else is found
The worth of faith and action that brings to man a crown
Mixed and confusing are the steps of the proud
Where outside is displayed jewels and coinage round
And deep within the heart poverty is found
Shouting, "shine and sparkle"
But nowhere it there found
Truth within the heart outshining gold's renown.
Rings and things gold capped teeth
Says to all with eyes, "This is what I advertise."
Like a stoic plastic smile
Trust placed in gold lasts only for a while.
It's a substance like any other's depth, speaking,
"Unfaithful will I be and from your hand shall pass."
For a moment all is well with struggles more or less
Absent what's most precious the house is left bereft.
Honesty.

A whitewashed wall a gold chain's talk a swaggering crucifix
Denounce the deeper meaning of structure's true intent.
Beneath the holy pretext of signals mixed and bent
Is found a cobweb teaming with unwanted guests.
Deception and hypocrisy blend as ornaments
And vie to capture focus in reflection's hollow stance.
Outwardly not needing is the picture opulence.
Understanding is not found in facet glint and ray

What is meant to capture isn't put out on display.
It's not meant to be weighed, coveted or fathomed
A man's best appearance is not found in gold and diamond.

Unless wisdom is the crown placed upon his head
All is just a picture of what was and will not last.
There's nothing that comes with us
Save the spirit's onward quest for the river ever flowing
Through the streets of gold so blessed
Be mindful of the signals we send to those we meet
In the end they find arrival at the Savior's feet.

Exodus 32:2-4 Aaron answered them. Take off your gold earrings that your wives, your sons, and your daughters are wearing, and bring them to me. So all the people took off their earrings and brought them to Aaron. He took what they handed him and made it into an idol cast in the shape of a calf, fashioning it with a tool. Then they said, "These are your gods, O Israel, who brought you up out of Egypt."

The Fool

The fool is easily duped.
He always shakes his head with an affirmative nod
But never really understands the words the wise impart.
He is very critical of all except himself
Refusing the material to improve his state
Thus he's heading nowhere save his sorry fate.

The fool will not acknowledge he is at a loss
He tries to take the lead in life as if he is the boss.
He has a problem that lives deep within his skin
It is the prideful mind of man that causes him to grin
Causes him to laugh out loud when nothing has been said
Life for him is taking place all within his head.

He knows not the truth of life explained
Within the Holy Scriptures that puzzles not the brain.

The word of God paints not a complex picture of what is too sublime
Nor offers to us paradox confusion by design.

Light and understanding is given for the asking
To all whose hand will knock or seek the way uplifting
Into understanding a fool has failed to grasp.

A light filled room he dares not comprehend
For in the darkness of his heart he doesn't want to understand.

Proverbs 9:10 The fear of the Lord is wisdom, and knowledge of the Holy One is understanding.

Rest

⌒⌒⌒

Can a leopard change his spots or man change his skin?
Can he run away from his self or outrun his sins?
Rest upon stone weary bones seek comfort close to the Rock.
Under skies revealing God's love find rest for the man alone.
Take some time to slow things down, let peace, knowledge and truth
unfold.
Know safety in the night and shelter from the sun upon a pillow of stone
Offered to the man on the run, from his past, his self and home.

⌒⌒⌒

Genesis 28: 10-12 Jacob left Beersheba and set out for Haran.
When he reached a certain place, he stopped for the night because
the sun had set. Taking one of the stones there, he put it under his
head and lay down to sleep. He had a dream in which he saw a
stairway resting on the earth, with its top reaching to heaven, and
the angels of God were ascending and descending on it.

Revelation

God reveals his character by showing us our need.
In the brightest light of day all we need is seen.
He speaks in tones of Father's love showing what is known
And brings a revelation that awakens heart and soul.

His act of saving power presented by his grace
Jesus, Lord, Redeemer, through him the desert blooms
In wonder of his majesty that gently says, "Come home."

A man knows when he is lost.
His view of life's landscape is desert dust and rust.
He stands and looks about him in wonder and disgust
And asks himself the question,
"Why has it come to this?"
The weight upon his chest makes it hard to breathe
And always on his mind is a constant need
To find an oasis the place where trees can grow
The place for one to rest his head and find the time to know
Where it is unending, the joy of peaceful sleep
Without the awesome bother of empty desert sand
That steals away his strength and lays waste to all his plans.

A man knows when he has been found
When his heart begins to race and tears of joy run down
Into tracks made from sorrow and no bitter taste is found.
When life is seen through a light that's shone with focus bright
Into the desert darkness that held him close and tight
With surety of a sharpened knife the gloom is cut away
And in the desert heat that burned with each heartbeat
The rain of revelation washed away defeat!

Psalm 23:1-4 The Lord is my Shepherd I shall lack nothing. He makes me to lie down in green pastures, he leads me beside quiet

waters he restores my soul. He guides me in paths of righteousness for his name's sake. Even though I walk through the valley of the shadow of death, I will fear no evil, for you are with me; your rod and your staff comfort me.

Night Vision

The spark that starts the flame housed within the lamp
Has within its substance fuel producing light
And power to intrude into the heart of night.

During the heat of battle when trials of life are hard
Though captured by illusions controlling time and space
With chains as broad as laughter's scorn and lies that bind our sight
The grace of God still marches on to defeat the night.

Winter's wind or coldest thought cannot prevent its flight
In purpose to redeem the lost wandering at the crest
With hearts that carry heavy loads allowing not a rest
Where none could reach before the cross
To be renewed and blessed.

In the night a thought is born that causes fearful rest.
From the heart a light is shone bringing vision's best.
Where all was dark and windowless the flight of grace does find
Captive man bound and gagged in just the nick of time!
Removing chains restrictive, cobwebs woven fine
And breaking down the prison that kept the man from God.

Psalm 118:7 The Lord is with me; he is my helper.

Forgetful

❧

O Lord, I am at tines forgetting your protection in life's storms.
The ones that grab hold of me and shake me to the bone.
Especially the storms of hurt
That kept me blind and lost and low.
Please help me to remain fixed upon your ways straight and true.
Like the fruit of forgiveness always present on the vine
Its flavor is increasing like an aging wine.
Let me not forget the cost you had to pay.
Let me never forget or allow my eyes to stray
Keep my heart fixed on you forever and always.

❧

Psalm 25:4-5 Show me your ways, O Lord, teach me your paths;
guide me in your truth and teach me, for you are God my Savior,
and my hope is in you all day long.

Open Up

Like a river rushing upon swollen banks
Speed my voice to heaven
With praise and loving thanks.
Straight to heaven upon the wings of faith
"Open up kingdom dwelling
Open up heaven's gate."

Like stars as beacons seeking
And mountains stretch to reach
My voice shall rise to heaven
With resonating speech,
"Open up kingdom dwelling
Open up heaven's gate
I know that you are near
Through the blessing that is faith."

No need for special visions
Or descending fire signs
As in the days of old
Your presence like the wind
Rushed into conscious minds.
Only touch the place within me
Let your Spirit fill the cup
And in joyful praise ascending
I shall cry, "Open up!"

Acts 2:1-3 When the day of Pentecost came, they were all together in one place. Suddenly a sound like the blowing of a violent wind came from heaven and filled the whole house where they were sitting. They saw what seemed to be tongues of fire that separated and came to rest on each of them.

Wild Honey

His voice had sweetness to those seeking God.
Like wild honey difficult to find.
His was a call to the sick and the lost
The bent and lame crying from pain
That cripples the soul at the core.
His was a call to a sin sick world,
"Repent, for the love of God!"

John's voice was not the refined kind.
Domestic honey with a taste that's hollow.
It wasn't difficult to swallow.

Like gravel, it hit like a gavel
To those who live by lies
A voice in the wilderness
Who could hear his call?
None in the desert of hardship and sand
But to those lost in the wilderness of life
It was wild honey, unrefined, strength filled and clear
Food for the soul, free of fear.

To those who would not repent
His voice stung like a bee and cut like a knife.
John had no fear of the sting of bees
And locust as a delicacy leaves much to desire
So it is not surprising he would raise the ire of snakes and vipers.
No matter to John, to boldly invade the heart of a beehive
For the sweetness of honey
Or steadfastly reaching into hearts for the sweetness of repentance.
He was focused upon pleasing God, not men.
A higher calling had John, "Repent!"

His message was consistently strong.
"Repent!"
He proclaimed the message and pointed the way saying,
"This is the Son of God."

❧

John 1:345 *"I have seen and testify that this is the Son of God."*

Charcoal Dreams

Carbon has it rough.
A hard time is this life.
Suffering's an offshoot of discord trouble strife.
It dreams becoming diamond escaping from this stuff
It schemes of finding peace by any means but love.
Always there is suffering on both sides of the track
As both know of movement forward and/or back.

Always there's a contest to dominate and bind
Capture unaware the naked and the blind.
A power play of subtlety from those who really fear
Revealing of the evil that stays awake to snare
Unsuspecting travelers who enter starlight's glare
Of promises of treasure to quench the heat within
Of embers burning quickly singeing at the skin!

Producing neither diamond nor a chest of gold
All of man's desire cannot bring a cup or drop.
Not barrier moat or wall can halt prevent or stall
Wishes dressed as promises upon the road a man is bent.
Motive fed by haughtiness in shadow sister greed
Decisions weighing heavy
For what is sown so shall be reaped.
After the peak is conquered the price of folly is in sight
Shining lures find capture like the fruit of thorny pride.

Conscience of the spirit sings a righteous song.
Notes put into action oft times come out wrong.
Fruit declares the worth of trees
A river's flow says, "Fresh."
Air is in the sky above

The sun and moon play catch.
Oceans team with many things of benefit to man
And still the charcoal dreams of diamond in its hand.

~~~

Proverbs 16:22 Understanding is a fountain of life for those who have it, but folly brings punishment to fools.

Heat

⌒⌒⌒

Volcanic undercurrents releasing poisoned heat.
Pollution's beat.
Vocal breath advancing threats
Chalkboard screech clanging bells
Emptiness of thought
From conflicts of the flesh
Friction's heat is wrought.

Drumbeats sounding for the lost
Focused on the battle and not what it will cost.
Voices shouting words of erupting threats
And we cry within ourselves as others beat their breasts.

We seek the place of peace and love.
Others build a fire stoked by raging hate.
No one thinks about
The earth the ground the trees
The one called into battle
Or the outcome of his fate
It's never really thought about
By those causing the rage.

The fire keeps on burning
In the heart of battle's fray
Until the flame of anger dies
And smoke is cleared away.
It's then and only then it's said
"What a price to pay."
A landscape of insanity not fit for man or beast.
The promise of a robin's song cannot be heard or seen
When the battle in the mind exits with its heat.

⌒⌒⌒

Matthew 5:44-45 But I tell you love your enemies and pray for those
who persecute you, that you may be sons of your Father in heaven.

Freedom

What does it mean?
To be free is a state of being complete.
Within a man's home and outside in the street
Within the heart and mind thoughts must be free to roam
Wherever it is right and it does no harm.

Freedom is given from God to man.
It must be protected in the heart and in the land.
When freedom is attacked a change is ushered in
By those who would be kings whose rule of law is sin.

Those who have found freedom in all of its forms
Have had the boulder lifted from the center of each breath
From deep within a tear filled rain where sadness came to rest
God spoke a whispered thought
Set the spirit free and filled a vacant heart.

O shower of light and love that rains upon the soul
Your mercy brought forth freedom in its richest form
It's the knowledge of you, O Lord, in a man who is reborn.

Psalm 95:7-9 Today, if you hear his voice, do not harden your hearts.

Presentable

How many hours are spent choosing perusing and posing?
How many hours are spent in reflective unrest?
Selecting appearance
We hope will endear us
To those the message is sent.
No matter the clothing truth is unfolding
In more ways than fashion or style
While we are choosing through closets confusing
Remember to check for the smile.
It speaks to what's in the suit.
Bright and clear to all far and near,
"Presentable person here!"

1 Corinthians 13:4-6 Love is patient, love is kind, It does not envy, it is not proud. It is not rude, it is not self-seeking, it is not easily angered, it keeps no record of wrongs. Love does not delight in evil but rejoices with the truth.

The Barrier

Human ability and natural laws place limits upon our thoughts.
They form for us a finite view giving power to what's lost.
The greatest of these barrier stones present themselves in caskets.
The seed must be transformed into something it was not
And cease to be seed but not to be forgotten.
Loss of limbs will not reduce my mind.
Will not diminish spirit now or over time.
And when my losses mount and body meets the grave
I still shall not diminish, no, not even for a day.

We see physical demise and no longer is there breath.
We have no doubt at all when we view the dead.
As witness we come and speak of life that's past
Accompanied by sorrow that calls with potent strength.
And all we have to lean upon seems to fall away
Into the night of emptiness where prayer alone can stay.

Cling not to me endurance friend
For gray the hairs upon the head
Point clearly to a better end.
Holdfast not days of youth
It's better now with nuisance aches.
It's better now with reduced pace
It's better still with love and grace.

O flesh and bones to no avail your moan.
Conformity is right a man must leave this life.
With hands upraised to God in praise death's illusion fades.
We will travel home to rejoice for countless days.
With angel voices singing joyful loud and clear,
"O God, Almighty, another son is here!
Through the barrier he's come without worry care or fear.
Hallelujah!"

Psalm 23:4 Even though I walk through the valley of death, I will fear no evil, for you are with me your rod and your staff they comfort me.

2 Corinthians 4:16 Therefore we do not lose heart. Though outwardly we are wasting away, yet inwardly we are being renewed day by day.

Ecclesiastes 7:1 A good name is better than precious ointment, and the day of death better than the day of one's birth.

Healing

꩜

Sorrow makes its mark indelible and stark
It finds each tiny hiding place and makes its presence known
Marrow flesh blood and bone are thrown into the mix
Cry's and screams from deep inside fly like hurricanes
Until the heart and mind and soul begin to walk again.

Into the mist of cloud filled sighs
The heart descends and spirit cries
Tremors race to temple's brace
Purchase heavy whispers "break"
Defense born at morrow's gate
Enter still the crashing waves of yesterday.

A word of courage emanates from a dark and gloomy place,
"Fear not the shroud and coffin pall ending day in westward fall.
See the clouds they bow above and through the misty haze
See the healer of the soul wash the hurt away.
With truth comes sweet surrender
To walk on water in the storm
To holdfast hope we have known
To find a place inside that knows
Where the Vine of Love resides
With leaves of green in sunlight reign
Etched in each the precious name
Of all God has saved."

꩜

Revelation 19:9 Then the angel said to me, "Write: Blessed are those who are called to the wedding supper of the Lamb!" And he added, "These are the true words of God."

John 15:5 "I am the vine; you are the branches. If a man remains in me and I in him, he will bear much fruit; apart from me you can do nothing."

In remembrance of the Twin Towers—9/11/2001

Might

⁓

The Potter breaks the pot for the defect it presents.
He who made the pot knows what to expect.
So it is injustice will flee in panicked flight.
Smashing into pieces grinding it away
Into the night of darkness forever it must stay.
With its brother pride and the evil in man's hand
The hidden things in hearts and plans produced at night
Will be brought to justice by the power of God's might.

Run to the mountains seek shelter in caves
Now the time has come when consequence does say,
"You played with truth and abused her every way
No longer is it time for you to think and pray
Now the time has come, the day you thought would never
Is here and with it beats the sentence of forever!"

The Lord of all creation has called an end to days
Of thoughts without the heart and spirit absent praise
"Look to the mountains
He comes upon the clouds
His Kingdom to sustain
With justice and judgment forever and a day.
O man of foolish pride repent-repent today!
Before the trumpet sounds before it is too late.
Before the Lord arrives and salvation's time does end
It's yours to see and choose majesty arrayed
Or to run and hide without hope of being saved."

⁓

Revelation 19:11 I saw heaven standing open and there before me
was a white horse, whose rider is called Faithful and True. With
justice he judges and makes war.

Revelation 6:15-17 Then the kings of the earth, the princes, the
generals, the rich, the mighty, and every slave and free man hid in

caves, and among the rocks of the mountains. They called to the mountains and the rocks, "Fall on us and hide us from the face of him who sits on the throne and from the wrath of the Lamb!"

Isaiah 2:10 Go to the rocks, hide in the ground from the dread of the Lord and the splendor of his majesty. The eyes of the arrogant man will be humbled and the pride of man brought low; the Lord alone will be exalted in that day.

Power

～～～

God's power is ability to safeguard and secure what is right and good.
The one who gave it from his throne says, "Blessing is approved."
When it is used to make suffering the norm
It appears on the world's stage as absolutely wrong.

No matter, it's yours to choose, tight fist or open hand
Demonstrating understanding of what belongs to man.
A grab for power is illegal in God's eyes
And when it loses luster it will surely die.
What is given to a man must be used according to God
Who placed it in his hand or else
It will also fade by numbering its days.

Tight fist closed mind cold heart blind eyes
Searching for a high place where privileged children play
Games of kings and queens, alas for but a day.
Tight fist closed mind imprisoned spirit gropes
And fails to bring the power that the unrighteous hope
Will gain for them an audience affirming world acclaim
Find their race for power has placed upon them chains.

Stone upon stone lock upon chain
Down beneath deep rock and hard place
Tight fist to the grave arrogance stays
On top of the bones as decorative death, meaningless!

～～～

Mark 9:1 And he said to them, "I tell you the truth, some of you who are standing here will not taste death before they see the kingdom of God come with power."

Matthew 5:5 "Blessed are the meek, for they will inherit the earth."

By Design

⌒⌒⌒

Before man could move forward in confident strides
Thought had to be given to fashioning hands
By project designers of competent plans
All of our efforts do not advance
When failing the truth concerning the past
Antiquity seekers of that which did last
Have unearthed such wonders we hardly can grasp
While digging one day they happen to find
The remains of a man and arrow so fine
They thought it created out of design
By one with a weapon in mind
The bones of the man they counseled for naught
No designer needed
No thinker of thought
No plan for the man to be wrought?

⌒⌒⌒

Genesis 1:26 Then God said: "Let us make man in our image,
after our likeness."

Tears

~~~

Just what are tears and what is their purpose?
No matter the cause, heartache or joy there is release.
Too much of sorrow will begin to rob our strength.
That's why we are told to mourn and then to let it end.
Of course no one has words that can bring to an end our powerless
condition
That calls with a voice weak as embers to the night that took our friend.

Is it really a loss? "Yes it is."
What then brings to us the joy of life again?
The knowledge of knowing it's not a permanent goodbye.
Yes, the knowledge of knowing is the key.
For when we know a thing is true the hurt and pain must leave
And in its place we find strength holding tight to our belief.

But it is more than faith or, "I believe."
It is the presence of our God that lives inside of you.
Tears are the healing way that God has placed in man.
In death there is sorrow and in joy renewal's spark
That carries the burden of a heavy hurting heart.

In time there is a healing when tears cease to flow.
No longer as a river to a place it does not know.
But in the quiet time of night and thoughts turn to those who've gone
We feel and touch the love they've left behind.
In this we are assured they live in spirit/soul.
The love that is present makes clear we'll meet again.
You see, only one thing never dies and that's the love of a friend.

~~~

Revelation 7:17 And God will wipe away every tear from their eyes.

John 15:14-17 You are my friends if you do what I command. I
no longer call you servants, because a servant does not know his

*master's business. Instead, I have called you friends, for everything
I have learned from my Father I have made known to you.*

*John 11:33-35 When Mary reached the place where Jesus was and
saw him, she fell at his feet and said, "Lord, if you had been here
my brother would not have died." When Jesus saw her weeping,
and the Jews who had come along with her weeping, he was deeply
moved in spirit and troubled. "Where have you laid him?" he
asked. "Come and see, Lord," they replied. Jesus wept.*

*1John 4:15 If anyone acknowledges that Jesus is the Son of God,
God lives in him and he in God. And so we know and rely on the
love God has for us. God is love.*

Windows of Light

⟨⟨⟨⟩⟩⟩

There are times when we receive clarity exploding with revelation.
It is at these times we must stop and understand it's something that's
given.
It is natural to ask, "Where does this come from?"
A stone tossed into the sky seizes the moment to fly.
It brings back to earth a far greater worth for its vision was that of a tree.

Should it return to a lake upon water it makes a statement suggestive
"he"
That gave to stone the vision of trees.
We too get windows of light sometimes from wondrous heights
And the things that we see cause visions of glee
Within hearts where lived only night.

Knowledge given contains power from the moment we receive.
Announcing to the spirit, "New life begins, now that you believe."
Now that you can see the truth of what you've been
The power to hold head up high declares, "Today you are a man."

There is power in the day freedom's breath we take
To do the things we knew as right but could not break away.
There is peace in the knowledge of he who sent his flame
That burned away the tyranny allowing truth to reign.

Like sanctifying embers engulfing us with love
You opened the window to your presence
Giving truth to common man and life giving water
Within a dark and barren land
That held a man rejected beaten chained and lost
Set free by God's mercy displayed upon a cross.

Truth shone with healing understanding
And spoke words all captives hope
"Pick up your mat and walk"

This day has come salvation to a house where all was dark.
O burning flame of power with torrents of God's grace
Saving rain from heaven to wash upon this place
Bursting through the veil with transforming light
Dwell in me forever and hold back the ways of night.

~~~

Acts 2:14 When the day of Pentecost came, they were all together in one place. Suddenly a sound like the blowing of a violent wind came from heaven and filled the whole house where they were sitting. They saw what seemed to be tongues of fire that separated and came to rest on each of them.

O God

It would be very nice to put an end to lots of stuff
The lies from crooked tongues
The war for power whose only aim is gain
And of course it would be great to see justice once again.
Let's put an end to philosophies causing blindness of the mind.
Let's remove deception that keeps a man from God.
Gone are the old ways when evil caused us pain
Let us remember to keep it buried in the grave!
Let's put an end to politics that tell us what's correct.
We know what is and is not good so what need is there for this?
A man must be competitive in order to achieve
And one must find the truth of life in order to believe.

O God, bring an end to time itself that step by stepped the grave.
It's a concept whose time has come and should now in turn be slain.
O God, bring an end to the cover-ups spin doctors velvet script
Surely it's a viper's tongue that caused us all to slip.
Bring an end to hands feeding man false passion and desire
Keeping man alive but never satisfied.
Desire it is said is like the world of the dead. "Always room for more!"
So bring an end to all that says, "This will heal and cure."
So say the street physicians whose offerings endure
The wind rain and weather as a plague upon the poor.

The same feeding hands capture children's hearts at play
With addiction that demands as a whistle of a train
Speeding toward the end with promise to escape
Marching as afflicted to the place they know not where
As cattle led to slaughter troubled by despair
They know that something's wrong with the way they're made to bow
To the drugs of broken promise on the streets of here and now!
O God, bring an end to death
That mocked and brought to us great sorrow.
Say goodbye to yesterday today and tomorrow.

O God, when you come again may all of this come true
Bring an end to all that is and beginning what is new.
Amen.

~~~~

Isaiah 61:1-3 The Spirit of the Sovereign Lord is on me, because the Lord has anointed me to preach good news to the poor. He has sent me to bind up the brokenhearted, to proclaim freedom for the captives and release for the prisoners, to proclaim the year of the Lord's favor and the day of vengeance of our God, to comfort all who mourn, and provide for those who grieve in Zion—to bestow on them the crown of beauty instead of ashes, the oil of gladness instead of mourning, and a garment of praise instead of a spirit of despair.

The Lion

Okay let's remember, when was the last time you laid eyes on a real lion?
I'll bet you were glad a cage separated him from you, or at least some
distance, right?
I'll bet his teeth made the immediate impression of, "Definitely, king of
the jungle."
It was not as if the lion could reach-out and declare you to be his lunch,
right?
Well it seems to me we should be taking stock of the terminology given to
Jesus.
He is called the, "Lion of Judah."
And when last I looked he was free to reach out to any of us.
Fortunately his ability to reach us does not mean he is looking for lunch.

The lion has such strength within his teeth and paws
All who view his majesty fall from his gaze
King has been his title throughout all of his days.
He lives a life free from all attack
And with confident ability he shows enemies his back.
Our lion is not hungry for our lives or our bones.
His purpose is seeking all of us to come home.

There is however, a lion of evil intent, a lion of stealth and darkness.
He is constantly hungry roaming throughout the earth seeking to destroy.
He is seeking everyone, but mostly the uninformed the unbeliever and the
know it all.
For these his palate is aroused and he takes time in their demise.
Slowly he digs a deep dark hole and places them inside.
Little by little he returns to nibble on his prize.

This lion also has a name that many scoff and laugh when heard.
They say it is an old wives tale like judgment and justice of God.
But many know the truth of him who will be chained in hell.
They name this snake the devil and many know him well.

Unfortunately this knowledge
Came to them
By ringing the dinner bell.

⌒ ᵕ ᵕ ⌒

1 Peter 5:8 Be self-controlled and alert. Your enemy the devil prowls around like a hungry lion looking for someone to devour.

Revelation 5"5 Then one of the elders said to me, "Do not weep! See the Lion of the tribe of Judah, the root of David, has triumphed; he is able to open the scroll and it seven seals."

Instruction

❦

There's a definite blockage in the mind of the young.
The more we say, "Listen" the deafer they become.
There's a malady under the sun, it seems,
No matter what we say they always say, "I know."
I've come to the conclusion a brick wall has been erected
Standing tall and unaffected by the consequence of, "know it all."
Is it preordained the youth must suffer scrapes and bumps at least
In order to recognize the truth in loving pleas saying, "Avoid these!"

As long as I have breath I'll keep on trying to warn and caution them.
With an old man's vision of what can and will happen when impulse
runs ahead.
You see, the old man's vision and the young man's dreams
Are different from the start, the old man sees the road ahead and knows
the trouble parts.
The young man dreams of future paths in hurried steps to take
But rarely heeds the warning signs of old man's mistakes.
This world has adopted a strategy that offers to our youth everything in
order to enslave.
Enslaved by debt and/or to substances that keep them from competing
Against deception's lies and the pulling manipulations of evil's
mechanizations.
Pay attention, O children of this life, and you will live in peace and not
in grief and strife.

❦

Proverbs 1:8 Listen, my son, to your father's instruction and do
not forsake your mother's teaching.

Psalm 78:1-4 Listen, my people, to my teaching, and pay attention
to what I say. I am going to use wise sayings and explain mysteries
from the past, things we have heard and known, that our father's
told us. We will not keep them from our children; we will tell the
next generation about the Lord's power and his great deeds and
the wonderful things he has done.

Restful fall

The affliction of hopelessness carries with it a heavy price.
Fear of living overcomes the fear of death.
The promise of a better life lures some to catch a comet.
There are those who clearly have evil intentions
Leading some to end it all with a communal drink.
All of these and more are but falsehoods
Masquerading as release from pain
"Go on why suffer any longer?"
Is said in many ways.
Fingers clutching precipice have tenuous existence.
Plunging into depths of unknown measure.
Darkness hangs like a shroud absent is reason here and now.
Depression the cornering venomous snake
That speaks lies and remedies that take the life we've been given
And slithers away to speak the words, "end it all."
To another whose life has found the edge darkness appears as a friend.

Torment sorrow guilt and fear as portraits in the clouds
Aching is a voice that whines,
"What purpose to prolong this mocking screech of deprivations song?"

A struggle this life we live.
Confronting hardships clinging to a handhold of hope.
Deny the voice of promised restful fall.
For letting go never ends it all.

Luke 4:9 "If you are the Son of God" he said, "throw yourself down from here."

Fill it up

⌒⌒⌒

Fill it up please, pressed down pushed together overflowing top
I don't want to sound insistent, but "Please fill it up."
Fill it with effervescent ebullience enough to rock the cup.
Add to it a turbulence releasing lots of joy
So I'll dance around 'til strength is spent like a little boy.

Fill it up, O Lord, until my insides ache
Until slain in the Spirit
Until my body shakes
Until the wonder of your presence overloads the place
Fill it up, O Lord, for goodness sake.
One kiss says acceptance enough to fill the space.
One word to the spirit is overflowing grace.
One vision of your smile will do it all the time.
So fill it up, O Lord, and rock this world of mine!

⌒⌒⌒

Matthew 5:6 Blessed are those who hunger and thirst for righteousness, for they will be filled.

Chains

They are still with us and in most cases there're necessary.
Prisoners are held in a state of inability to cause harm.
And some chains hold heavy weights adding mechanical advantage.
But the most troublesome are those that demand of us action
Otherwise a penalty of noncompliance will be imposed.

Years ago, chain gangs were forced to produce
Along roads of states that decided their fate
For them there was not a choice
Failure meant beatings or worse.
Motivation was fear present and clear
The rule of the gang was remembered through pain,
"Under penalty, break not the chain."

Today they are present in name borne by letters possessing false claims.
Its message still clear containing fear, "Under penalty, break not the chain."
To some this is cause for concern for they have not received and/or heard
The letters containing God's word, bringing not a troubling verse
Rather, promises meant to be claimed, for all to be free of life's chains.

2 Timothy 2:8-9 Remember, Jesus Christ raised from the dead, descended from David. This is my gospel, for which I am suffering even to the point of being chained like a criminal. But God's word is not chained. Therefore I endure everything for the sake of the elect that they too may obtain salvation that is in Christ Jesus, with eternal glory.

High Heat

The world is filled with troubles that come and go as thieves.
Unexpected as the rumbling earth and heart attacks of pain
They appear as either loss of life or else eternal gain.
The heart of man has trouble deep within, caused by truth rejected
Conflicting with his sins.
The one who is selected and blessed with words to heal
Has not the option silence in compliance with the world.
Truth cannot be buried or shut inside a vault
As in volcanic action high heat bursting from the crest
Will burn away deception and always win the test.

❧

Jeremiah 20:9 But if I say, "I will not speak anymore in his name," his word is in my heart like a burning fire, shut up in my bones. I am weary of holding it in; indeed I cannot.

Don't Worry

Sometimes it's just easier to keep quiet.
Really, there are times when words are just not adequate.
You've lost your job and savings?
You've lost a great uncle pal?
Lost your house?
And somehow, "Don't worry" brings the sunshine out?
Of course, "Don't worry" is meaningless if we are not prepared to help.
It's an easy thing to say.
Yes, everything has consequence, a price to pay.
No matter joy or sorrow, loss or gain, there will always be a price to pay.
The rich lose the ability to walk among common folks.
The poor go unnoticed and the workman is too busy to see either one.
"Don't worry," means nothing to all classes of society.

"Don't worry" makes not pain to cease.
It causes not serenity or brings to life real peace.
It doesn't begin to dispel fear and offers not a
Shred of hope to wipe away the tears that always will accompany
The heart and soul of fears that keep a man awake even when asleep.

I ask you, who worries when there is nothing left?
Where is the confidence that power issues forth?
Where is the message for those whose hearts are lost?
Where does a man place his head and heart?
When all about him appears crest fallen sun up 'til dark.
When all there is and nothing more cries deeply in the night
Where is the strength to carry on the struggle of this life?
"Don't worry" takes on a mocking uncaring tone
That penetrates the heart and infects the bones
Of all who suffer loss in the confusion zone!

Our Great hope is God.
Almighty God and Father,
When you say not to worry your voice fills the soul

For you, O Sovereign Lord, are always in control.
In you there is the confidence to step into the night.
Knowing your hand is with me and your rod is truth and might.
Your kindness fills the body with food fit for a king.
You place a robe upon my shoulder and speak to me the things
That makes the sadness run as restoration sings,
Hallelujah, to the Lord on High who brings peace of mind again!

Matthew 6:25 "Therefore I tell you, do not worry about your life, what you will eat or drink, or about your body, what you will wear."

Matthew 6:34 "Do not worry about tomorrow, for tomorrow will worry about itself. Each day has enough trouble of its own."

The Pendulum of Change

It has always been a two way street.
Grinding teeth posturing grins flexing peacock's walk
If it were not so serious comics would have a ball.
Is it really so bad nowadays or has the pendulum swung the other way?
Seems to me those who did the suffering have passed away
And the only one's complaining are the street hustling organizers.
Insatiable screaming organizing and teaming-up
In order to fill the pocket and not the beggar's cup.
Let's face it if racism was gone they would be out of a job.
Community organizer is another way of saying blackmailer.
They just won't go away, O my, someday.
Like a socialist that's never satisfied, their demands are never quelled.
"Give me more or else, I'll cause disharmony hatred and social unrest."
And the more they get the more they want from us who never gave them
hell.
Again, it seems we are made to pay for those who've left the scene
Are buried long ago with their dream of living free.
There is nothing that I can do to undo the injustice of the past,
Except to safeguard the present.
The color of my skin marks me as a racist, really?
And soon they'll monitor my thoughts, O gosh!
I'm maligned, placed behind and monitored in all my speech.
As if I'm a disease waiting to break out
And advocate slavery of those already enslaved by the state.
Unless a man finds peace, unless he accepts himself,
He will always want more laws to justify his existence.
Everyone should know it's the evil in a man
That makes him desire more and attempts to dominate all he sees.
Who is listening to a common man when the voice of truth is gagged?
The microphone called media is more like, "Ministers of Propaganda!"
Amazing how these tombstones actually have a voice.
Are fashioned from materials not of common stock.
Are made of different colors of every shape and size
With visible foundations hollowed out by pride.

Prepared illusions facades perceived as clean
Hatred poured as mortar supporting shallow beams.
Ignorance the catalyst forging bitterness for seams.
The parapets are raised without a level line
By the uneven setting of bigotry's design
Prejudice the architect from the tower waves
Sending misdirection to those who have no sight.
All the change and agitation has been constructed in the night.

Galatians 4:1-7 What I am saying is that as long as the heir is a child, he is no different from a slave, although he owns the whole estate. He is subject to guardians and trustees until the time set by his father. So also, when we were children, we were in slavery under the basic principles of the world. But when the time had fully come, God sent his Son, born of a woman, born under the law, to redeem those under the law, that we might receive the full rights of sons. Because you are sons, God sent the Spirit of his Son into our hearts, the Spirit that cries out "Abba, Father." So you are no longer slaves, but a son; and since you are a son, God has made you also an heir.

Zoom-Zoom

Listening to a racecar engine's exhaust is like a lion's roar.
The jet plane's power is evident of speed.
So many things are fast, especially in the animal kingdom.
The slow poke ends up on the menu.
Light is supposed to be the fastest thing of all
One hundred eighty six thousand miles per second
Zoom-zoom couldn't catch it on a good day.
The fastest thing is, "thought,"
Zoom, I'm on the moon as quickly as can be
"As quickly as can be" cannot be measured.
Light is still traveling on the speed of nature's wings.
It is no wonder prayer is a calling card that rings heaven's bell.
As quick as all get out faster than a comet's tail.
God anticipates our calling at every twist and turn
Because the life that we've been given must be quickly learned.
Traveling at the speed of thought is mind-boggling.
But still we can't out pace eternity no matter how we try.
I suppose forever is the place that left us behind
When first we thought to listen to the allurement of a lie.
Someday we will come face to face
With the place that's called eternal
When yesterday is gone
When the past is all forgotten burnt up in the sun
When today is left remaining untouched and free from harm
And no longer is it measured by the tick-tock of alarm.
Since God's thoughts are so much higher than our own
So much faster than ours, then truly,
His salvation and justice is speeding faster than our comprehension.
Feeble are our thoughts that travel at snails pace
Marching as in concert to a rhythm men compete
Never finding time to hear life's symphony.
Faster than thunder's clap and faster still again
Lightning sends its message and his hand parts the cloud

Revealing the last chapter in the book that's called, "The Man."
And then the second printing begins it all again
Except there is omitted the brokenness of sin.

⌇⌇⌇

Luke 11:9 "So I say to you: Ask and it will be given to you; seek and you will find; knock and the door will be opened to you."

Isaiah 51:5 "My righteousness draws near speedily, my salvation is on the way, and my arm will bring justice to the nations."

Isaiah 55:8 "For my thoughts are not your thoughts, neither are my ways your ways," declares the Lord.

Measured Man

A man is measured by the conduct of his life
Scrutinized by those he meets and knows
They listen to his speech and judge the appearance of his clothes
The bearing of his stature, pronouncement of his words
All come into question as a man is judged on earth.

The imperfection of a man judging another is destined to fail.
Dust to dust sin to sin a perfect judge is not in man.
Flawed and corrupt is the gavel in his hand
And none can throw a stone unattached to sin.
And so it is with understanding a man's judgment is mighty thin.

We can say, "His heart is heavy," but who can weigh such a thing?
Neither can the soul and thoughts find a scale.
The perfect Judge does not measure a man.
He weighs him,
And finding his heart as stone his mind rigid as pride
He then seeks to find a spark of good hidden deep inside.

The wisdom of such a Judge sees the errant ways of man.
Such wisdom wants to bestow mercy to make him understand.
He does not force a man to find and trust what's right.
He could make him bow to the awesome power of his might.
Instead he speaks to him as one who has lost a son.
And in convincing wisdom forgives him all his wrongs.
At the very moment such mercy strikes his soul
Tears of pure contrition break out in mighty shouts!
For the man then finds his measure is the same inside and out!

Proverbs 16:2 All the ways of a man may be pure in his own eyes, but it is the Lord who proves the spirit.

Proverbs 16:11 Balance and scales belong to the Lord; all the weights used with them are his concern.

Daniel 5:27 Tekel, you have been weighed on the scales and found wanting; Peres, your kingdom has been divided and given to the Medes and Persians.

Necessity

There are so many things I can do without.
Every one of them is a negative that will not be missed.
I have no need for gambling, as once it was a friend
And there is no need for alcohol to make my headache spin.
What use it there for hip-hop songs that denigrate at will?
And what about the movie shows that glorify high crimes?
There is no need for all of these once truth becomes our guide.

There are so many things I cannot do without.
The blessings of the Lord are too many to account.
His righteous light bathes away the gloom.
His sacrifice now mocks the empty tombs
That called to us with laughter
Are muted as the stone was rolled away
And in resurrection promise we live free to watch and pray
Unfading and untarnished as the robes we'll wear that day.

Without understanding of the one who called us home
This life's a brief encounter, a flickering of light
A dance that offers movement then in silence brings the night
To stumble in the darkness of unknowing and in pride
Clouding life's true vision of the spirit trapped inside.

Without knowledge ignorance would reign
None could know his plan to breath life into the man.
Without his mercy dressed in love
His word revealed in precious blood
His truth dispelling ignorance
This world of ours would make no sense!
So much for independence within the life of man
It's a diversion of illusion that captures all who stray
Away from all that's necessary in a world of errant ways.

413

Proverbs 19:2 "Without knowledge even zeal is not good; and he who acts hastily blunders."

Ephesians 2:12—remember that at that time you were separate from Christ, excluded from citizenship in Israel and foreigners to the covenants of the promise, without hope and without God in the world.

Revelation 7:9 After this I had a vision of a great multitude, which no one could count, from every nation, race, people, and tongue. They stood before the Lamb, wearing white robes and holding palm branches in their hands, They cried out in a loud voice: "Salvation comes from our God, who is seated on the throne, and from the Lamb."

A Question

Everywhere we go we are faced with questions.
Our line of work knows no limitation of inquisitive nature.
It's our job to answer questions that solve problems.
Sometimes we are faced with an external injury requiring a hospital visit.
"Please fill out the form, answer all of the questions as best you can,
I'll be with you shortly."
As fate would have it
A nuisance of affliction flew into my eye.
The triage nurse was helpful by directing me at first
To the kind receptionist with whom I must converse,
"What is your religion?" she asked.
Among other questions that identify
"Christian" was my answer to which came no reply.
I guessed she'd heard it all before from lots of other guys.

After being treated and receiving status good
I thought about that question and reasoned it this way:
Not wanting to paint a picture of a lost and sinful world
It's hard to believe many are identified
As followers of the evil one, the father of all lies.
And so, to my way of thinking I am given to conclude
For that religion question not all are telling truth.
I can imagine the truthful answers that should be given.
Religious to the point that descriptive application
Fits inside the box, asked to be checked.
Thief.
Magician.
Atheist.
Cult leader.
Politician.
Liar.
Comet chaser.
And the list goes on and on and on.
You see, it is clear

415

The road that leads to salvation is narrow.
Neither wide traveling groups marching together
Or singular stepping fools are permitted through the door
That opens without effort, for all who hear God's call.

～～～

Mark 7:6-7 He replied, "Isaiah was right when he prophesied about you hypocrites; as it is written: These people honor me with their lips, but their hearts are far from me. They worship me in vain; their teachings are but rules taught by men.

Relating to Others

〜✦〜

Advice to others is sometimes good.
And at times it is better to just keep quiet.
One of the most difficult times to speak
Presents itself in caskets, they don't answer back.
They don't have the capacity to hear
And frankly at this point they just don't care.
But those of the living are awaiting something that says it all.
"He was a good father and grandfather."
"He was a good provider."
"God loves him."
And so the accolades continue as if never said before.
They could be said with a megaphone and the same result is born.
"The man is dead what else can we say?"

O that sounds too callous to me.
Why not try to let others see acceptance on your face?
We have to be delicate because sadness is like a wild animal
It takes to running and troubles hitch a ride
And in the heat of day is when they learn to fly.
Like a stampede confusion sets it off.

All of us deal with it differently, but we should learn to listen.
Listening for the arrival of the place of open skies
Where happiness unmeasured speaks the word, "Alive."
Residing in the heart of God, where all that's his survives.
Try to listen and not explain to those who tremble deep within.
All our efforts are really shallow since we don't reside
Within the saddened spirit of loss personified.
Sometimes our efforts are better left undone
At least for a moment give this time to a friend.
In due time a light will shine inside
The hearts of those who suffered loss
They will hear the comforting
Voice speak the words so clear

"I heard your cries and know your pain,
Entertain no longer fear
Rejoice as would a day of birth
For the one you love is here!"

Revelation 7:17 And God will wipe away every tear from their eyes.

Thirst Conquest

We thirst for so many things and nothing offers permanence.
My tongue is dry and parched and water brings temporary relief.
Hunger is a thirst that takes on many forms
Power greed position, craving a chance to orchestrate a vision
Where sits atop the mountain those whose egos gloat
And laugh aloud at people who live in lands below.
What is consequence to those whose lives are sheltered?
A mannequin in a storefront put on for display?
They don't understand it and flat out reject it.
Their thirst for wealth and power is really a thirst for escape
From the dominance of others whose motives resemble snakes.
In turn they find the venom a tasty bit of hate
And in time it's the very form they emulate and take.
They speak to those without wealth and power,
"A snake's life can be great!"
A jutting jaw of hissing rage that sends out an alarm
Speaking with a judgment sound and a prideful tongue
No matter the condition, living in a lake, or on a snow capped mount
The snake of wealth and power
Will never quench his thirst for he's tasted lying venom
From the pool of foolish pride
And waded in the waters that promised him the earth.

So many distractions that claim to quench our thirst
Claim to leave us feeling good when we're at our worst.
There's a longing in the soul of man that doesn't scream or shout
It doesn't cry with deafening sound, "Get me something now!"
Still, when we come to understand the language that it speaks
We'll have no need for searching for our thirst will be complete.

Romans 12:20 Rather, *"if your enemy is hungry, feed him; if he is thirsty, give him something to drink; for by so doing you will heap burning coals upon his head."* Do not be conquered by evil but conquer evil with good.

Following

⌒⌒⌒⌒⌒

Following requires trust.
No one would follow or allow himself to be led
Without first believing, "He knows what's best."
Many a leader has proven to be foolish at great costs to others.
It's no wonder when asked to follow into action or battle
Confidence and trust is the first to step forward.
Setting aside our ability and self preserving thoughts
As if to say, "This plan sounds righteous and just."
When it comes to Jesus, all who believe follow his teachings.
It is we, who say, "Lord, we must follow,
For only you have the words that lead to eternal life."
When we suffer abrasions to our being from the loads we choose to bear
At times they bite the heart and soul causing us despair.
We hear cries from the poor-in-spirit seeking truth in this great-war
They long to know the way but find doors are always closed.
It's then we're brought to deeper thought propelled by your great strength.
It's then with every step advancing the loads seem lighter still.
We see you there before us and mountains turn to hills.
Who are we to share this honored place?
It seems but for an instant in the span of this brief life
With the promise of eternity the paradox is clear
Only you could have conceived a way to make man hear.
We have been given to know it's not by chance we carry heavy loads.
Hardships appear differently through the eyes of love.
Who would deny a helping hand to a man who asks?
There was a time we were bound and gagged
And in our hour of need God reached out his hand.
"To which ever you choose stretch forth your hand."
Fire or water bringing life or death to man.
It's the clear and potent message God wants us to understand.
Lord, we follow your example forged in sacrifice.
We know the earthly fire unrelenting in its aim,
To keep a man in bondage suffering enslaved.
We have watched in great sorrow your suffering for men

Displayed upon the stage of worldly witness eyes
You came to end the mockery of potent empty lies.
Until this very day your truth is healing many
Freeing all held tightly in the grip of mankind's enemy.

⌒⌒⌒

Matthew 8:21 "Another man, one of his disciples, said to him, "Lord, first let me go and bury my father." But Jesus said to him, "Follow me, and let the dead bury their own dead."

Sheep

⌒⌒⌒

Little sheep listen carefully.
There are animals in the field that look at you as food.
They'll surround and come together and drag you into woods
And in no time at all you'll be dead and gone
No one will ever miss you since you never said, "Goodbye."
If you haven't noticed there's a man that's called, "Shepherd"
He leads you to clean water and grass beneath your feet
And keeps you all from harm when the wolf decides to eat.

Some sheep love to travel in the dark.
They love to travel widely to visit other flocks
And sometimes in their bleats criticism knocks.

They won't submit to shearing complaining of its pull
And so we never really know what's underneath their wool.
Pay attention to the Shepherd you widely traveled few
Lest you be unprotected and end up in the stew.

Yes, a sheep is not the brightest of animals.
But they do love the company of others of their kind.
In fact, they don't have as much worry like a chicken or other meaty
friend.
They share their wool with everyone and grow it back again.
I suppose they do not mind too much since there're protected
But once they start to roam around outside the sheep gate pen
There is no guarantee they won't be cut and fried
By the wolves who'll not miss the opportunity
For sheep, and potato on the side.

⌒⌒⌒

**John 10:1 "I am the good shepherd; I know my sheep an my sheep
know me,"**

Command

As I look back on my military days of service
I don't ever remember having been given the option to decline a command.
The command was cut and dry, "Aye aye sir," was the reply.
It meant, "I understand and I will comply, sir."
There was no room for debate, especially when on a wartime footing.
General Quarters meant more than a place to hang around.
It spoke to everyone in specific terms, "Go to your station and prepare for war."

Commanded compliance implies there's a need that's risen.
Some have failed to understand the one who is speaking is, "The Great I Am."
Holy is the Lord our God images and nothings are not allowed.
How cool is that, "You shall not worship a nothing."
That makes a lot of sense!
Keep clear of idol images and the nothing craft
It gives the wrong appearance
That God can be diminished, and we know that's bad.
Again, this sounds like not only good advice but it is a command to be followed.
After all who wants to worship an idol made of stone or other material?
That too makes sense!
It's not like you are going to get an answer,
Might as well talk to a stuffed animal.
Of course I have but have never worshipped one.
The reason God does not allow certain things is simple.
Because he does not want us clouded by a world arrayed with traps.
It's really a lack of understanding in he who is commanding
When we know, "nothing" means just that.
"Nothing from nothing leaves nothing," and so the song goes.
So let us not waste our time causing undo stress for God and mostly our selves.

Misplaced faith finds deception as a guide.
He falls into a pit and expects to be rescued?
In time the truth will dawn on him,
The pit was dug before the foundations of the earth.
It is called anticipation with a dash of predestination.

Exodus 20:12 I am the Lord your God who brought you out of Egypt, out of the land of slavery, You shall have no other gods before me.

1 Kings 18:16-18 So Obadiah went to king Ahab and told him, and Ahab set off to meet Elijah. When Ahab saw him, he said, "So there you are—the worst troublemaker in Israel!" "I'm not the troublemaker," Elijah answered, "You are—you and your father. You are disobeying the Lord's commands by worshiping the idols of Baal.

Revolving Doors

❧

These doors are user friendly they operate both ways
So entering right or left is perfectly okay
There will always be someone
With a fixed state of mind
Unaware of the movement against their way of life
The maker of the doors has made it plain
"Pay attention lest the wrong approach cause you hurt and pain.
By rigidly assuming it must operate your way."

Throughout the world of men there are voices heard
Loudly applauding God, who sent to us his Word.
He who created you and me and trees
The heavens and the universe
With brightly shining stars
Wants all to recognize the love within his heart.

Pay attention those of you who
Gamble with your very life
The God of love and truth
Is right before your eyes.
As with many things
Deception's here and there
But when it comes to God
Creation's mark is clear.
Pay attention,
There is in no other motive than to show to you God's love.
To be again united with those who've said goodbye.
Sharing then eternity with he who is, Most High.

❧

Proverbs 12:15 The way of the fool seems right to him, but a wise man listens to advice.

Locksmith

We call a locksmith to change or fix a lock
It either has been compromised or cannot do its job.
Many locks have combinations and others have a key
But each and every one of them has authority.

A combination of numbers keyed in a row
To the right and the left in order must go
Gaining entrance to chamber releasing the gate
Unlocking the bolt preventing the way.
Locks are like the order of days
Rise with the sun until work is done
Sleep under a blanket of stars.
Sorrow sets the spring
Hurt can harden parts
Betrayal slides the deadbolt
But love unlocks the heart.

Matthew 5:10 "Blessed are those who are persecuted because of righteousness, for theirs is the kingdom of heaven."

Life's Solution

Even the very wealthy have problems.
There is no escaping the hazards of life.
Sickness can snap some people right back to what matters.
Addictions speak more to the slave than one free to travel the earth.
Yes, even the rich can find mental decay and in this
No matter what they own it fades away.
The poor are not much different
They have problems of a more immediate need
Eating, shelter and yes even brushing of teeth
Can pose a problem to the poor living in the streets.

A poor man named Lazarus
Found all he could ever imagine
When upon entering paradise he was greeted by many
They knew of the hardships of his life
All of the troubling days he went hungry
And how he was, viewed as nothing by a rich man.

Within all of his confusion and suffering
He knew what many had not
God was always with him
From the morning to the night
Obstacles as mountains daily he did climb
To keep his self alive, but with all of his sometimes confusion
He found solutions only wisdom could provide.

He was not a rich man
Neither could he buy or sell
But he heard the call of wisdom
And avoided the fires of hell.
Now Lazarus, it is said was rich indeed
For he knew of the God who loved him
And to his voice he paid heed.

Lazarus was the richest poorest man alive
But within the walls of heaven's gates
He was treated like a king
In the bosom of Abraham he lacked for not a thing.

~~~

Deuteronomy 15:7 If there is a poor man among your brothers in any of the towns of the land the Lord your God is giving you, do not he hardhearted or tightfisted toward your poor brother.

Matthew 5:3 "Blessed are the poor in spirit for theirs is the kingdom of heaven.

Double Talk

We don't recognize it until we gain some years
It's then the double hidden standard becomes a bit clearer
It's then I have to stop and think
Just what's happening here? Its not making sense!
The younger I am the less I'm given trust for lack of experience.
And the older I become the more I'm showed the door.
As if to say, "We don't want you any more."
I live half of life too young of this I have been told
And in the latter part of life they tell me,
"I'm too old!"
I admit, I sought a balanced place in time
Where it would come together and make sense to my mind.
To my chagrin I'll begin to tell of this farce,
Forget the ideal settings they don't exist upon the earth.
There is no age the suit will fit.
No special date of birth.
And most of all there are no limits for
Bull-dinghy to clog receiving ears
With efforts to confuse us with worldly cares and fear.

This world is a battlefield of intense bitter fibs
And the faster we find the truth
The sooner we begin to live.
I've seen the double talk in the workplace
In the churches of our God
I've even found it much alive hidden in the heart,

But if you want to know the truth
It's God alone who cares
It's he whose word is constant steady true.
And when we come to know this truth
All lies and double-talking are exposed and tossed into the air
Life then finds the balance that sweeps a righteous path.
In God's truth alone

Double speak is not allowed
Straight and forward "yes or no"
Keeps both feet upon the ground.

❧

John 8:43-44 *"Why is my language not clear to you? Because you are unable to hear what I say. You belong to your father, the devil, and you want to carry out your father's desire, He was a murderer from the beginning, not holding to any truth, for there is no truth in him. When he lies, he speaks his native language, for he is a liar and the father of lies."*

Adam and Me

〜〜〜

In the beginning God made it plain
Earth to the man is given to reign.
No restrictions save one,
"Adam, pay attention, Eat not from the central tree.
Heed not the call of its promising song touch not nor taste what is right
and is wrong."
One act of rebellion and man did gain days that are numbered lived in
regret
Filled with troubles and ending in death.

First stroke of the whip was meant for Adam and me.
Hammer and nail should have pierced our hands and feet.
But even with that it would not be complete.
You see an unblemished Lamb was the ransom demand.
Sinful man could not redeem himself.
Lost then were we in the place we were not meant to be.
First we were lost on the earth and then under it.
Nothing mattered, for no matter what we did
The Pawnbroker wins without redemption of sin.
Many a man has said to his self,
"I live a good life, I love my children and my wife.
I go to work each day and give to the poor.
I do all that is required and sometimes even more!
What have I done that calls me wrong?
It all sounds unjust, there must be something more."

Yes there is something more it's called sin.
Sin is the thing that God abhors.
It's not allowed to venture forth into his presence, eternity's throne.
For all that is sinful needs cleansing through blood
Shed on a cross in torment and more.
Unless we believe God is right we remain lost.
He declared the truth
To admit he is right and we are wrong.

To acknowledge his Son's redeeming grace.
To see his resurrection in your heart mind and soul
Will bring directions to the place we call home.
With Adam and me and multitudes strong!

❧

John 3:15-16 So that everyone who believes in him may have eternal life. For God loved the world so much that he gave his only Son, so that everyone who believes in him may not die but have eternal life. *GNB*

Blackened Core

❧

Silently it begins until it is formed.
It's then it tests its strength by risking a small roar.
As a poisoned rain it stings and penetrates.
With the evil of its ways it grows inside a man.
Works of dreadful hurt as if a caustic bath.
Burns away the truth and swiftly grips a man.
Deceptive hiss from viper's lips intending only harm.
Unity portrayed as caring peace and love
Was never really there in nations absent God.
Like the growth of a tree wide its range becomes
So too the evil that beckons man, "succumb."
Reaching with its branches and digging with its roots
Holding tight upon a man from his head down to his boots.
The snake within the leaves
Is then revealed to man
No longer pretense needed
Evil then declares,
"I am the darkest night you chose in place of truth.
The poisoned blackened core of lies pretending good.
You gave away God's light in favor hope and change
And now you're left bereft in shackles made of shame.
Don't act surprised or as if you did not know
You tasted rebel stew and allowed a curtain call.
Now you live in memory of when you had your way
Alas the days of prominence are gone away to stay.
Misery loves company and there's always room for more
In this the blackened core where you first learned to roar."

❧

Job 28:28 And he said to man. "The fear of the Lord—that is wisdom, and to shun evil is understanding."

Lions of Stone

Fire and water is there at your feet
Life or death is for you to decide
Believe in God's Son or simply deny.
Lions guarding a door are but stone and cannot roar.
They cannot hunt the living or rest in the shade
Tear away flesh or stalk prey
They can't move have no need for rest
Not bothered by heat because they don't sweat.
We have a choice to become alive
Or stay as stone with the appearance of life.

Lions of stone
Neither flesh nor bone
They have no cares for heaven or hell
No troubles in life to ponder or tell
No choices to make of consequence binding
No God to obey or to heaven find climbing.

Lions of stone
Are not intended to praise the God of the living.
The Savior of Man was not meant for them.
They had nothing to lose from the beginning
It's not a question of losing or winning.

We are not stone and our purpose is clear
Accept his forgiveness that showers the soul
Stretch forth your hand and in water you'll find
A life of peace and love that's divine.
In fire destruction a terrible choice
Like a lion of stone,

No heart.
No soul.
No voice.

❦

Matthew 12:13 Then he said to the man, "Stretch out your hand."
So he stretched it out and it was completely restored, just as sound
as the other.

Desire

〜〜〜

Fire to flame death to graves desires underscore
Their stated position upon fruition, "There's always room for more!"
In man they are moving intent upon proving power and riches of worth
Effort and plan within his hand to demand satisfaction from earth.
Deceit from the start they bring troubles to hearts of impetuous thought
In truth they are calling to those who are falling.
"Make ready a place for your God!"

〜〜〜

Matthew 3:2 In those days John the Baptist came preaching in the desert of Judea saying, "Repent, for the kingdom of heaven is near."

Reaction to mercy

〜〜〜

My God, I love you, you know it's true.
O my God I love you, because you are Truth.
My God, I love you and for you alone I live.
O My God, I love you for the blessings that you give.
My God I love you for the mercy you have shown.
O My God, I love you my mind and heart you own.
My God, I love you for your guidance through the night.
O My God, I love you for your unequalled might.
My God, I love, if I could I would kiss your feet.
O My God, I love you for making me complete.
My God I love you for allowing me to share
A little bit of heaven in knowing that you are really here!
My God I love you Lord I love you I confess.
Yes, My God I love you.
You're the best.

〜〜〜

Mark 12:30 "Love the Lord your God with all your heart and with all your soul and with all your mind and with all your strength."

Only Jesus

Who can know the mind of God?
Who can conceive of his plans?
Who can envision what God has in store for those who take hold of his hand?
Who can explain to the dust of the earth the miracles of trees flowers rebirth?
Who can lay claim to the knowledge of heaven's infinite expanse?
And who can tell of the seasons that bring harvest and rest for the land?
Who can offer prayers to God with praise sufficient of worth?
And who can express the love that God has bestowed upon earth?
Who can know why God loves mankind so much
He gave his Son to die on a cross?
Who?
Jesus.

1 Corinthians For since in the wisdom of God the world through its wisdom did not know him. God was pleased through the foolishness of what was preached to save those who believe.

Masterpiece

The world is depicted through great works of art
They capture perception not commonly thought.
The masters inspired by nature's pose
Present on the canvass her excellent form images from what's known.
All are but copies inspired by he who painted the heavens the color of
thought.
The universe wrought by his powerful Word
Inspired the books of wondrous verse
For all to see the work of his hands
The work of his Word and marvelous plan.

Psalm 19:1 The heavens declare the glory of God the skies
proclaim the work of his hands.

Always

⌒⌒⌒

Muffled voices spinning room machine's humming breath
One foot within the living and the other laid to rest.
Another voice now is heard inside the temple walls.
Above a light is seen filled with love and confidence.
Acknowledgement dawning reinforcing fabric spent
Strengthened and uplifting the fragility of a man.
His voice a cadence to the ear, ***"I am always with you,***
Have no fear."

⌒⌒⌒

Matthew 28:20 "And surly I will be with you always, to the very
end of the age."

Hidden Vision

"Step ahead," footfalls to test, in cobblestone shimmer reflection begs,
"Rest."
Outside the gates of city walls tall, shaking as a bowstring blur
Mockers and weepers witness sublime
Hidden the meaning, hidden the time, hidden the call in decibels high
Hidden the tears hidden the cry from hidden eyes.
"Step again." The Spirit speaks,
With humble persistence dragging his feet
Past the faces shock and shame
Symbolic the flames and smoke of this place
Hidden the meaning redemption and grace.
Crackle the fire as dancers of pain
"Place of the skull," its name
Much more the forest of this arid place
Hammer and nails hands of a man
Fruit of the tree naked and pale
Bleeding away life into sand
The love of God presented to man.

Matthew 27:50 At that moment the curtain of the temple was torn in two from top to bottom.

Different Vision

Mockers watched the Temple desecration
Victory expectations deserving worldly thought
With evil generations they looked upon the Lord.
His eyes closed shut earth rumbled forth its ire
Tombs gave up their dead
The sky became a pyre
Earthquakes parted ground
Tremors rushed the source
Awaiting movement
At the foot of the cross
In resurrection triumph
The call of God remains:
"Come to me all of you, eternal life to gain."
Victory of the cross
Quiet now the voice that mocked
The King of Kings
"O death, where now your sting?"

Matthew 27:54 When the centurion and those with him who were guarding Jesus saw the earthquake and all that happened, they were terrified, and exclaimed, "Surely he was the Son of God!"

What we know

~~~

We know without anger the blood slows.
Give time to think before an action grows.
We know to have a poor spirit pride cannot find a place.
In this humble knowledge understanding rests in peace.
We know our nature to be wrong
It sings and laughs and plays the game
But deep inside what's found is the uneasy feeling
That God is not around.
We know to be humble causes change underneath the skin.
When we look into the mirror it's the same outside as in.
We know there's a friend in repentance for its tears water faith
Producing the trees where the fruit of truth prevails
Bringing into focus all of life's details.
We know there's a center of all truth
And of its own volition with power it does move!
At the heart of truth there is love with outstretched hands,
Bidding us, "Do enter into the promised land."

~~~

**Matthew 5:3 "Blessed are the poor in spirit, for theirs is the
kingdom of heaven."**

A new day of focus

We must always look forward into a frame of mind
Keeping us focused on the eventual prize.
There will always seem to be a mist hanging low.
A wall to block the rays of the sun
Hinting within borders the added weight of days
Impending gloom as sounds pronouncing rain.

Even when we carry a torch to light the way
In readiness for battle with what can harm
A greater light is wanted to make the journey strong.

In the event of lost sight we never lose our heart.
God is always with us when each new day is born.
Ending the deceptions that chill us to the bone.
Blown away are they
These mists of shortcut wrongs
They seek to make a day grow longer
When we awaken with no thought of God.

2 Corinthians 4:6 For God who said, "Let light shine out of darkness," made his light shine in our hearts to give us the knowledge of the glory of God in the face of Christ.

Sharp

～⌒～

Being sharp in your mind
Strong in your heart
Wins acceptance with men
And pleases God.
This is the way to ward-off the threats
That plague us from the time we awaken until the time of our death.

～⌒～

Psalm 57:4 I am surrounded by enemies, who are like man-eating lions. Their teeth are like spears and arrows; their tongues are like sharp swords.

A friend's question

*We have known each other for fifty-years
And he asks me, "I have a strong mind, why then am I so poor?"
Of this I reply, "What do you consider rich?"
"You know," says he, "Financial stability and no worries for the kids or
grandchildren."
"O that kind of rich," I said.
"Well if that is the category,
You are now looking at the richest poorest man in history.
You see my friend an outpouring of wealth is reported every day.
The sum of our lives in Christ is always in the black.
It's like a river overflowing the bank upon dry and parched land.
There is a table set for all of Christ's guests
At the, "Wedding feast of the Lamb."
All of those we love will be reunited again.
Our invitation to the feast has been given in our hearts,
And let me remind you this feast is prepared for us.
Prepared for us by the Lord!
There is no one more generous or rich.
Of this there is no doubt
Just look at all the good that he's given in this life throughout.
Yes, our kids and grandchildren are who top the goodness list.
After the feast we will settle down forever in our new homes.
Yes, I said, 'forever' and nothing will wear out.
No painting of the walls or loud garbage dumping sounds
Just praise and glory for our King
From every heart and mouth.
Repeatedly resounding applause is heard:
"Praise him!
Praise him!
Praise him!
Praise God,
For his wonderful Word!"*

**John 14:2 "In my Father's house are many rooms; if it were not so,
I would have told you. I am going there to prepare a place for you."**

Deep Dive

We can dive deep with heart mind and soul.
With aqualung we explore places we did not know.
As with all things we do there are laws contained therein
Break just one and end up with the bends.

We need to recognize what is too deep for us.
We must know what is beyond our strength.
In this, we come to understand
Limitation is a form of wisdom.
What is too deep seek God,
What is beyond our strength, permit God,
What we are given belongs to God,
Acknowledge him and all he has he'll give.

Matthew 13:35 So was fulfilled what was spoken by the prophet: "I will open my mouth in parables, I will utter things hidden since the creation of the world."

Be happy

～～～

Where is this happiness to which you say, "Comply?"
"Where again, is this joy that transcends troubled sighs?
When do the clouds get blown away replaced sunshine's healing rays?
Show to me the scalpel that cuts away despair.
Don't try to speak to me of happiness or try to show me joy.
I'll show to you the broken place where all of it has died."

"Take a moment broken heart to hear distant voices praising.
The source of all our joy protects and surrounds
The heart the mind and soul of man from top to bottom ground.

Take another breath troubled one let truth dry your eyes.
Take a look above the clouds see light filling up the sky?
Look past the thunderous cloud heed not its vocal cry.
It's only desperation's morning moan awakening with lies.
It loves pronouncing certain doom to those in earshot range.
You need only concentrate on the one who keeps you safe.
Jesus."

～～～

Matthew 13:44 The kingdom of heaven is like treasure hidden in a field. When a man found it, he hid it again, and then in his joy went and sold all he had and bought that field.

Shepherd

"Boy, the flock is buzzing today.
We got a new Shepherd and it has been heard
He choked a wolf in the second watch with just a single word.
Lots of us have been saying the time has come to prosper
Sure, we'll keep up the shearing and distributing the wool
To all who can't afford it, but now we can live in luxury."

"I see, what you are saying, and yes,
We can expect to be prosperous.
But not as you suggest
You see he is our guardian
And he will do his best.
He's not making promises of trinkets made of gold
Or fancy little bells that when wandering he knows.
Just plain old-fashioned common sense
That speaks to sheep in ways that take away
The glittering of star-struck worldly ways."

"The Lord is my Shepherd I shall not want."
He brings me to the reality I hoped for.
Beside the quiet waters the storms of life cannot overcome me.
Hardship can only visit from a distance because my life is filled with joy.
Sadness and mourning has to cease because our Shepherd is truth.
Even though we walk into the valley of the illusion of death
Into the deep places of the unknown, he knows what to expect.
I shall not fear or desire what there is no use for.
All I need is Jesus.

Hebrews 10:32-35 Remember those days after you received the
light, when you stood your ground in a great contest in the face
of suffering. Sometimes you were publicly exposed to insult and
persecution; at other times you stood side by side with those

who were so treated. You sympathized with those in prison and joyfully accepted the confiscation of your property, because you knew that you yourselves had better and lasting possessions. So do not throw away your confidence; it will be richly rewarded.

Reinforcement

All things in life need to be reinforced replenished or renewed.
We ourselves require occasional shoring-up of the walls of faith.
In this regard, Lord, you are great!
All of our praise ascends confirming faith that lives within.
All emotions sealed with love, says, "You are here with us."
Every breeze kissing the heart is as a rushing wind
Speaking the words and works of love, "I live within."
Throughout marrow flesh and bone healing heat of faith unfolds.
With knowledge wisdom confidence
We look above with loving gaze
Toward you O Lord for all our days
Reinforced by love and grace.

Isaiah 41:10 "So do not fear, for I am with you; do not be dismayed, for I am your God. I will strengthen you and help you; I will uphold you with my righteous right hand."

Sweet Lies

No matter how we approach truth
There is always one thing that eventually happens,
Healing.
It's always better to hear a caustic truth
Than to ingest a sweet lie.
So many songs written, past and present
Asking for, "sweet lies" in order to avoid rejection.
So much rejection, even falsehood is respected.
This is really cruel confusion
Objective movement denying what underlies,
Motive purpose and illusion
Into what's known as, "sweet lies."

Healing from the warmth of words
Whose weight of truth stands-tall and binds
The hurts and cares of this life's trials
Whenever hurt arrives.
Captured within its breath
Released in loving eyes
It doesn't come in increments
Designed to duck and hide,
It's courage and empowerment
Lives in the light, not hides.
Lives within the heart of God and the soul of man
Rejecting such as, "comfort zones" avoiding all there is.
"Sweet lies" are but a buffer added to a pill
Disguising pain's discomfort
As a bandit seeks to hide
All the ways a man can fall
With help from one, "sweet lie."

Psalm 101:6-7 I will approve of those who are faithful to God and let them live in my palace. Those who are completely honest will be allowed to serve me. No liar will live in my palace; no hypocrite will remain in my presence. GNB

Shipwrecked

Today we don't call it a shipwreck.
It's more like a bad credit rating.
Or else it is a bad reputation that sinks us to the bottom.
It is true: God forgives but the world never does.
Well, the world plays by different-rules that compensates according to the
world.
It makes it clear and plain, to all whose lives went wrong.
"We'll let you back into the game, but there's a price to pay."

I suppose that's because we gravitate toward self-destruction.
The behaviorist thinkers don't need to devise intricate plans
Concerning the demise of man.
We do it on our own through incessant demands.

We don't need a rudder shaft to fall from its bearing post.
Or else, a turbine reduction gear to screech us to a halt.
In the final analysis, it is, "we"
Who've done the damage of self inflicted wounds
Without the outside help of unseen jagged rocks
Absent siren call to lead us fast astray,
"Mirror, mirror on the wall" is all we have to say.
Will tell us where it all went wrong
When sitting at the bottom of the life we live today.

Proverbs 13:6 Virtue guards one who walks honestly, but the
downfall of the wicked is sin. *GNB*

Choosing to listen

There's a legacy of sin in part
The experience of choosing wrong
Breaking a man's heart.
Causing him to doubt and live this life without God.

All of us have this carryover knowledge
It digs into our flesh and bites into the soul
This failure that we chose has marked and made us sad
Living in this world separated from our Dad.

All of us have this understanding it mocks us throughout life.
It's the knowledge of right and wrong.
Experience has shown the way and God prevents our fall.
Everyone has said, "I'll do what I want!"
Until the hurt of life drives home the wisdom part.
"Heed his righteous voice," is the call across the ocean time.
Or else relive the hurts that come with a prideful mind.

My children listen to your father's advice:
"Love is not a novelty that shows up now and then.
It's been with you from the beginning, since God created man."

Isaiah 49:1-3 Listen to me, you islands; hear this you distant nations: Before I was born the Lord called me; from my birth he has made mention of my name. He made my mouth like a sharpened sword, in the shadow of his hand he hid me; he made me into a polished arrow and concealed me in his quiver. He said to me, "You are my servant, Israel, in whom I will display my splendor."

Brooklyn snapshot

Every neighborhood had a hangout or two. Ours was a place called Leo's located on fourth-avenue and Butler Street. The jukebox had all of the hits of the time, (late 50's and early 60's) and everyone sang along. Just up the street was Joe's luncheonette and it too was a hangout for the neighborhood kids. When I look back on those times in my life the thing that stands out as most pronounced is this: These places were more than just a hangout for us but a refuge from the streets that at times could be very mean. Joe and Molly along with Leo and many of the other parents always watched us as if we were their very own. I suppose it is a part of the parental code, to look after kids, but they did it in a manner that never infringed upon our daily routines. It is comforting to me to know there will be a reunion of all of these wonderful folks, and I am proud to have been a small part of their lives.

Leo's and Joe's Luncheonette

*A vanilla egg cream
Counter stools that spun all around
Hamburger grill and ice cream bins
Steel handled doors lifted up to the eyes
Releasing the cold in visible streams
So long ago it seems.
Kids sat sipping drinks at table and chairs
As if real customers were sitting there.
Six plays for a quarter and everyone knew the words.
Yes, this place was theirs.
T-shirts rolled at the sleeves with garrison belt legal through two loops.
Who made up that rule?
Pomade raised hair as spikes and later came the duck-back
With curls that drooped between the eyes
Baseball at the "parade grounds" diamond one had grass, but not for this team.
"Twisters" was our name it took two years before we won a game.
Today it's a tennis court, and the diamonds have all turned into a kickball sport.
Dirty uniforms could always pass through the doors of, "Leo's and Joe's."
We got clean for a party at Joe's, slow dancing lights low, little cares,
They were ours and we were theirs.
Back in the borough called Brooklyn
On the street we called home
Friendships have lasted a lifetime
No matter what direction we roamed.*

Mark 10:13-14 People were bringing little children to Jesus to have him touch them, but the disciples rebuked them. When Jesus saw this he was indignant. He said to them, "Let the little children come to me, and do not hinder them, for the kingdom of God belongs to such as these."

New Life

Whitecaps kneel to the conductor of the wind.
A white rose in blooming deepens strength.
White stars shining as streetlights in the night
Endless is the journey of light.
Seeking and searching bending wrong to right
Always there is the truth of God pulsing in our veins
Capturing and letting go into the world again
As a sparrow leaves the nest and tree that gave it sheltered birth
The love of God has brought new life to all who call him friend.
Has brought a breath of clean fresh air underneath our wings.

New life erases pain that gripped and held tenaciously
From the beginning of man's days
A cleansing stainless steel would envy
Purity of a brand new start without the baggage
Of a lost and heavy heart
That wandered aimlessly in the land of gloom and dark.

Revelations 2:17 He who has an ear, let him listen to what the Spirit says to the churches. To him who overcomes, I will give some of the hidden manner. I will also give him a white stone with a new name written on it, known only to him who receives it.

Forgiveness

⌒⌒⌒

Of all the hurtful things we do to others we must love
And later find remorse that's stirred, to advance an offering
Of reconciling salve, rejection of the offering is just as bad.

⌒⌒⌒

Matthew 6:12 Forgive us our debts as we also have forgiven our debtors.

Brothers

⌒⌒⌒

You have displayed genuine love.
You have gone the extra mile.
Lit the lamp for all to follow.
Made my heart smile.
Walked inside my shoes.
Given memories without end.
Prepared a table fit for kings.
Outshone the brightest star.
In warmth and love as gentlemen
My thanks with strength without end
Your kindness will be missed.
My prayer will always be:
"O Lord, of Lord's watch over them
Who broke this bread with me."

⌒⌒⌒

Psalm 23:1 The Lord is my shepherd, I shall not want. He leads me beside quiet waters, even though I walk through the valley of the shadow of death I will fear no evil, for you are with me; your rod and your staff they comfort me. You prepare a table for me in the sight of my enemies.

Retirement day with coworkers.

Obvious

❧

Right and wrong perfection and flawed
Points out a concept that can't be ignored.
Absent this truth why have any laws?
Why label as criminal the ways of man?
Why are some things accepted and others condemned?

The conscience assaulted by folly-deaf to the soft voice within
A trip to the outer fringes bends to all blowing winds.
What is apparent cannot be denied.
Truthful conditions are not in debate—neither is man's inevitable fate.
Good is no doubt a much better state.

What then is a man who sees not the gate?
Who knows not the signs of errant 'til late?
Who denies the truth placed into his hand?
A moment in time breath quickly exhaled
Unknowing denying the clear view ahead
Is a life that has failed eternity's test!

❧

Proverbs 27:18 Take care of a fig tree and you will have figs to eat.

Blood Sweat and Cheers

I saw Christ on bending knees his face upturned to heaven, saying,
"Father, take this cup from me."
Human fear divine tears sweat in precious blood
I tremble at the sight I see and marvel at the Lord.
In the moment I thought weak, again I heard him speak,
"Father, not my will, It is your will I seek."
Worn by fear, for just the other day, "Hosanna" he did hear.
Palm branches paved the road and children strained to see
The coming of, "Savior King," the, "Man of Galilee."
Glistening spears in torchlight night, voices seeking one called, "Christ."
"I see a friend walking with this band, pointing with a kiss."
Armor has its sound and silver has a ting but only Jesus knows the sound
betrayal brings.
I remember many things but only an inkling of understanding remains.
Only he knew, it was hidden in the brilliant light of day.
The first Passover: "lintel and doorposts" set apart by blood.
Head hands and feet marked by love.
The cross was written at the entrance door.
A child's game of, "Connect the dots" made the sign of the cross.
From the time of his birth in a town called, "House of Bread."
He was laid in a manger where animals were fed.
Manna sent from heaven, rich in mercy's eager ways.
Seeking out the lost and captured by the grave.
Conversing with the elders inside the temple walls.
Speaking words of wisdom to all who'd hear its call.
Innocence of a child sending truth into the heart
Portrayed by wondrous healing and raising of the dead
The casting out of evil the crippled made to walk
The blind and deaf find meaning the dumb speak words of love!
Miracles and deeds of good producing great expectant joy
The Savior King has come to earth, announcing, "Life," to the world.
As in the beginning and will be at the end
From a time perfection to a place unending joy
I see a new day dawning—a ray announcing song

A herald's voice proclaiming, "A child to us is born!"
I remember many things that come in waves and throngs
But nothing overshadows resurrection morn
Energizing power filled with awe!
I remember many things now, and marvel at the complex simplicity of
God.

***

Luke 18:31-34 Jesus took the twelve disciples aside and said to them, "Listen! We are going to Jerusalem where everything the prophets wrote about the Son of Man will come true. He will be handed over to the Gentiles, who will make fun of him, insult him, and spit on him. They will whip him and kill him, but three days later he will rise to life." But the disciples did not understand any of these things; the meaning of the words was hidden from them, and they did not know what Jesus was talking about.

In memory of the attack upon the World Trade Center in New York City 2001

Emergency 911

〜⌒〜

Once the sound of peaceful pace busy feet from place to place.
Within an instant hope is forced to halt in silent marvel gaze
At courage racing in the Brave
In the Finest thoughts as flint faced the beast for innocence.
EMT healing hands joined the Boldest in the task presented to the
Tower's Best.

Bells and preacher disbelief forestall movement of the feet
"All is well return remain," halts the flight of downward gain.
Hope laid stricken bound in tears as truth in windows gripped despair.
Heart to heart and eye to eye as a beggar's bowl advanced,
Ignites the bond in common man.

Determined feet in turnout coats through the heat and blinding smoke.
Hope renewed in just a glance of axe and strength in hero's hand.
Of light in crowded stairwell floors
Of steadfast hearts beating grace
Into the maw of hell they raced to meet the beast face to face.

Angels marveled in refrain, "No greater love can man display."
Flashing lights and sirens prayed as courage faced the beast.
Falling beams of crippled steel as arrows to the heart
Concrete sighs afflict the eye and all things fed the heat.
Flashing lights and sirens prayed as courage faced the beast.

A moment in the sun's retreat children's laughter turned to gray.
"O my God!" All voices speak through crashing sounds and panicked feet.
Flashing lights and sirens prayed as courage faced the beast.
"Haul away now lads haul away fast
With hope in your helmets and strength in your hands!
Haul away now lads haul away fast
From the top of the rubble to a pocket of chance!"

Remember, truth is freedom's key.
Hold to the breast thoughts long past of what life used to be.
A captured thought of what was lost is food to keep us free.
The mind reasons separation brief.
Yes, in paradise united still the heart weeps.
Have mercy, O Lord, on us who remain and into your Kingdom
Embrace the Brave.

❦

Proverbs 11:21 "Be sure of this: The wicked will not go unpunished, but those who are righteous will go free."

Retrospect

Childhood speaks to me of sidewalks and of streets.
Of tenements with many floors whose top we never reached.
Of baseball bats and ill fit gloves dusty fields and brotherhood.
Of school bell moments and homework maze all of which filled our days.
With innocence our realm of play, unspent, except for rips scrapes.
Adolescence came in stages, crew cut hair and sudden rages.
This and that was better worse as neighborhoods formed and burst.
As we grew and learned to shave we found in all a common trait.
A capacity to love and hate and thirsting for a truthful place
To feel secure to rest our faith battered bruised and tested great.
It halted laughter soft and sweet from the sidewalks and the street.
The windows shuttered sealed from fright to guard against deception's
bite.
Caution signs on streetlight corners, blinking lights defining turf as
nation's borders.
Distrust was gained in storms that beat the windows, as if to say, "Stay
indoors."
Yes, once we lived in pain and life rushed silently overhead.
Deep was the place of hidden dreams and planning
Of longing to be free from the onslaught of madness
Intent and focus cared not for childlike faith
But found deception's moment could satisfy the race
To gain grasp acquire what others did not want or see
Within a world of water, and fire, that offered life or death
We had a choice to touch its flame or else to walk away.
In time fire as eternity grew strong
And came announcing to its owner,
"What you sowed is reaped what you gained is yours!"
Lasting are the scars until you stand before the Lord.
A shout in midnight's calm, remembrance of its cost
Neither wealth nor blanket can bring to life some warmth.
Remember, in pursuit of vanity the fire burned deep within the pit.
In time it spread outside and burned the tender skin.
Like driven embers flying in direction impulse knows.

Adulthood brought new avenues to roam.
New friends to call upon
Responsibility to family to right a listing ship
To focus on the other, with fun and games replaced
By those whose trust was written in smiles of offered chance
To regain the loss of moments spent without a thought
To save the last of dignity we our self thought lost.
Thank God for his grace!
Allowing me to see that sad and lonely place of
Cold captivity of a never-ending race!

❧

2 Peter 1:12-15 So I will always remind you of these things, even though you know them and are firmly established in the truth you now have. I think it is right to refresh your memory as long as I live in the tent of this body. I know that I will soon put it aside, as our Lord Jesus Christ has made clear to me.

Childhood snapshot

Shootings stabbings and toy nabbing
Such was the days of my youth.
Young muscles ready to flex.
All without knowledge of what would come next.
Gang wars rumbling streets shouts and screams
Mixed in between homework and neighborhood games.
Punch ball stickball stoopball basketball hardball and soft
All with a rounding of testing what a kid is made of.
Friendships bonded within heartache and joy
Some of us taken before manhood arrived.
Captured by the insistence of wars
Born in the streets and within the pores
Plaguing conditions of all rich or needy
In the place called, "Brooklyn" where summers gave rise
Imaginations of action only a child could devise.
School days were filled with work
Only a few short hours were given to street.
The weekends found as magnets attract
All of the kids as wolves in packs
Not for the purpose of harm as one might suspect
But for sharing as family and friends
A bottle of soda in the hangout of Joe's
An egg cream from the counter of Leo's
A dollar earned selling daily the news
Printed on paper without words that confuse.
Before all of that a foundation was laid
Made up of truth that no one would doubt
For all of it came from the singular mouth
The God of Creation
The one who had said,
"You are my child and don't ever forget."
Yes, the sixties was a decade of come of age things
So long ago it seems.
Retrospect is a nice kind of word

Remembering the past and all that occurred.
That we have this memory can only mean
We were spared from the death others had seen.
We were given the chance to become fathers of sons and daughters
And later on to become grandparents
Such a blessing none could imagine back then
With all of the shootings and stabbings
And yes the one time toy nabbing so tempting for us kids.

⌒⌣⌒

Matthew 5:9 "Blessed are the peacemakers, for they will be called sons of God."

Eternity

In the beginning God spoke:
"Let there be light."
So began the journey into night.
Perhaps it was then eternity seized its moment?
Reality and concept intertwined.
Beginning the reality of God's intent for man
And the concept man cannot understand.
Because God is the great, "I Am"
I accept both reality and concept within God's plan.
Deep as eternity's day deeper still the concept arrayed.
Vast is eternity's day brought into existence and sent out to play.
Grabbing hold of the mind that can't comprehend
A universe without limits time without meaning life without end.

Eternity's day is shining intent
Awaiting the words, "Let man understand."
It opens the eyes of the heart and the mind of the lost
Illuminates darkness into heavens of time
Sending its message tic-tock sublime.
Makes clear to all since light began, it is a gift to man.
Eternity climbs into everywhere producing sighs
As a child asking the question, "why?"
So it is eternity bobs and weaves and dances
Searching and seeking to give us the answers
The present is forefront proof for the will
But eternity's concept troubles us still.
Existing to fill reminding through sight
God spoke, "Let there be light."
Bringing joy into darkness strength into clay
Praising Creator from its first ray
Forever and lasting and with us to stay is eternity's day.

Perhaps this is part of the reason
We sometimes have difficulty with faith?

We know the reality of God as seen in the light
Through things we experience have seen and believe
But to glimpse the infinite eternal forever we cannot conceive.
Here in the present his word still speaks, "Let there be light."
So all may see and believe.

John 1-5 In the beginning was the Word, and the Word was with God, and the Word was God. He was with God in the beginning. Through him all things were made; without him nothing was made that has been made. In him was life, and that life was the light of men. The light shines in the darkness, but the darkness has not understood it.

Final Vision

People following a walking tree.
It falls against cobblestones as if seeking rest.
What could this mean?
O yes, it's the Nazarene.
He's beaten bleeding battered and lean.
I know what this means.
Jesus, yes that's his name.
I can imagine what he's thinking.
"It feels like rain damp and chilling
Why can't I see clearly?
Is that a soldier walking toward me?
What is he saying?"
"You, take his arms!
You, take the tree!"
His features are speaking loudly.
Dripping from a crown fingertips and feet
His face says, "enough" but it's not as yet complete.
Crucifixion sends its message strong:
"Walk talk and think in the ways of the world
And you will not be bothered by whip spear or nail
You won't find the pain that loves to make one wail."
I want to run from here but I must see what they will do to him.
I see a well formed by tears of love,
Mixing with the streams of his precious blood.
Eyes searching vacant skies in loneliness he cried,
"My God, my God, why have you forsaken me?"
Words that brought surprise to those
Who hammered the nails and gambled for his clothes.
One last cry to heaven's host
He bowed his head and released the Ghost.
Determined efficiency.
Dishonor guard impersonal at best.
Few mourners save the cloud overhead.
Fog caresses the earth a gentle covering for the interred.

"Guard the tomb!
They shall not enter to steal him away!"
Third day, grip broken.
"Look not for the living among the dead."
Sunrise conducting the chorus, nature's witness in awe
Resounding echoes of wave breaking news, thunderous applause!
Death lamenting, "He lives!"

⌒⌣⌣⌒

Isaiah 53:5 But he was pierced for our transgressions, he was crushed for our inequities; the punishment that brought us peace was upon him, and by his wounds we are healed.

Maintenance Vision

⟳

How shall we approach service to God, life?
We are as tools in the toolbox of God, some for special use and others not.
All must be ready for usage, kept clean and free of rust
Preventing operation and the drag it brings to us.
How can we become that special tool?
Desire most the hand of God to tighten and unwind
Join with others who seek the same, who call to God in faith.
No matter what our usage may be
The joy of knowing we played a part in God's plan
Is far greater than can be imagined
No matter what tool we may have been.

⟳

2 Timothy 20:22 In a large house there are articles not only of gold or silver, but of also wood and clay; some are for noble purposes and others ignoble. If a man cleanses himself from the latter, he will be an instrument of noble purposes, made holy, useful for the Master and prepared for any good work. Flee from evil desires of youth, and pursue righteousness, faith, love and peace, along with those who call upon the Lord out of a pure heart.

Refresh

⌒⌒⌒

Remember the voice that struggled to be free?
Remember the cold captivity?
Red and raw the heart endured tears that fell inside
Valleys meant to echo joyous cries.
Remember the tight mooring lines of pride?
How we were taken by turbulence and fire
That gnawed the inner halls
Like driven embers flying in direction
Only impulse knows?

Remember the cinders adding to the blindness
That caused stumbling and falls
Adding to the blindness of eyes in waterfalls?
Remember when we lived in pain that came in waves overhead?
Deep was the ocean bottom we could never view
Deeper still the sadness of aftermath remained
"How could all this happen" was constant in refrain.
Remember lifting heavy loads that bore into the soul?
I do.
Forgetting invites a chance of doing it again
Of visiting the places we have known and some that appear as new,
Remember where we've been and there will be no chance of a redo.
Memory is a gift that sometimes may be hard
And when it too shall end depends upon our God.

⌒⌒⌒

2 Peter 1:12-15 So I will always remind you of these things, even
though you know them and are firmly established in the truth
you now have. I think it is right to refresh your memory as long
as I live in the tent of this body, because I know I will soon put it
aside, as our Lord Jesus Christ has made clear to me.

Hypocrisy

~~~

What the lips proclaim
And the heart denies is a lie.
It's clear to see
A twinkle brings a smile
A glisten calls a tear
Surprise invites a stare
And anger loves to glare.

Hypocrisy tries to hide but in the eyes its there
A window to the heart that speaks with broadside words
As a company dancing tap or microphone with volume peaked blaring
out a rap.

A single-minded man stands upright with his eyes
As children look to parents with love trust and smiles.
A double-minded man hides deep within his lies
Like a corpse not having breath light or life.

~~~

Luke 11: 37-39 When Jesus finished speaking, a Pharisee invited
him to eat with him; so he went and reclined at table. But the
Pharisee, noticing that Jesus did not wash before the meal, was
surprised. Then the Lord said to him, "Now then, the Pharisees
clean the outside of the cup and the dish, but inside you are full
of greed and wickedness. You foolish people! Did not the one who
made the outside make the inside
also?"

When you feel alone

Look outside yourself
Look for higher strength
Feel the warmth inside
When found you won't forget.
Some things are hard to handle
Grief stress and strife
We need only ask to take away life's bite.
The heaviness of heart can weigh us down inside.
When loved ones pass a void is formed as night
A void as static noise from deep inside the heart
It's then I hear you calling to lessen hurt and pain:
"Be still,
Take hold my outstretched hand.
The tears will fade away.
When grief and strife are no longer tightly bound.
When they are a memory no longer dragged around.
Smile and rest your head in the Kingdom of the found."

Hebrews 4:15 Our high priest is not one who cannot feel sympathy for our weaknesses.

Revelation 21:4 He will wipe away all tears from their eyes. There will be no more death, no more grief or crying in pain. The old things have disappeared. *GNB*

Capture

⌒⌒⌒

A passing glance
A blink within a stare
A beat of recognition
A smile dissolving sad
A storm quickly passing
A multitude of thought
A million beating drums
Sending sound into the air
Life, reaching as a prayer
Never to find doubting
Your intended ear
Overtures demanding
With force of bitter tears
Bidding without asking
In knowledge you are here
O God of love and truth capture my despair.
Wipe away the tears take hold my outstretched hand.

⌒⌒⌒

Hebrews 4:13 There is nothing that can be hid from God; everything in all creation is exposed and lies open before his eyes. GNB

Power

〜〜〜

It's your to choose tight fist or open hand
To demonstrate understanding of what belongs to man.
Upward reaching embracing all in sight
Finds power given by God's light.
Tight fist
Closed mind
Cold heart
Blind eyes
Searching for a high place
Where privileged children play games of kings and queens
Alas, but for a day.
Tight fist
Closed mind
Imprisoned spirit gropes
Fails to bring the power that the unknowing hope
Will gain for them an audience affirming world acclaim
Find their race for power has placed upon them chains.
Stone upon stone
Lock upon chain
Down beneath deep
Rock and hard place
Tight fist to the grave
Arrogance stays
On top of the bones
As decorative death
Meaningless.

〜〜〜

Isaiah 41:4 "Who was it that made this happen? Who has determined the course of history? I, the Lord, was there at the beginning, and I, the Lord God, will be there at the end."

Peter F. Serra

America

America what happened to you?
There was a time when unity was true.
Even politicians hid their inner thoughts.
Position power greed was kept behind closed doors.
Cracks in the foundation peeling paint so dry
Columns leaning left comrade members speaking
Attempting to deep set with talking points repeating.
"Never waste a crisis distraction is the key
No one will remember the day the lie the crime
As long as we keep speaking with words that seem to rhyme."

They fill the air with change that failed to fill the promise
They want our God erased so they can hear their thunder.
They want him six-feet under.

The hope is pure illusion and the change from what to where?
All is but confusion in our land that was so blessed.
Dear leaders are obsessed with a world where none can breathe.
The lies and tyrant's rant in the land that hoped for change
Is now unmasked to see evil's tight fist hand.

"I pledge allegiance to the flag-one nation under God."
This pledge has rubbed into their flesh and always do they moan:
"Remove him from the heart in the schools and in home!"

Red has found a new home where anger now resides.
White is still standing for some good she still provides.
Blue is still the color of the blood that's shed for her.
Stars that shone of brilliance have seemed to lose their way
But God is always faithful to those whose voices speak
The truth and hope of men and the flag of stars and stripes
Silent now it weeps in the quiet of the night.

Our flag has found corruption of evil's dirt and grime
Rotting at the fabric of body heart and mind!
The wind of change has ripped and has gathered many storms
With hope to silence voices beneath its winsome roar.
Voices speaking truth they would very much have gone.
Never shall they hear it fade for truth does stand-alone!
Hallelujah!

~~~~~

Proverbs 11:7-9 "When a wicked man dies, his hope dies with him. Confidence placed in riches comes to nothing. Honest people are safe and secure, but the dishonest will be caught. Someone who holds back the truth causes trouble, but one who openly criticizes works for peace." GNB

ABOUT THE AUTHOR

Author Peter F. Serra was born in Brooklyn New York, in 1946. He was born again at the age the age of thirty-three through the grace of God. He is a husband, father, and grandfather and has been married to his lovely wife since 1967. Without her patience this work could never have been accomplished.

Mr. Serra was (is now retired) a licensed Stationary Engineer with the City of New York, and was also employed in many private hospitals in Brooklyn. He is a United States Navy veteran, enlisting in the Navy at age seventeen, and served aboard the USS Cambria APA36, from Feb. 1964 through Oct. 1967. As a "Gator Navy" sailor (Amphibious forces) he learned many things that have carried over for the remainder of his life. As a Navy boiler man this initial training was honed and built upon until ultimately becoming licensed to operate such high pressure vessels within his chosen civilian profession. He received an honorable discharge for his service at the completion of his military obligation.

Mr. Serra was an active civilian member of the New York City Police Department for many years, including the attack upon the World Trade Center. As such he has included in this work three poems (Emergency 911, Healing and Justice) dedicated to those whose lives were taken away and to those who gave everything in their valiant efforts to save others. The concentrated efforts of everyone to rescue, heal and restore was (I suppose) not seen since the devastations accompanying the last world war. As an eyewitness to the trade center devastation from the viewpoint of "ground zero" and from within the inner workings of The New York City Police Headquarters, there was tremendous compassion toward everyone. There was awesome unity and focus upon the safety of the city's resident and commuter populations, so much so, it resembled a wartime setting with regard to police checkpoints of entry into the city and even more so within the lower Manhattan areas. I've been honored to have worked with such brave and selfless men and women whose sole purpose at the time was to "protect and serve." With regard to the serving of others, throughout my working life I have been equally blessed to know many within the vast hospital system of this great city of compassion. Whether within the private sector or the city hospital system one thing stands as a beacon of man's endearing qualities, his love for his fellow man shown by the dedication to others. In this motivational love is reflected the love of God for his creation. Today I am occupied with perhaps only two main areas of life, being the best grandfather possible (grandma really does all the work) and the desire to pass along to family and others the mercy shown to me by God.